THE LIFE and WORK OF

DR. ALISTER MACKENZIE

Tom Doak / Dr. James S. Scott / Raymund M. Haddock

Sleeping Bear Press

It was the summer of 1995, a rare hot day in St. Andrews, Scotland. I was there for the Open Championship, and as with any major championship at St. Andrews, many books on golf were published for the event. Alister MacKenzie's lost manuscript, *The Spirit of St. Andrews*, was stealing the headlines on publishing. Greg Norman was reading it every night, Peter Jacobson told me he loved everything MacKenzie did and in a London paper's story on Arnie [Palmer], over half of the story was about MacKenzie's book.

MacKenzie's stepgrandson, Ray Haddock, the finder of the lost manuscript, was attending the championship and he asked me to lunch to meet with his new friend, Dr. James Scott, who had been doing an inordinate amount of research on MacKenzie.

It was a great day; the spirit of the town, the excitement of the championship, had caught us up in the spirit of the game. It was perfectly appropriate that in this setting, the three of us agreed that a book on the life and work of one of the greatest golf architects of all time would be a perfect project. Little did we know that it would take over six years to finalize the book, as tracing the man's complete life was an arduous task, only accomplished with the effort and determination of Dr. Scott, a non-golfer with an enquiring mind and academic's ability to carry out such a complete research and Tom Doak, the one architect who understands more about MacKenzie's work than anyone else.

We are proud to be able to share with you *The Life and Work of Dr. Alister MacKenzie.*

Brian Lewis
Sleeping Bear Press

Sleeping Bear Press
310 North Main Street
P.O. Box 20
Chelsea, MI 48118
www.sleepingbearpress.com

Printed and bound in Canada

10 9 8 7 6 5 4 3 2 1

Library of Congress Cataloging-in-Publication Data
ISBN: 1-58536-018-X

Doak, Thomas.
The life and work of Dr. Alister MacKenzie / authors, Thomas Doak, James S. Scott, Raymund M.
Haddock.
p. cm.
ISBN 1-58536-018-X
1. Mackenzie, A. (Alexander), b. 1870. 2. Golf course architects-Great Britain-Biography. I. Scott,
James, 1924- II. Haddock, Raymund, 1932- III. Title.
GV964.M316 D63 2001
712'.5'092—dc21
2001001041

Why do a biography of Alister MacKenzie? After all, *The Spirit of St. Andrews*, written just before he died, is a perfect recap of his philosophies of golf and of life, and his genius endures in great courses on four continents.

But Dr. MacKenzie remains something of an enigma. He hailed from Leeds, England, but was a Scotsman through and through. He always proudly used the title of "Doctor," but his practice as a physician was small and unfulfilling. His interest in the use of camouflage in the military made him one of the leading experts in the field, but his ideas were ignored by his commanders and his writings on the subject were published anonymously. He spent years as a golf architect around his base in England—where his courses were both renowned and controversial—but a bitter divorce made him unwelcome at his home club, not only in the last years of his life but for a generation thereafter. He spent his final years designing golf courses around the world, yet he spent only a few weeks here and there with the design partners who carried out his plans. Many modern architects consider him their inspiration, yet he died in relative obscurity and financial distress, pleading to collect fees from the very club that would ultimately make him famous. He was the genius behind such great courses as Augusta National, Royal Melbourne, Crystal Downs, Lahinch, Kingston Heath, Royal Adelaide, Titirangi, and The Jockey Club, but he never played any of them nor even saw them in their finished form.

The authors of this book each know Dr. MacKenzie in a different light. Dr. James Scott has meticulously researched MacKenzie's life. Golf architect Tom Doak has studied Alister's courses and is one of only a handful to have seen all of them. Because of his expertise, he has also been entrusted with restoring MacKenzie courses such as The Valley Club and Pasatiempo. Ray Haddock is the stepgrandson of the good doctor, and was the discoverer of MacKenzie's famous lost manuscript, *The Spirit of St. Andrews*.

Thanks to their efforts, golfers the world over will learn why Alister MacKenzie is considered by many to be the greatest course architect of them all. ✍

Table of Contents

Chapter One
Early Golf Architecture: United Kingdom

THE FIRST GOLF COURSE IN LEEDS, ENGLAND, WAS HEADINGLEY GOLF CLUB, ESTABLISHED IN 1892. A SECOND COURSE, LEEDS GOLF CLUB AT COBBLE HALL, FOLLOWED FOUR YEARS LATER. Alister MacKenzie—in his early to mid twenties at the time—was a member of both clubs, if not from the day they opened, certainly not long after. Even in his early golfing days, he had strong ideas as to how a course should be developed. The first evidence of this was in the disagreements he had with the committees of the two clubs as to what should be done with their territory.

Over the next few years, MacKenzie gave a lot of thought to the subject of golf course architecture. It became something of a hobby for him, as it did for one of his close friends, Arthur Sykes. Along with several other golf enthusiasts, they became convinced that Leeds deserved a better course. Consequently, in January of 1907, both men were at the formation meeting for Alwoodley Golf Club. The meeting was held at the Leeds Club, a distinguished city-center gentlemen's social and dining club that ultimately provided many of the founding members of the new golf club being considered.

A permanent committee was formed during this initial meeting, of which Alister and Sykes were "made" members. The use of the word "made" rather than "elected" makes it clear that the club's founders believed that oligarchy was the best way to run a golf club. Membership in the committee was by invitation of that body and it was for *life*. Alister was also named Honorary Secretary.

Throughout most of his career as a golf course architect, MacKenzie had trouble dealing with committees—especially if they weren't permanent committees. Commenting on Alwoodley in his book *The Spirit of St. Andrews*, written in 1933, MacKenzie said that he and Sykes thought "we had more chance of getting our ideas through a permanent committee of friends ..." He continued:

During the last twenty-four years, the committee, except for death or emigration from Leeds, has remained the same as it was the day the club was founded.

Notwithstanding our disputes in the early stages, we would strongly recommend every club to have a permanent committee. It is the only way a policy of continuity can be adopted, and this is particularly important in the case of green committees.

The history of most golf clubs is that a committee is appointed, they make mistakes, and just as they are beginning to learn by these mistakes they resign office and are replaced by others who make still greater mistakes, and so it goes on.

Despite his impassioned case for continuity, Alister showed no interest in limiting his role in golf to that of Honorary Secretary at Alwoodley; within two years he had resigned the post. This may have been a political matter because there were arguments within the committee over design issues. MacKenzie recalled that, "Every committee meeting was a dog fight and on many occasions we nearly came to blows." Since he remained a fixture in the committee, however, it could

be that his involvement in designing Moortown and other courses simply made him too busy to continue in the role of Secretary. In any case, he was still held in some favor at Alwoodley. In 1912, he was elected Captain of the club for the year.

Credit for the design of Alwoodley is frequently given to MacKenzie alone. In 1914, golf writer Bernard Darwin said Alister already had Alwoodley "as a memorial." But it is also widely known that soon after MacKenzie became Honorary Secretary, the club approached Harry S. Colt for his advice on the layout. As MacKenzie remembered, "We managed to persuade the committee to call in Harry Colt to settle the disputes, and he decided in our favour."

During Colt's visit he stayed at MacKenzie's house, and his description of their meeting in the foreword of MacKenzie's 1920 book *Golf Architecture* makes it clear he recognized MacKenzie as a man of ideas:

After dinner he took me into his consulting room, where, instead of finding myself surrounded by the weapons of his profession as a Doctor of Medicine, I sat in the midst of a collection of photographs of sand bunkers, putting greens, and golf courses, and many plans and designs of the Alwoodley Course. I found that I was staying with a real enthusiast, and one who had already given close attention to a subject in which I have always been interested.

Colt, like MacKenzie, did his designs rapidly and left a lot of the detail to be worked out by the contractor on-site. So he was back in London while MacKenzie, living nearby, was frequently on hand during construction. This meant that Alister could have had control of the

TOP LEFT: FIFTH HOLE AT ALWOODLEY GOLF CLUB. THE CLUB WAS FORMED IN 1907. **TOP RIGHT:** THE 17TH GREEN AT HEADINGLEY GOLF CLUB, LEEDS, ENGLAND. **BOTTOM:** THIS WAS MACKENZIE'S HOME FOR MANY YEARS IN LEEDS.

Length of Holes (approximately)

	ordinary	medal			ordinary	medal
1.	368	370		10.	356	390
2.	273	320		11.	125	135
3.	400	422		12.	325	355
4.	407	472		13.	370	410
5.	315	355		14.	154	154
6.	295	35		15.	354	382
7.	145	15		16.	388	400
8.	444	500		17.	411	433
9.	196	19		18.	377	400
	2843	316			2860	3059

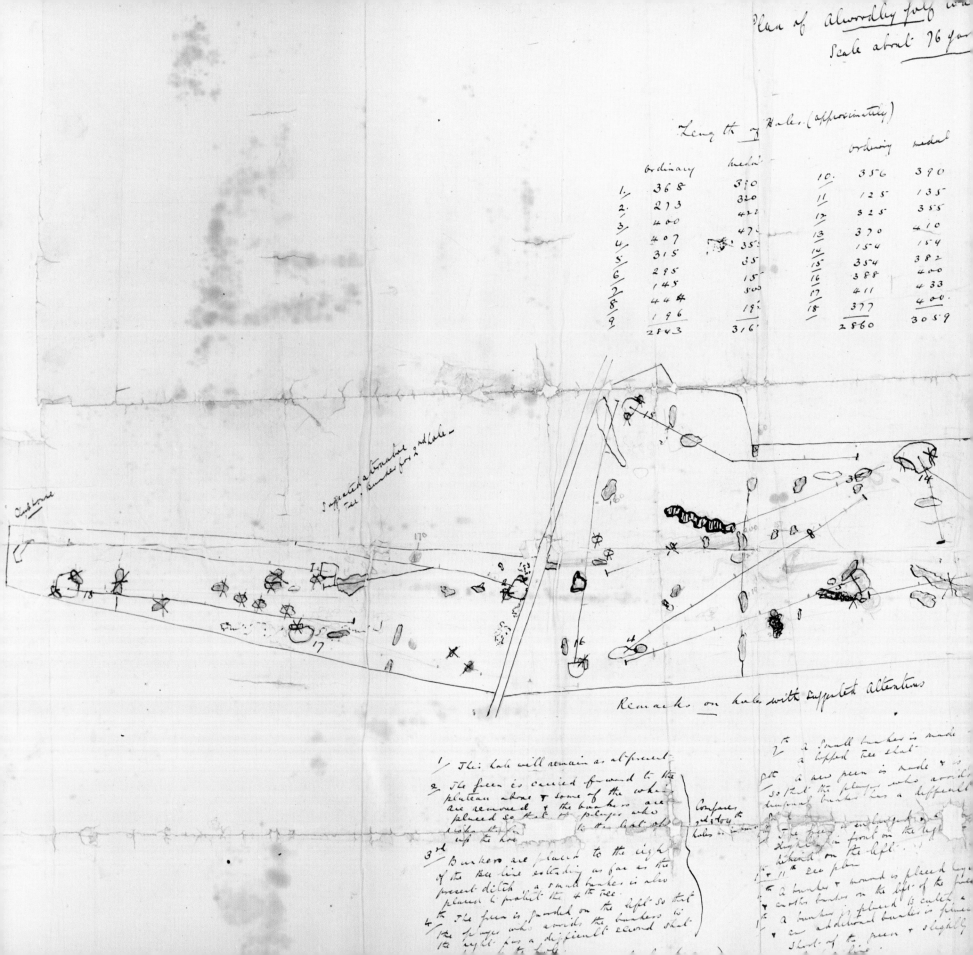

Remarks on holes with suggested Alterations

1/ This hole will remain as at present.

2/ The green is carried forward to the plateau above & some of the [ ] are removed & the bunkers are placed so that the players who [ ]

3rd Bunkers are placed to the right of the bee line extending as far as the present ditch & a small bunker is also placed to prohibit the [ ] tree.

4th The green is guarded on the left so that the players who avoids the bunkers to the right has a difficult second shot.

[ ] a small bunker is made [ ] a lipped tree that

[ ] a new green is made & so that the players who avoid [ ] bunker has a difficult

[ ] the green is enlarged & slightly [ ] in front on the left behind on the left.

[ ] & 11th see plan

[ ] a bunker & mound is placed [ ] another bunker on the left of the [ ] a bunker is placed to catch [ ] an additional bunker is placed short of the green & slightly

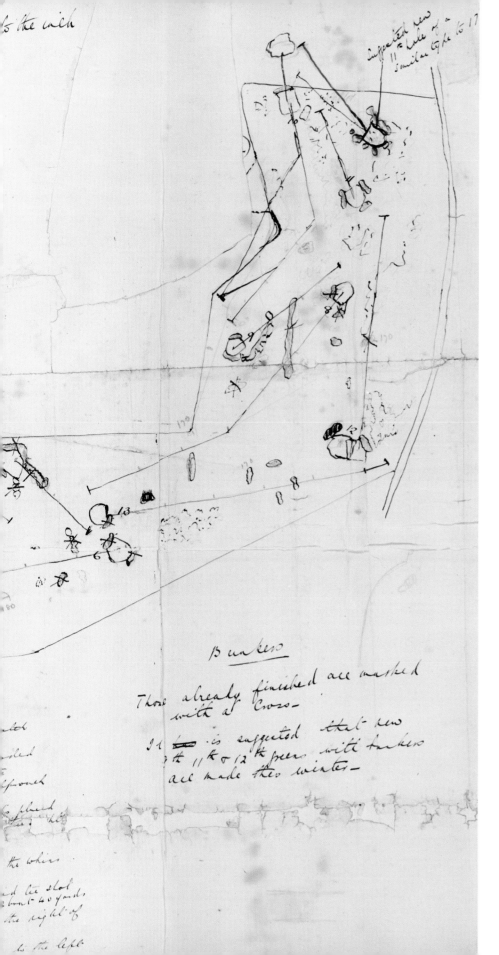

detail work of greens and bunkers if he were interested. There were additional arguments within the committee over diversions from Colt's suggestions, but during a hard winter Sykes and MacKenzie were the only officials who made the effort to visit the course regularly. Since the greenkeeper—a man named Brown—had never seen a golf course before, he basically did everything Alister told him to do. In the spring, when the other committee members saw what had been done without their knowledge, more arguments broke out. Perhaps due to Providence, a good summer of enjoyable golf eventually caused the members to accept the work that Alister had directed.

Whether the routing of the Alwoodley course was completely or only partly Colt's, its construction was certainly Alister's first opportunity to get many of his ideas on golf course design onto the ground. Similar to a first love, a first golf course reveals much about a designer's passions and priorities. Alwoodley had many features that were very different from those found on inland courses of the day, and they became an element of Alister's style from that point forward. Among the most important were:

MACKENZIE'S ROUTING MAP FOR ALWOODLEY GOLF CLUB, 1907.

∾ *Undulating greens.*

Alwoodley's putting surfaces certainly were not as bold in their contours as those eventually built at Augusta National and Royal Melbourne. However, they were large greens divided into different flagstick placement areas, with undulations prominent enough that the golfer hitting an approach had to take into account where the cup was and then adjust his shot accordingly. This concept, taken for granted today, was a common feature on the Old Course at St. Andrews with its huge greens, but on almost no other course up to the time of Alwoodley's construction. Inland courses were generally distinguished by smaller, flatter, purely functional greens; the only challenge was to put the ball *somewhere* on the putting surface. The need to put the ball on the green and in the right spot was different. Among the more distinctive greens at Alwoodley were the par-5 third, with a punchbowl left half and a plateau on the right, and the par-4 15th, where an upslope running diagonally through the front part of the green would carry a weak second shot from the left away into a front-right greenside bunker.

∾ *Long and narrow greens angled from the center of the fairway.*

Most of Colt's green designs can fairly be described as squarish or rectangular in shape. MacKenzie's, on the other hand, tended to be long and skinny—even accented with an interior curve or a kidney shape. The result was that a player who hit his drive to the proper side of the fairway was presented with the length of the green for the approach. The player who drove it on the wrong side, however, was often presented with a broadside approach over a hazard into a green with little depth. Alwoodley is full of variations on this concept. The second and third greens favor a drive to the right; the fifth favors an approach from the left-center, but the slope of the fairway tends to carry balls away to the right; the 17th is only visible after a long drive down the boundary on the left; and the aforementioned 15th actually presents its full length to an approach from the left, though the slope within the green favors a pitch from the right.

VIEW FROM THE 18TH TEE AT ALWOODLEY GOLF CLUB.

Fairly large and free-form bunker shapes.

On inland courses of the day, the bunkering left much to be desired. Most fairway bunkers were ramparts across the line of play that were designed to penalize off-line or topped shots, with no thought at all to making the bunkers beautiful or natural in appearance. This was probably a remnant of links design, where most bunkers were kept quite small to keep sand from blowing out of them. In addition, because most were half-hidden in folds in the ground, visual scale was not an issue. Alwoodley's bunkers not only were visible to the player, they had a flourish to them and enough size to make them prominent, yet in scale with the broad landscape of the property. MacKenzie was also quite sparse with his fairway bunkering at Alwoodley, preferring to let wing bunkers around the green and hazards up to 50 yards back from it make life more difficult for the player who had driven into the rough or out of position. The majority of holes either have just one bunker or none at all, and only one hole has bunkers on both sides at a landing area.

Additional contouring.

In addition to the features he gave to the bunkers and the putting surfaces, Alister did contour work *around the greens* as well, creating little mounds and moguls and hollows. The reasons for this were both to add interest to greenside play *and* to "tie in" the edge of the green to the natural contours around it. That way, it would be less clear where the artificial work began and ended—and that was the first principle of camouflage,

15TH AT ALWOODLEY, A 415-YARD PAR 4. A STRONG DOGLEG TO THE RIGHT, WITH AN OUT-OF-BOUNDS FENCE VERY CLOSE TO THE CORNER OF THE DOGLEG. THE GREEN IS SET A BIT AWAY FROM THE BOUNDARY, WITH A RISE IN THE GREEN SET DIAGONALLY ALONG THE LINE OF PLAY THAT SHEDS SHORT SHOTS OFF TOWARD A BUNKER ON THE RIGHT.

a subject that had fascinated MacKenzie during the Boer War. Once covered in the heather and bracken of the native Alwoodley rough, it was nearly impossible to determine that the work was artificial. MacKenzie recalled with great delight that even members of his own committee were fooled into thinking that the contours were all natural in origin.

Though MacKenzie's first design should be recognized and hailed as a landmark in golf course architecture, Alwoodley has avoided the limelight. This was not the isolation of exclusiveness that eventually developed at Augusta National, but reflected a sense of corporate embarrassment when MacKenzie and his first wife, Edith, were divorced in the late 1920s; they had been at the heart of the club since its embryonic days. Indeed, the members seemed to make an attempt to avoid acknowledging that Alister ever existed. His portrait, which had hung in the clubhouse, mysteriously disappeared and his name is conspicuously missing from everything written about the course during the 1930s and 1940s. It has been only recently—now that the club members of his gen-

eration have all passed away—that pride in MacKenzie's achievements at Alwoodley is again evident at the club where he began his career.

His successful efforts at Alwoodley raised it far above the level of other courses in the area and it made Alister the leading authority on golf course development in his home city. He soon had another chance to put his ideas into practice, just across the road on the site of some old nurseries.

In November of 1908, a group commissioned Dr. MacKenzie to design 18 holes for a new course to be called "Moortown." Only $500 was available for the entire project, however, and that caused MacKenzie's practical sense and genius for marketing to first be displayed. Alister suggested that the money be used to build one fine golf

OPPOSITE PAGE, TOP: MACKENZIE PLAYING THE 15TH HOLE AT HIS HOME COURSE, ALWOODLEY GOLF CLUB. **OPPOSITE PAGE, BOTTOM:** MACKENZIE PITCHING TO THE FIRST GREEN AT ALWOODLEY. **ABOVE:** MACKENZIE TEEING OFF THE EIGHTEENTH AT ALWOODLEY.

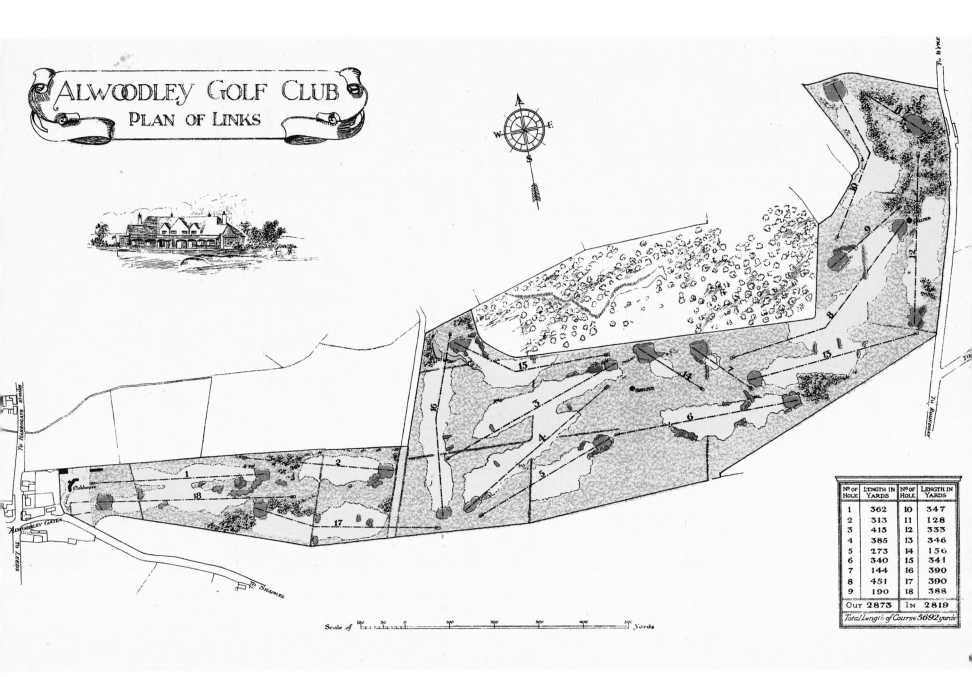

ALWOODLEY GOLF CLUB
PLAN OF LINKS

Nº of Hole	Length in Yards	Nº of Hole	Length in Yards
1	362	10	347
2	313	11	128
3	415	12	333
4	385	13	346
5	273	14	156
6	340	15	341
7	144	16	390
8	451	17	390
9	190	18	388
Out 2873		In 2819	
Total Length of Course 5692 yards			

Scale of   Yards

TOP: GIBRALTAR AT MOORTOWN. BERNARD DARWIN SPOKE OF IT AS A HOLE "OF ALARMING EXCELLENCE." **BOTTOM:** OFFICIAL OPENING OF MOORTOWN GOLF CLUB ON SEPTEMBER 24, 1910.

hole in order to show any interested parties the potential of the course. MacKenzie selected a natural site for a short hole. When it was completed, the hole was of such high quality there was a rush to join the club.

That first short hole would today be considered the "signature hole" at Moortown. MacKenzie christened it "Gibraltar" because the raised platform that constituted the green sat atop a large rock outcrop. A par 3 of about 170 yards, the Gibraltar hole was somewhat similar to the famous par 3 at North Berwick in Scotland called "Redan" (although Alister claimed later that he was not familiar with the Redan at that time). A large bunker dominated the left front of the green, and an entrance for run-up shots was provided to the right. There was a tier in the green to hold up weaker shots, and the approach was subtly crowned to turn less than well-struck shots into bunkers on either side. Heather and birch on the bank to the right and rear of the green completed a most picturesque and demanding hole.

With the Gibraltar hole attracting investors throughout 1909, the construction of the rest of the course was begun that fall and finished a year later. On Saturday, September 24th, 1910, Moortown opened with an exhibition match between James Braid and Harry Vardon. MacKenzie—by that time Vice President of the club—served as referee. While Alwoodley was to become known as a place for informal match play among members, Moortown from its early days sought out and successfully hosted top-flight championship events, most notably the 1929 Ryder Cup matches.

With slightly less natural undulation than nearby Alwoodley, the Moortown property did not offer as many natural golf holes. Consequently, MacKenzie perhaps spent more time on the shaping of the bunkers, which are more refined at Moortown. Then again, perhaps this is because Mr. Franks, the superintendent (of whom Alister spoke most highly) had a better knack for bunkering than Mr. Brown at Alwoodley. Since many of MacKenzie's designs relied heavily on the talents of those who carried out the work after he had left, that may have been the case at Moortown.

OPPOSITE PAGE: 1929 RYDER CUP. THE FINAL DAY OF THE MATCHES WAS THE BEST AT MOORTOWN. **ABOVE:** MOORTOWN'S CLUB PRESIDENT, THE HONORABLE RUPERT BECKETT, HITS THE FIRST TEE SHOT AT MOORTOWN.

Chapter Two
MacKenzie the Scotsman

MANY OF THE GREAT EARLY ARCHITECTS OF GOLF COURSES WERE SCOTSMEN. OLD TOM MORRIS, THE LONGTIME ST. ANDREWS PROFESSIONAL, WAS THE FIRST CALLED UPON TO LAY OUT COURSES professionally. Donald Ross, of Dornoch, was the most prolific, designing more than 400 courses in America after emigrating in 1899. Others, including James Braid of Elie, Willie Park of Musselburgh, Alex Smith of Carnoustie, and John Duncan Dunn of North Berwick, made their mark as designers as well as players. But perhaps the most influential of all was Alister MacKenzie, who in the late 1920s placed outstanding golf architecture on the global map—Britain, Ireland, Australia, New Zealand, Argentina, and America—paving the way for world-class golf in each of those countries.

MacKenzie's work was special because his background was entirely different from that of his contemporaries in the design field. They all grew up in a golf professional's shop while he had a university education. In addition, because of an injury as a teenager, Alister's involvement in golf got off to a slow start. Even when he reached his twenties, he hardly played the game. Thus he didn't approach course design from the perspective of "rewarding expert play," as most professionals did. He was the first to celebrate the beauty of golf courses, and his goal in placing hazards was to make the game more interesting for the average golfer.

Something else that was different about MacKenzie was that he wasn't born in Scotland. He was born on August 30, 1870 at the family home in Normanton, near Leeds, England, and much of his youth was spent there. However, he was raised a Scotsman from the start. Although christened Alexander MacKenzie after his paternal grandfather, his parents chose to use the Gaelic form of "Alister." His mother, Mary Jane Smith MacKenzie, was the daughter of a prosperous ship's chandler in Glasgow. His father, William Scobie MacKenzie, was a physician born and raised in Lochinver in the western Highlands. Dr. William moved to England to find a medical practice big enough to support his family, but the family's spiritual home was in the Highlands, where they returned every summer.

Normanton was a coal mining town in the midst of a boom. In 1840, Normanton's population was 750. By 1880, it had grown to 15,000. Dr. William was one of the town's most prominent citizens, not only as Medical Officer for Health for more than 30 years, but also for campaigning to improve living conditions; many homes still lacked running water. In spite of the doctor's high standing, however, Normanton didn't have a big influence on the lives of the MacKenzie children. There were few professional families in town with whom to mix, and most of their parents' social lives centered on Leeds, about ten miles away. For Alister and his four siblings, summers in Lochinver were far more interesting and memorable than the dreary life of Normanton.

Lochinver is the largest community in Assynt, a large parish with a small population in southwest Sutherland, Scotland. Lochinver lies on the west coast on a small sea loch from which it takes its name. Most coastal hamlets nestle at the mouth of a stream. Lochinver is superior in that regard in that it has two fine salmon rivers. At the north end of the

CERTIFIED COPY of an ENTRY OF BIRTH
Pursuant to the Births and Deaths Registration Act 1953

CI 774505

village, the Inver pours out a torrent of water. A hundred yards to the south, the Culag brings water from Glen Canisp.

Surrounding Lochinver are some of Scotland's most imposing and beautiful mountains. To the southeast is the remarkable form of Suilven; to the northeast are Quinag and Ben More Assynt—all rising starkly from the undulating moorland with a unique profile. Suilven is closest to Lochinver and is known to sailors as "The Sugar Loaf." As seen from the sea, it seems similar to the mountain that towers over Rio de Janeiro. William Daniell's famous 1820 engraving of Suilven was actually done from the site of the future MacKenzie homestead, "Inver."

Inland from the sea loch lie a myriad of fresh water lochs fed by the extremely moist climate of the western Highlands. A hundred years ago sheep farming, deer stalking, and lobster fishing were the main "industries" of Assynt. More recently the harbor has been used by deep-water fishing trawlers from all over Europe.

TOP: ALISTER MACKENZIE'S BIRTH CERTIFICATE OF 1870. HIS REAL NAME WAS ALEXANDER. **BOTTOM:** SEVERAL OF SCOTLAND'S LARGEST MOUNTAINS ARE NEAR LOCHINVER, WHERE ALISTER GREW UP. SAILORS CALL SUILVEN "THE SUGAR LOAF."

All this had been the MacKenzie clan's ancestral land from about 1670 until the 1745 rebellion of Bonnie Prince Charlie and the decisive defeat at the Battle of Culloden. The title to the land was then passed over to "lairds" from the south of Scotland or from England, who proceeded to relocate most of the historic inhabitants to tiny rented homesteads to clear the way for vast sporting estates or large sheep farms. Many of these people were later driven from the land by exorbitant rents and emigrated to America or Australia.

Lochinver eventually passed into the hands of the Duke of Sutherland, one of the most ruthless of all the incoming landowners. The MacKenzies held on and prospered in Lochinver, however, thanks mainly perhaps to Alister's grandfather. Alexander "Meal Mhor" MacKenzie became the Duke's "ground officer" for Assynt.[1] In this position, his duties included the agronomy of keeping the estate in good shape for deer stalking, the unenviable task of collecting rent from his fellow residents, and the carrying out of other orders of the Duke. Thus "Meal Mhor" is remembered in the area with a mixture of respect and fear.

As a consequence of his job, though, "Meal Mhor" acquired for himself and his family entree into a level of society that was strictly denied to his ancestors and friends. The MacKenzies took advantage of this as the next two generations indulged in salmon fishing, deer stalking, and other pursuits usually reserved for the aristocrats. "Meal Mhor" was also able to send his son, William Scobie MacKenzie, to medical school. In turn, Dr. William reared children who distinguished themselves in professional life. All of this, in combination with the marriages of both Doctor William and Alister (which could be described as "financially fortunate"), led to the family becoming well established several rungs higher on the ladder of life. By the time Dr. William retired and returned to Lochinver, he was comfortably part of the laird's entourage.

Alister's father always considered Lochinver his true home. He is buried there and it was Alister's own wish—one that was not to be fulfilled—that he also should be. Dr. William's training in Glasgow and practice in Normanton were only temporary absences while he made his way in medicine. As soon as he could afford to, he retired from practice in Normanton and moved back to Lochinver. Even though Dr. William was retired, many residents sought medical care from him rather than from the local practitioner.

[1] *Meal Mhor is Gaelic for "Big Man of the Hill."*

Like his father before him, Dr. William was a figure of authority and respect. Upright and handsome with a speckled beard, he regularly wore a cloak, often of tartan, and a "double-snooter" (Sherlock Holmes) hat. Once back in Lochinver he purchased a fine 40-foot yacht, *The Gipsy*, for his family. He sailed his boat, dealt with the medical practice forced upon him, and entertained friends from around the district. He also went for long tramps around the countryside, stopping to chat with every local he met. Following his death in 1917, his burial was the last in the family grave at Nedd.

The activities of the MacKenzie family members were catalogued by Alister's niece, Mary Bowman (she died in 1999).[2] She recorded this forty years ago for Henry Longhurst, the distinguished golf writer, who had asked for information about Alister's life. At the time, she was both the last surviving participant in those holidays and the last member of the family with a clear, and fond, memory of Alister. The relevant section ran:

Dr. MacKenzie's father was tremendously keen on open-air pursuits for his children and the whole family used to migrate to Sutherland, on the NW coast of Scotland for holidays. An old Highland friend tells of the envy she and her brothers and sisters felt because the MacKenzies enjoyed so much freedom. "They were so athletic and were always to be seen swimming, canoeing and

fishing in the bay," she said recently. Dr. MacKenzie [Alister] was also a good shot and learned the art of stalking at an early age. Indeed, the head of a fine 'Royal' (twelve-pointer stag) shot by him in 1912 still hangs in the old family home in Sutherland.

Alister was the eldest of the surviving children (one died at birth). He had two younger brothers, William and Charles Atkinson, and two sisters, Marion Ellen and Mary ("Mabie"). As the eldest, he was the

[2]*To get the flavor of the wonderful times experienced by the MacKenzie children, one could do no better than read Arthur Ransome's books, beginning with* Swallows and Amazons, *describing such real adventure sailing holidays. Ransome's family lived close to the MacKenzies in Leeds, though his own childhood holidays were set in the Lake District of northwest England.*

OPPOSITE PAGE, LEFT: WILLIAM DANIELL DID THIS ENGRAVING OF SUILVEN IN 1820. **OPPOSITE PAGE, RIGHT:** THE FAMILY GRAVE AT NEDD. **ABOVE, LEFT:** WHEN ALISTER'S PHYSICIAN FATHER, WILLIAM, RETIRED FROM PRACTICE IN ENGLAND, HE MOVED INTO THIS HOUSE IN LOCHINVER. **ABOVE, RIGHT:** THE MACKENZIE CHILDREN LAUNCHED BOATS FROM THE DOCK AT PORT ARTHUR.

leader of this adventuresome group throughout their childhood. He was also involved in the field sports that abounded in Lochinver.

At one end of the compact Inver area occupied by the MacKenzie family was Port Arthur. From here, the children could launch a boat to simply row or to fish in the sea. They could go out to *The Gipsy*, and, given permission and the services of the crew, sail out into the broad seas of the Minch, between the Outer Hebrides and the Scottish mainland.

Mostly, though, the voyages of *The Gipsy* were to neighboring islands and bays, such as Enard Bay in Coigach—reachable in a day. Going north was something of an adventure, because it meant rounding the hazardous cliffs of Rhu Stoer promontory. But *The Gipsy* was quite capable of sailing to distant waters. She not only had sleeping berths and

an auxiliary engine, a great rarity then, but also—something of a marvel in those parts in those days—a flushable toilet. This was an era when Dr. William was campaigning for a proper main water supply for the Lochinver community. John MacRae, son of *The Gipsy's* skipper at the time, recalls seeing this toilet on board before he had ever seen one on dry land. He was instructed on how to manipulate the levers to achieve a flush. When it happened, it was such a torrent that he panicked, thinking the vessel was going to sink!

The Gipsy is also remembered for the fact that malt whisky was always freely available on board; ten-year-old whisky for the crew and

THE MOUTH OF THE INVER RIVER IN LOCHINVER.

15-year-old whisky for the MacKenzies and their guests! (Years later, when writing about the appropriateness of water hazards on golf courses, Alister quipped: "Being a Scotsman, I am naturally opposed to water in its undiluted state.")

Away from Port Arthur, going inland, only a few steps would take them to the wonderful salmon pools and leaps of the lower reaches of the Inver River. There was some of the best and most beautiful salmon fishing to which ordinary mortals would have great difficulty in gaining access. Following the beautiful riverside path upwards for a mile or so, they would eventually emerge from the trees to a moorland landscape where lochs of all shapes and sizes awaited their fishing rods. Longer paths were also available when the children wanted to climb the Suilven and Canisp mountains.

In addition, Dr. William established a shooting range that allowed targets set up on the Inver side to be addressed across the water from the village side where a War Memorial now stands. From here, not only did he teach his family to shoot, but any of the local lads who were keen to learn as well.

Once skilled in the handling of a gun on the range, there were plenty of opportunities for using it on live targets. Rough shooting abounded, but the serious business was the stalking of the red deer during autumn. The forests of Assynt have long been famous for deer and have served as a magnet for rich southerners or foreigners to come for the stalking and later to seek possession of the land. Alister certainly undertook the sport of royalty and millionaires, and the head of the twelve-pointer he shot in 1912 is testimony.

Stalking is a sport that is, in large measure, an exercise in using human cunning to outwit the natural camouflage of the red deer. The animal's coloring renders it invisible to all but the most skilled eye, even when assisted by all possible magnification. So stalking can be seen as something that probably had a central role in Alister's development in later life. Stalking/camouflage/golf course design constituted a logical progression, although Alister never seemed to have expressed awareness of the stalking and camouflage link.

While Alister was a happy participant during the Lochinver visits and the activities in his youth, when the next generation came along—having no children of his own—he probably felt out of place. He had a great affection for Marion's children, but it is likely that he visited less often. It is reasonably certain the last years that he was at Lochinver were 1912 and 1919. In 1912 *The Gipsy* made a circumnavigation of northern Scotland and took part in the regattas on the Firth of Clyde. The last voyage of the ship under the MacKenzies was in 1919, taking her to a new owner in Ireland. It involved Alister and one of his brothers (probably Charles). One version of the trip is that it ended in shipwreck; another version is that it nearly did so.

Surprisingly, the only sport that Lochinver did not offer was golf. It was as far away from a golf course as it is possible to get in Scotland. Royal Dornoch, 50 miles to the east, was the closest. The MacKenzies were apparently too busy with their other pursuits, that they ignored it. Alister never even mentioned Royal Dornoch in his writings. It's possible, of course, that it was because it was the home of a competitor [Donald Ross]. More likely, it is because he never played there. Dr. William had not grown up around golf either, and though he took up the game later in life as a social pastime, he was far from hooked on the sport. Whatever early interest Alister may have had in the game was curtailed by a rugby injury at school that left him with a permanent wrist injury. Therefore, if he hadn't become so mentally stimulated by the game, it is doubtful he would have played at all.

For someone who became so famous in the world of golf, it is remarkable how difficult it is to find first-hand accounts about Dr. MacKenzie's personality. He made his mark around the world, and yet—except for his time at Pasatiempo in his later years—he seldom stayed long enough anywhere for people to get to know him. Nearly all of his partners and contemporaries were dead by the end of World War II before the interest in golf architecture had its renaissance. And around Leeds, where Alister's career started and where people knew him best, there was a strange reluctance to talk about him due to a consequence of a family disruption. The Alwoodley Club, where he had his introduction to course design, refused to acknowledge his role for half a century. It is also odd that in Normanton and Lochinver, Alister's father is more readily remembered than Alister himself, even though Dr. William died in 1917.

While Dr. William is remembered fondly wherever he lived, there is a marked difference between his image in Lochinver and that in Normanton—which may give us a revealing slant on Alister's personality. Around Normanton, sporting a tartan cape as he drove his pony and trap, he was something of a "character," with a cheerful quip for most citizens he met.[3] In England this bold, outgoing way might have been offensive to some; in Scotland, a similar personality is admired. The Scots have a word for it: "gallus"—a jovial, roguish, outgoing, confident personality with a scorn for convention and a fearlessness. (It derives from the expression "gallows humor" to describe someone who can laugh in the face of any adversity.) This might also be a good description of Dr. William's eldest son Alister, because he, too, could be taken either way.

This personality may have had a lot to do with the slow start of Alister's design career—the confidence Alister exuded on the world stage may have been interpreted as arrogance by the reserved English who paid for his advice early in his career.

[3] *The story lives that one day he had some form of collision with a lady pushing her baby in a pram. An altercation followed that Dr. William concluded with this pithy line: "Madam, you can get a new baby much more easily than I can get a new pony!"*

~ MacKenzie the Doctor ~

In his writings, MacKenzie made repeated references to his training as "a medical man." Several magazine articles about him, and even a book, have also referred to him as "The Good Doctor." All of this, of course, raises the question: was Alister a good doctor?

Apart from his service as a Civil Surgeon during the Boer War of 1899-1902, and as a medical officer for the Territorial Army (reserves) from 1910 through the middle of World War I, Alister's medical career was less than memorable. A review of his scholastic career provides unusual insight into MacKenzie, the so-called "Good Doctor."

Alister began his pre-clinical medical training at Gonville and Caius College, Cambridge, on October 1, 1888. In 1891, he passed the Cambridge Natural Sciences Tripos Part I, Class III. Since Cambridge did not have a clinical medical school, however, Alister chose to continue his studies at Leeds.

In 1895 he entered the British medical register by passing the examinations for the Membership of the Royal College of Surgeons and the Licentiateship of the Royal College of Physicians. Two years later, he obtained the Cambridge medical degree: Bachelor of Medicine and Surgery. Yet even after his role as a "Civil Surgeon" in the Boer War, Alister was still registered as an undergraduate student at Leeds. This lasted until he passed the school's examinations in 1905—17 years after he'd begun his studies—on the first occasion on which Leeds University awarded its own degree independently.

Being a "medical student" is not the same thing as being a "student of medicine." The latter implies endeavoring to advance medical knowledge. However, there is no evidence to suggest that Alister was ever so involved. Being a medical student, on the other hand, can be a completely passive state that only requires annual matriculation and payment of the necessary fees.

This was a time when "chronic" medical students were common. Many offered variations on a story about a rich but rather naive aunt who—in her confused wisdom—endowed the favored nephew with a generous annuity to be paid "while he continues to be a medical student." Such a situation could account for a reluctance to relinquish the student status.

Alister was an unusual long-term student in that he had no serious examination problems. He might merely have wanted to collect more letters to put after his name. He was much more interested in practical achievement than in scholarship in his later endeavors as a camouflage expert and as a golf course architect. On the other hand, he certainly liked to use "Doctor" before his name in golfing circles and emphasized his medical background in all his writings, fully aware that it was impressive to many people.

In fact, MacKenzie's medical career was not very impressive. From 1895 until 1907, he worked as a doctor around Leeds, first assisting his father in Normanton. After his stint in the Boer War, he managed to obtain numerous titles. He was House Surgeon at Leeds General Infirmary and, for a spell, anesthetist there. He was also Medical Examiner to the New York Mutual Life Association and Honorary Medical Officer at Leeds Public Dispensary. The reality is, the titles sounded much more important than they really were.

In 1907, he was appointed "Consultant Surgeon" at St. Monica's Hospital in Easingwold. St. Monica's was an outpost about 40 miles from Leeds that was so small it only had a total of 11 beds. Throughout this appointment he continued to live in Leeds at Moor Allerton Lodge. During this time he became involved with the development of his first golf course designs at Alwoodley and Moortown, which were close to his residence.

Based on existing information, there is little to suggest that Dr. Alister MacKenzie was particularly interested in medicine. In spite of his plethora of lower medical qualifications, he never reached for anything higher; in contrast to his numerous writings—not only on golf course architecture but on camouflage as well— he wrote nothing on medicine.

Interestingly, his most profound reference to his own medical career came in his 1920 book, *Golf Architecture*, when he wrote:

How frequently have I, with great difficulty, persuaded patients who were never off my door-step to take up golf and how rarely, if ever, have I seen them in my consulting rooms again.

No evidence exists that Alister even considered the possibility that any of these patients—when presented with golf as a prescription for their illness—felt they were not being taken seriously and sought the opinion of a more conventional physician.

What seems clear is that Alister preferred to work outdoors and with the land, as his grandfather had done, rather than work with sick humans like his father. It seems he strayed into the profession because it was "in the family." To measure his medical career in golfing terms, one could fairly say that he never got off the first tee.

And golfers around the world are better off because of it.

Chapter Three
Prewar Contracts in the North of England

IT IS A COMMON PERCEPTION THAT MACKENZIE REMAINED IN MEDICINE UNTIL HE WAS "DISCOVERED" BY A MAGAZINE COMPETITION IN 1914. IN FACT, WITH HIS REPUTATION FIRMLY ESTABLISHED by the twin successes of Alwoodley and Moortown, Alister found himself in demand as an architect throughout the north of England even before the first World War. Today, his name is attached to more than 75 courses in the British Isles (see Appendix).

It is important to note, however, that the development of golf courses in that era was much different than it is now. Therefore, to what extent this early work continues to be (or ever was) a testament to the doctor's design theories is difficult to pin down. It had only been a few years since Willie Park, Harry Colt, and Charles Blair Macdonald helped cause the term "golf architect" to be coined, and in Britain—where golf had always been a game played across the natural ground—many clubs viewed a golf course architect as more of a luxury than a necessity. Previously, good local players were trusted to suggest how a course might be improved. The design of Douglas Water Golf Course in Scotland, for example, is credited in *Donald Steel's Golf Course Guide to Britain and Ireland* to "striking coal miners in 1921."

MacKenzie twice published extensive lists of the courses that he had designed as part of brochures for his business, and these are the basis for the courses that we are documenting in this book. At first, we treated these lists with skepticism because it was good business for an architect to claim as many successes as possible. Therefore, many were tempted to stretch the truth. Alister's various partnerships over the years allowed him to "claim" many courses on which his personal involvement was negligible. His business brochure from 1928, for example, proudly lists Pebble Beach alongside Cypress Point as one of "his" works, when it was originally laid-out by Jack Neville and Douglas Grant. MacKenzie's claim was probably based on the redesign of several holes by H. Chandler Egan, who was MacKenzie's partner for a short time. But further research revealed that MacKenzie was, in fact, personally involved in the remodeling of Pebble's 8th and 13th greens.

With many of his early commissions, MacKenzie's advice was made during a single day's visit. That was the case at Darlington Golf Club, which hired MacKenzie in preference to Willie Park and authorized his fee of "Ten Guineas for the first day (about $50) and Five Guineas for the second day, if necessary." And that was to design eighteen new holes!

Due to the time and budget constraints he was under, it was difficult—if not impossible—for Dr. MacKenzie to express his bold ideas fully. And even if construction was carried out, it may not have accurately followed his thoughts. Several courses where he actually supervised the work have been abandoned or relocated, including Wheatley Park Golf Club in Doncaster and Fulford Golf Club near York. Illustrations of bunkers at Fulford were proudly displayed in MacKenzie's 1920 book, *Golf Architecture*.

Bunker work of MacKenzie's that has *survived* that was also included in his book can be seen at Headingley Golf Club in Leeds and the City of

THE 380-YARD PAR-4 18TH AT MOORTOWN. AN ANGLED GREEN PROTECTED BY DEEP BUNKERS AT THE RIGHT-FRONT REWARDS A STRONG DRIVE UP THE LEFT SIDE. BUT OUT-OF-BOUNDS IS IN PLAY FOR A PULLED TEE SHOT. THE GREEN IS SET IMMEDIATELY IN FRONT OF THE CLUBHOUSE AS AT LYTHAM AND TROON.

Newcastle Golf Club. The redesigned 16th and 17th greens at Headingley are also top-quality MacKenzie. However, perhaps his best surviving prewar work after Alwoodley and Moortown is to be found at Reddish Vale Golf Club in Cheshire. While its rollercoaster routing over undulating valleys is one that some might dismiss as "sporty," many of the holes capture the spirit of pleasurable excitement that MacKenzie's holes aimed for.

A portion of Dr. MacKenzie's pre-1914 work also displays a creative, "seat-of-the-pants" approach to design and construction frequently seen in the designs of contemporary architect Pete Dye. Garforth Golf Club near Leeds, for only one example, was once the site of an old mine working. MacKenzie used some of the mining debris to build up tees and greens and covered other 'pit heaps' with long grass and sand to imitate dunes. (After the war, he took a similar approach using old mine workings at Cleckheaton & District Golf Club in West Yorkshire.) At Sitwell Park in England, the local paper reported on an unusual method of construction, perhaps inspired by MacKenzie's service in South Africa:

Holes have been drilled in several places and explosives inserted which were then fired by electricity. One of the most experienced shot-firers in the district has been put in charge of the work which had so far been carried out with gratifying success. These runaway bunkers are placed in the fairway . . . When the shots are fired the earth is ripped up to a depth of 3-4 ft and the soil is blown out. These are left in the rough state and will be turfed over, the pans being slightly sloping away from the tee.

MacKenzie would later comment in his camouflage writings on the usefulness of shell craters as hiding places, noting that a captured enemy trench was a most dangerous position because enemy artillery knew its precise range: "These captured trenches acted as dummies and absorbed the attention of the enemy's artillery while the attacking force remained in safety in front of them." He was already finding the parallels between his two interests.

In England, however, MacKenzie's work is stereotyped not for his knack for finding interesting golf holes on undulating property, but for his penchant for multitiered greens. In the north of England, almost any two-tiered green is called a "MacKenzie green," and the odds are good that Alister had a hand in its creation. On a trip to Cavendish—made simply because it was reputed to be a MacKenzie design—a researcher was assured by the assistant professional that "we have several MacKenzie greens here." All of them, in fact, were MacKenzie's—but only six or eight of them were two-tiered! MacKenzie acknowledged in

The Spirit of St. Andrews that the situation annoyed him when he said that "every freak green in Britain is termed a MacKenzie green." He continued:

During the championship at Hoylake, I was returning to Liverpool by train in a railway carriage with a number of golfers who were discussing Hoylake and other greens.

None of them knew who I was, and one of them turned to me and said, "We have some of these infernal MacKenzie greens on our course." I remarked, "Was Dr. MacKenzie responsible for them?" He replied, "Well, they are called 'MacKenzie greens,' so he must have made them." I asked him what was the name of his course, and he mentioned a course near Liverpool. Much to the amusement of the other occupants of the carriage, I remarked, "I happen to be Dr. MacKenzie. I have never seen or even heard of your blasted course, so how I can be responsible for your greens I don't know.

MacKenzie's fondness for severe greens reached a new peak in 1913, and one can speculate as to the reason. In 1912, Harry Colt built a third 18-hole course in St. Andrews. It was called the Eden Course, and it was a commission that naturally brought great prestige. The two men would not become partners until 1919, but Colt was friendly with Dr. MacKenzie from their time together at Alwoodley. Though MacKenzie in his writings was always quick to give Colt the full credit for the Eden

Course, it is very likely that MacKenzie spent a lot of time in St. Andrews during its construction. (MacKenzie had to have spent several weeks in St. Andrews learning the finer points of The Old Course in order to write about them so well in his 1920 book. Since he was quite busy during the Great War, this would appear to be the most likely time.)

For various reasons—to make room for larger practice facilities, for example—the Eden Course has changed somewhat over the years. Originally, all of its four short holes featured stunningly contoured, outlandish greens, just as severe as some of those on The Old Course, if not more so. (In fact, they're actually more like the famous "Himalayas," the St. Andrews Ladies' Putting Green that adjoins the second tee of The Old Course and which MacKenzie admired in *Golf Architecture*.) What's puzzling about these Eden course greens—today's first, fifth, and 14th—is that they are much more severe than anything Colt ever designed, before

OPPOSITE PAGE, LEFT: THE FIRST HOLE AT REDDISH VALE GOLF CLUB IN CHESHIRE. OPPOSITE PAGE, RIGHT: 10TH AT CAVENDISH IN THE NORTH OF ENGLAND. ABOVE, LEFT: ANOTHER "MACKENZIE GREEN"–THE 15TH AT CAVENDISH. ABOVE, RIGHT: THE OLD THIRD GREEN (NOW THE FIRST) ON THE EDEN COURSE AT ST. ANDREWS.

or after, and quite out of character for him. Consider this excerpt from Colt's "Some Essays on Golf Architecture," written in 1920:

If a player is conscious that he has gauged an approach putt well and that he has struck it truly he likes to see it go in or dead, and it is nothing but a torment to watch his ball, guided by powers which are beyond his control, go rushing down a steep place like swine possessed by a devil. . . . Mortals should bow to the inexorable law of gravity.

It's possible that this statement was meant to distance himself from his new partner, MacKenzie, but it is also unmistakably the viewpoint of a good player—which Colt was and MacKenzie wasn't. So how to explain the first green on the Eden Course? If MacKenzie didn't strongly influence its creation, it very well may be that the design of that green influenced *him*, because from 1913 onward he became known for undu-lating greens so severe that they set his work apart.

The first course that MacKenzie built after the completion of Colt's Eden course was his layout for Sir George Sitwell at Sitwell Park, Rotherham, South Yorkshire. It galvanized MacKenzie's reputation in England. For MacKenzie, it was a watershed moment in his career. Sir George was MacKenzie's first private client. Until this point he had been dealing with green committees, except at Alwoodley and Moortown, where he was among the founders. Sir George was really the first client who provided the doctor with both the money and the freedom to let his ideas run wild. Sir George also appointed Sir Edward Lutyens, architect of many famous buildings including the Viceroy's House, New Delhi, and the British Embassy, Washington DC, to design the clubhouse, and Hamilton Temple Smith, a director of Heals, the famous furniture makers

THE GOLD
∼ CHALLENGE CUP ∼

Whatever rivalries and frictions that may have existed between Alister MacKenzie and Harry Colt when they were alive, it is nice to be able to report that long after their deaths, the memory of each is honored through competition of a different kind. The Gold Challenge Cup is an annual competition between winners of the Colt Cup (played for by members of clubs designed by Harry) and the MacKenzie Medallion (played for by members of clubs designed by Alister).

In the year 2000, Camberley Heath Golf Club (winners of the previous Colt Cup) played a friendly match against Sandmoor Golf Club (winners of the previous MacKenzie Medallion). Sandmoor came away with both the victory and the Gold Challenge Cup, the trophy having been generously donated by Stoke Poges Golf Club (appropriately enough, a Colt/Alison design).

THE OLD SEVENTH GREEN (NOW THE FIFTH) ON THE EDEN COURSE. **OPPOSITE PAGE:** THE 140-YARD SHORT HOLE AT SITWELL PARK.

of Tottenham Court Road, London, was appointed to design the furniture for it. So Alister was in very top-class company on this project.

Sitwell Park eventually came to fruition, but not without some growing pains. The winter of 1913-1914 was a wet one and it put construction behind schedule. Then the war intervened, suspending hopes of establishing an elite membership club. There were problems with the course's drainage system as well, perhaps stemming in part from MacKenzie's more extensive construction of greens and bunkers. Finally, the club secretary began to question the severity of some putting surfaces and the ability of the greens superintendent/foreman. The superintendent had been appointed by MacKenzie and had defended the doctor's work.

Sitwell Park took MacKenzie's elaborate contouring of greens into a new and steeper dimension. From his surviving sketches, it is clear that

MacKenzie intended that the contours of the green and its surrounding bunkers should determine the play of the hole. At Sitwell Park, he built greens that were more undulating than anything before seen on a man-made golf course. The most graphic example of this was a 140-yard par 3—illustrated in golf architecture books of the day—with a putting surface that fell off more than ten feet from back to front in several distinct levels. Apparently, several of the other greens were also heavily contoured.

When the course finally opened, it was immediately controversial. A few professional golfers (some of whom were starting to compete with Dr. MacKenzie for design commissions) were very critical of the greens, insisting that they were unfair to play on and out of place for an inland course. MacKenzie was not at all surprised by the reaction; his later writings made it very clear that he knew his ideas on design were different,

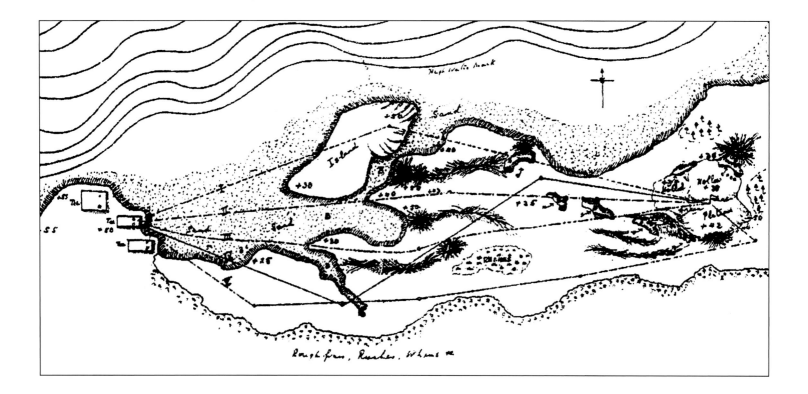

and he expected criticism by those of the "card and pencil" fraternity. His client, on the other hand, was not at all prepared for the outcry. He also did not share MacKenzie's thick skin, and wondered whether what Alister had built was making him a laughingstock. By the mid-1920s, the course was closed and several of the greens were leveled, taking the teeth and the interest out of the layout. MacKenzie duly noted in *The Spirit of St. Andrews* that changes to the course had made it insipid and dull, and that the membership had dwindled. However, the economic troubles of the day could also have had some bearing on the latter point. To the very end, though, he was convinced that the course had been a bold move in the right direction.

Some aspects of the course remain intact today, but what made Sitwell Park controversial and noteworthy—for better or worse—was long ago erased.

In the spring of 1914, the London periodical *Country Life*, whose golf editor was Bernard Darwin, (grandson of Charles), announced a one-

time competition in golf architecture. The best design submitted for an original two-shot hole would be used as the finishing hole on an American course being developed by Charles Blair Macdonald at Lido, Long Island, New York. Horace Hutchinson, Darwin, and Macdonald were to be the judges.

The August 1, 1914 issue illustrated the prizewinning design of Dr. MacKenzie, with commentary by Bernard Darwin:

The First Prize Design

Dr. MacKenzie is very well known as a golfing architect, more especially in the North of England, where he has one striking monument to his skill in the Alwoodley course, near Leeds. His design has been clearly thought out with the greatest care, and is most ingenious. In the memorandum attached to his drawing he explains the principle on which the hole is laid out: "An effort has been made in designing this hole to produce the old type of golf in which a player has no fixed line to the hole, but has to use his own judgment in playing it according to varying conditions of wind, etc. In this respect it is somewhat similar to the long hole coming in at St. Andrews. The green is guarded by bunkers and a large hillock (15 to 20 feet high) on the right side of the approach, and is tilted up from the front to the back and from left to right, so that the approach from the left is an easy one and from the right necessitates such a difficult pitch that the player is likely to overrun the green into the bunker beyond." This idea has been most successfully carried out, for the five different routes open to the player are all interesting; and his choice must vary from day to day, according to the state of the weather and under no condition could the hole be of a cut-and-dried nature. It is highly entertaining to follow out the different roads that lead to the hole and see how skillfully all sorts of possibilities have been foreseen. The short driver who sneaks round by the right-hand road is forced to tack to the left before he can approach the green, since a mountain effectually blocks his path on the right. He who takes the left-hand road by way of the island can get home in two, but in order to do this he has to run a very considerable risk with his tee shot, for the island is uncommonly narrow in its narrowest part. It is a possible criticism that it is just a little too narrow, but it may be observed that the ground rises towards the end of the island; the ball is likely to fall tolerably dead rather than to run away into the sandy desert on either side. Even the man who takes the boldest line of all and drives a fine ball straight on the hole, through he reaps a proper reward, has still plenty of interest in the shape of bunkers to carry. One criticism that has been suggested is that with so very large an area of sand the green keeper might often be tearing his hair over the problem of blown sand. Dr. MacKenzie has thought out everything so carefully that very likely he has thought of this point and has an effective answer. In any case the flaw is a very small one in a design of the utmost ingenuity.

MacKenzie may have also drawn inspiration from the rocky, island-strewn coast around Lochinver in western Scotland where his family returned every summer. Alister's entry was a stunningly complex design; such ideas as an alternate fairway or an island fairway were completely original at that time. Most of all, the suggestion that it was a hole like those in the early days of golf (where there was no predetermined best route to the hole) was very radical in a profession whose members normally attempted to define just that.

A closer inspection reveals just how severe the design really was. The plan shows a three-level green with the rear portion eight feet above the front. At the front right edge of the green there's a twenty-foot sand hill that completely blocks the approach from that angle, so that weaker players might have to swing around the back of the green before chipping on. The island landing area itself has a 20-foot rise to stop shots from bounding over it. The elevations, however, have been carefully thought out so that all of the hazards are plainly visible to the golfer wherever he may be on the way to the hole.

Even though there is a common perception today that MacKenzie was merely dabbling in course design while practicing medicine, it is clear from the 1914 *Country Life* piece that Darwin recognized him as a golf architect. By this time, MacKenzie had at least eight new courses and eight major renovations already to his credit, and it was clear his passion was with golf architecture. But by using the title of "Doctor" in its piece, *Country Life* gave the impression that MacKenzie was someone on the same level as its distinguished readers. This was not lost on MacKenzie, who proceeded to take the hint and trumpeted his medical training in all of his public relations from then on.

Winning first place in the design competition and the realization that he could compete on the international stage was a huge boost to MacKenzie's confidence. (*Country Life* not only was read by the upper crust society in England but also in every English-speaking country around the world.) Unfortunately, it would be some time before he could capitalize on his new fame. The announcement in the August 1, 1914 issue that he had won coincided with another major event: declarations of war across Europe.

MacKenzie, as a Surgeon Captain of the Territorial Army reserves, was immediately called up to active duty.

Chapter Four
War and Camouflage

LANDSCAPING TAKES SEVERAL FORMS, ONE OF WHICH IS CAMOU-FLAGING. INVOLVEMENT WITH THIS WAS A BIG STEP IN ALISTER'S CONVERSION FROM DOCTOR TO GOLF COURSE DESIGNER. HE WAS introduced to civilian (natural) camouflage while stalking red deer around Lochinver. His military involvement with camouflage (artificial) was spread over three conflicts: the Boer War in South Africa, 1899-1902; World War I in Europe, 1914-1918; and the "Troubles" in Ireland in the early 1920s.[1]

During the Boer War, MacKenzie saw the irregular Boers (Dutch immigrants who had settled South Africa more than a hundred years earlier), with small resources, repeatedly make fools of the vastly stronger British forces—particularly at the Battle of Colenso. He attributed this to the Boers' intelligent use of landscape features to disguise their activities as opposed to the British stupidly ignoring the protection that nature offered.

Long after, MacKenzie wrote the following in *The Military Engineer*:

My own interest in camouflage was aroused while I was serving in the Boer War and particularly during the black week of the war when the Boers, by means of ambushes, wiped out the British at the battles of Colenso, Magersfontein, and Stormberg. At the Battle of Colenso, with which I was best acquainted, the Boers by means of dummy fortifications behind, and concealed positions in front of the Tugela River, annihilated Buller's army with the loss of only five wounded men.

The brilliant successes of the Boers were due to a great extent to their making the best use of natural cover and the construction of artificial cover indistinguishable from nature. I made a close study of the subject because it was obvious that if similar ideas were developed along scientific lines even greater results could be attained.

At that time, MacKenzie was giving medical support to the infantry and would "mess" in their company rather than with the medical staff. He came to realize that the infantryman's concern with the terrain on which he operated had many similarities to the golfer's concern with the terrain on the golf course that he played. The sand table is the experimental base of the infantry tactician: on it he can construct models of territory, modify them, and conduct TEWTs (Tactical Exercises Without Troops) to his heart's content. The same sort of kit can be adapted for

[1]*In view of MacKenzie's very extensive and highly unconventional military involvement, it is remarkable that despite many inquiries to army record offices, nothing had emerged to formally confirm the fact that he had served. Then in 1997, Major R.S. Cross, Assistant Secretary to the Light Infantry, made a very astute observation: On a silver statuette of a soldier in Boer War uniform presented by a group of officers in memory of those who had died in the war was the engraved name of "Civil Surgeon A MacKenzie" as one who had contributed to the cost. "Civil" apparently stood for "civilian" to differentiate him from the common "uncivil" variety of doctors. He was serving with rather than in the Somerset Light Infantry.*

golf hole design. MacKenzie did his own adaptation for greens using plasticine models rather than sand. In a military offensive, the aim is to capture an objective with minimal casualties; in golf, it is to get the ball into the cup in minimal strokes. MacKenzie's simplification of the analogy was to state that the military *camoufleur* (practitioner of camouflage) tries to set up insolvable confusions for the enemy, while the course designer uses the same skills to set up solvable puzzles for the competitor. Bunkering is common in both activities.

During World War I, MacKenzie again faced the hell of trench warfare. Although the conditions were entirely different from those in South Africa, he was aware that the Allied Forces were again suffering unnecessarily heavy casualties because of a failure to organize even the simplest camouflage. He found this continuing stupidity difficult to endure and came to realize that few of the professional soldiers had as wide an experience of camouflage and manipulation of ground appearances as he did. Eventually, in 1916, he resigned from the Royal Army Medical Corps (giving up the rank of Major) in order to become a Lieutenant in the Royal Engineers and to do camouflage work. To take this step, he must have been firmly convinced that he had more to contribute to the war effort as a camoufleur than as a practicing doctor.

Unfortunately, this highly unconventional move—typical of the man—did not turn out happily, at least in the short term. It seems his friend from his Boer War days, General Sir Henry Wilson, had led him to believe the he would have the opportunity to develop his own ideas and, at the new camouflage school then being considered, to train others in their application. This did not work out.

Alister's earliest military camouflage exercises during World War I have been reported to have involved trench digging around the Moortown golf course at Leeds. In time, he was posted to the new British Army Camouflage School in London. It was located at Kensington Gardens, an appendage of Hyde Park. Since MacKenzie had anticipated that he would be in charge, it's easy to imagine his reaction when he learned that General Sir Douglas Haig (then Wilson's superior) had selected from civilian life one Solomon J. Solomon, an artist of distinction, to undertake this task.

Several years later, in an article in *The Military Engineer,* MacKenzie

claimed that he was the head of the camouflage school, but the records of the Royal Engineers make it clear that Solomon was in charge. Alister, though, may have been responsible for cajoling the military to set up the school, and this would not be expected to appear in the records. It is said that MacKenzie's demonstration of trench digging and concealment in Hyde Park resulted in admiration by King George the V. Even if true, it would be of little consolation.

Here was MacKenzie, someone with the experience of two wars and who had sacrificed rank in order to do camouflage work, having as his senior a novitiate to military affairs *and* someone who had been presented with a higher rank. But not only rank rankled MacKenzie. Solomon was an established portrait painter in London society and became a Royal Academician, commonly abbreviated to *R.A.*[2] As a consequence of Solomon's portraiture activities, he had contacts with people of importance in almost every sphere of London life, including generals and cabinet ministers (without whom it is unlikely he would have obtained his position). The relevance of having painted portraits of the regal, the noble, or the merely wealthy to teaching military camouflage may not seem immediately obvious. What needs to be realized is that the portraitist must develop a certain skill at disguising features—even if it is only to hide the warts, blemishes, and scars of his sitters in order to satisfy their vanity.

Solomon's military role involved little disturbance of his private and very active social life: home and studio were within walking distance of Kensington Gardens. This surely added to MacKenzie's irritation. Solomon, as might be expected, tried to recruit fellow painters to the school with similar ideas to his own. This left MacKenzie subordinated and isolated on matters of camouflage, and it is doubtful that he was very congenial to his "comrades in brushes."

For the ideas of camoufleurs to be realized on the battlefield, it requires acceptance by the commanders on the ground. This was not readily forthcoming during World War I and, even if they were accepted,

[2]*At the time of the ceremony for Solomon's admission to these exalted ranks, a wag was heard to say, "Come along and see Solomon R A'd in all his glory!"*

ADDING FUEL
~ TO THE FIRE ~

There was a subplot to the relationship that MacKenzie had with Solomon and his painting that may have contributed to it being such a poor one. In Leeds, Alister had been acquainted with members of a family named Bacon, owners of a flourishing business in photographic portraiture (they were responsible for the frequently produced photo-portrait of Alister in his dress kilt). Another member of the family, John Henry Frederick Bacon, ARA, was a rival of Solomon's in painting portraits (Alister was to become step-father-in-law to one of Bacon's daughters when he married Hilda Sykes Haddock in 1930; her son, Tony, married Joan Bacon, John's daughter in 1928). In 1911, John Bacon received an important but very time-consuming commission to "The Coronation Luncheon Given to Their Majesties King George V and Queen Mary in Guildhall." Unfortunately, despite his labors to create acceptable likenesses of all the assembled royalty and nobility, the painting was still not complete when Bacon died in February of 1914. Solomon was commissioned to finish it. Obviously, this produced a situation of some delicacy between the Bacon and Solomon families. When Solomon chose to discard what John Bacon had done and start over—especially since all that was required to complete the painting were finishing touches to some of the individual figures—the situation changed to outright animosity.

In 1922, eight years later, Solomon finally finished the painting.

the troops were not qualified to implement the plans. Alister relied on a combination of subtlety and encouragement of general untidiness to obscure what was on the ground. He wrote at some length on the infantryman's systematic "bullshit" training to do things in an orderly, tidy manner, which made him incapable of implementing camouflage that was the antithesis of this. In his view, a trench dug in an irregular manner by an agricultural laborer was safer than one dug by a trained soldier. The soldier would dig to the precise measurements prescribed in the military manual ("… to the nearest thousandth of a millimeter," Alister wrote) with straight, neat edges—all of which made detection by the enemy easier, particularly from the air. Solomon's ideas, on the other hand (as might be expected from a painter), involved creating enemy confusion with the use of painted screens, some of them on a very grand scale. Neither MacKenzie's nor Solomon's approaches found much favor with the infantry commanders.

Many years after the war was over, MacKenzie and Solomon found common cause in expressing their sense of outrage at the frustration of those wasted years in camouflage. Solomon vented his fury at military jealousy and what he saw as disparagement of the artist in *Strategic Camouflage*, a book published in 1920. After Solomon's death in 1927, MacKenzie expressed his own wrath—much of it directed at the painter—in articles that eventually appeared in *The Military Engineer* after Alister died. This mutually posthumous arrangement was probably fortunate for MacKenzie because many of his comments were close to libelous.

The rest of MacKenzie's World War I military service seems to have been wasted as far as being able to make the contribution to the war effort. However, perhaps his mind turned to thoughts relevant to the course designing that he would be doing when the war ended. His frustration would then be turned into miraculous fulfillment.

The strange episode of Alister's later involvement with camouflage in Ireland has received little attention. It happened at a dangerous turning point in Ireland's troubled history, and it now stands as an extraordinary story involving the lives of Alister and two other Boer War veterans over twenty years. These three not only survived that war, they survived the protracted massacre of the First World War—which was even more remarkable. They then became associated, in very different roles,

~ MacKenzie the Military Critic ~

Two pieces of MacKenzie's writing have recently come to light that throw a new and revealing light on his camouflage activities during World War I. The first was in the March 6, 1915 issue of *Country Life*, the magazine that had given his golf design career such a boost only nine months earlier by awarding him the first prize in the competition to design a hole for The Lido Golf Club in New York State. This article, entitled "Military Entrenchments," presents in a well-illustrated way Alister's ideas on military camouflage while roundly criticizing the practices of the officers then in charge. Not surprisingly, there was much counter criticism. In the May 1st issue of *Country Life*, MacKenzie responded by continuing to criticize "Army officers" in general for their failings. To publish criticism of military techniques in the middle of the war seems both brave and foolhardy—editor and writer might have found themselves charged with high treason, punishable by execution if convicted. Luckily, however, events took a different twist and MacKenzie's published comments probably contributed to his getting transferred to the Engineers. The principle that may have applied here is, "The best way to deal with a critic is to embrace him into the fold."

The second piece of Alister's writing that has recently been discovered was done in the United States. It was found in *Professional Memoirs Corps of Engineers, United States Army and Engineer Department at Large, Vol. IX, 1917,* and entitled "Entrenchments and Camouflage; Lecture by a British Army Officer Skilled in Landscape Gardening." It had been known that this piece of writing, not under MacKenzie's name, existed. In *The Spirit of St. Andrews,* MacKenzie indicated that at some time he'd given a senior U.S. officer permission to use his lecture material. The cloak of anonymity was transparently thin; at one point in the article he says, "I wrote on this subject in the winter

MACKENZIE FREQUENTLY CRITICIZED HIS MILITARY SUPERIORS FOR IGNORING HIS CAMOUFLAGE IDEAS THAT HE'D DEVELOPED DURING THE BOER WAR. THIS ARTICLE, ENTITLED "MILITARY ENTRENCHMENTS," APPEARED IN THE MARCH 6, 1915 ISSUE OF *COUNTRY LIFE*.

of 1914-1915 in *Country Life*." The style of writing is his and the details accord with his other writings on the subject. The word "Lecture" in the title is misleading because the piece clearly represents the distillation of several lectures covering much of the camouflage field. Toward the end he incorporated questions he had received after delivering the lectures and the answers he supplied. Asked about the connection between the construction of trenches and golf courses, he replied, "In golf course construction not only do similar revetting problems, construction of breast works, etc., come in, but also an eye for country, imitating and making the best use of natural features, and a similar trend of thought in devising traps for the enemy."

These articles suggest that for some considerable time before he transferred to the Engineers, MacKenzie had been deeply into practical camouflage. How this became possible is hard to comprehend. A doctor in the Medical Corps dabbling in practical military matters not only cuts across the normally rigid boundaries of army units, it is contrary to the Geneva Convention of 1864 which, in theory at least, granted immunity from enemy fire to medical staff entitled to display the Red Cross symbol.

The articles also indicate that when MacKenzie and Solomon met at the Camouflage School, it was not a question of a meeting of the minds—two people new to the camouflage field—that might together have produced some fresh ideas. MacKenzie's mind had clearly been steeped in camouflage for years. The injustice of MacKenzie's position, therefore, seems even greater than had been evident before. Camouflage, MacKenzie's third profession and regarded as a minor one, now comes to rank as a major one. In fact,

the strength of his expression of views on the subject is such that it appears that it was an obsession.

The American paper also raises the question of a fourth MacKenzie profession: Landscape Gardening. The accreditation of his American article does not mention the author as being a camoufleur, a physican or a golf course designer, but states he was "A British Officer Skilled in Landscape Gardening." His Leeds letterhead about this time carried reference to this as something he offered to do, although there isn't any evidence of his having done such work. Perhaps a search of garden designs in Yorkshire from early in this century would reveal more about this activity. All this serves to emphasize the closeness of MacKenzie's work to that of "Capability" Brown, the doyen of British garden and estate landscapers.

with the internal fighting in Ireland in the early 1920s.

The senior was Alister's military mentor, General Sir Henry Wilson, the then Field Marshall, who had made possible his move from the medical corps to the engineers. An Irish Protestant, Wilson had risen to be the senior officer of the British army from 1918 to 1922. Like Alister, he had been deeply affected by the Battle of Colenso when camouflage won the day for the Boers.

The second man was Erskine Childers. Like Alister, he had been born in 1870, but to a well-to-do London family. Contemporaries at Cambridge, Childers followed Alister to the South African war. In 1903, he acquired some fame by writing a best-seller called *The Riddle of the Sands,* an adventure story of yachting and amateur spying set in the Frisian Islands off the northwest coast of Germany. A blend of truth and fiction, as well as being a gripping yarn, the story gave warning to the British public of the build-up of German forces and aggressive intent that culminated in World War I. These predictions earned him a favored position when the war became reality. While most British soldiers had to endure the misery of chronic trench warfare, Childers experienced the

excitement of being a passenger on one of the earliest air raids; a sea plane attack on the German naval base at Cuxhaven on Christmas Day of 1914. Then came intelligence work, followed by more raids using—for those days—futuristic torpedo boats. But there was a deep conflict simmering within Childers that related to the "Irish problem." Of the many Irishmen serving in the British forces, few seemed to have serious concerns about mounting tensions at home over Irish republicanism. For Childers, although English by birth, it was the obsession of his life. (Just before the war began in 1914, he had, with his Boston-born wife, Molly, used his yacht to deliver a cargo of small arms and ammunition for use in the Republican cause into Howth, a little port just north of Dublin.)

Alister was the third of the trio and there are obvious similarities between himself and Childers. Neither was a professional serviceman but, in war, both were considered "loose cannons" (for them, the rigid service organization hardly seemed to exist). Yet, even when holding relatively junior ranks, each seemed to have a mysteriously easy and casual contact with the "men at the top"—Field Marshalls or Admirals.

The little drama came to a climax in 1922, the year when Michael

Collins, the Republican leader and hero was assassinated. In February, just a month after the Irish Free State had come into existence, Wilson completed his time as Chief of Staff and, freed from the constraints of military office, entered politics and got elected to Parliament for North Down, Ulster. His forthright speeches, pressing for radical measures against terrorism, immediately marked him as an enemy to Sinn Fein. The Ulster Unionists, on the other hand, welcomed him and asked him to advise on military matters. Wilson then approached Alister on a personal basis for help with camouflage. Before MacKenzie could become involved, however, Wilson was shot by Sinn Feiners on the steps of his home in London's Belgravia. The assassination triggered the start of the Irish Civil War which, independence from Britain having been obtained, was fought for a year between rival Irish factions.

Childers the Englishman, after serving in World War I, returned to fight for Irish Republicanism. But his contribution was not entirely welcome, even after becoming an Irish citizen. On the run from the Free State forces as a hard-line Republican, he was captured, convicted of possessing an automatic pistol, and shot at dawn on November 24, 1922. Thus Alister was the only one of the three to live to see New Year's Day of 1923. The bullet that killed Wilson possibly saved MacKenzie's life. Had Wilson lived longer, Alister's loyalty to him was such that he would have done all in his power to provide help. Alister might have then become a target for another Sinn Fein bullet.

That even this episode in his life was not the end of Alister's concern with military camouflage is obvious from the posthumous publication of his papers in *The Military Engineer*. His intense interest in the matter has come to the fore through a recently discovered letter that he'd written to the President of the United States (presumably Franklin D. Roosevelt) and certain other major political figures of the day, including the head of the League of Nations. Alister's letter is undated, but from the reference to the completion of Augusta National Golf Club it must have been written shortly before his death:

"The League of Nations has failed to stop the China-Japanese War. I am prepared to submit to you, as President of the United States of America, the League of Nations and both the Chinese and Japanese Forces, a means by which the aggressor in land warfare, even if he is ten times as strong as the defending force, is certain to lose.

These principles do not apply to war at sea or in the air but only to land warfare. I refer to what has become known as camouflage—real camouflage does not exist, as is popularly supposed, in paint. It consists in concealment of the real fortifications & men & the construction of dummy fortifications to divert the enemy's fire from the real forces. These invisible and dummy fortifications are equally effective when viewed from the ground or the air.

It is clear that neither the Japanese or Chinese know anything about real camouflage as the photographs of their defences show that they are both using sand-bags. If both sides made commonsense camouflaged defences, the aggressor would lose so that the war would cease. Sand-bags should only be used for dummy fortifications so as to attract the enemy's fire from the real defences.

My only object in writing this is to assist in the prevention of wars. If the world is convinced the aggressor will lose, war will stop. The efficiency of real camouflage is making defences invulnerable was proven during the Boer War and scores of times since.

If you desire a conference to give me the opportunity of proving my contentions I will be pleased to visit you in Washington. Please do not dismiss this letter from your mind as the ravings of a man who does not know what he is talking about—I have many photographs and other evidence to prove my contentions—I have studied the subject for over 30 years.

During the Autumn of 1914, I implored the British War Office to allow me at my own expense to give demonstrations of new methods of concealing men, gun positions & fortifications but had a terse communication to the effect that the engineers had already given a considerable amount of attention to concealment and they did not consider I could teach the Engineers anything.

Two years after I was brought up to London to give the identical demonstrations which I had offered to give two years previously, and those demonstrations to the Duke of Connaught, Sir Wm. Robertson and many leading generals and members of the Army Council, men largely responsible for the formation of the School of Camouflage in Kensington Gardens in London, England. General Lassiter of the US Army visited the School in its early stages and General Dawes has also seen some of my photographs. Neither of them saw enough to obtain a clear conception of the value of camouflage, nevertheless they both appeared to be impressed.

I am prepared to prove conclusively that a small body of civilian sportsmen with a few weeks training in camouflage on the defensive can defeat with certainty an attacking regular army of ten times their numbers.

My contentions can be easily verified in Army manuals. The proof is easy, as in these days cameras can be substituted for firearms as in mimic warfare between airplanes.

Bitter experience has taught that it is useless submitting this to a War Office or a jury composed entirely of soldiers. It would be as responsible to submit a question regarding the stoppage of religion to a jury of clergymen.

If my contention is right it means the disbandment of all land armies and few soldiers would be in favour of this. Moreover, with the exception of a few brilliant intellects such as Baden-Powell, soldiers are obsessed with the glamour and glory of war and opposed to the filth and deceit of camouflage. They look upon it as a cowardly method of defeating the enemy. They oppose a training in it in time of Peace, & it is only the bitter realities of War which make them reluctantly adopt it.

It is with extreme reluctance that I write this letter. I am in advancing years and happy in my own work & wish to spend my remaining years in peace. I hate being again dragged into the controversies, jealousies and suspicions of ulterior motives that will doubtless arise regarding a civilian who has the temerity to attempt to overthrow existing military practices. Nevertheless it has been pointed out to me by my friends that it is my duty to give to the world, photographs and other data possessed only by myself, which would help to ensure Peace.

I shall be passing through Washington shortly, as during the next few weeks I shall be with Robert Tyre Jones Jr supervising the finish of the Augusta National Golf Links. My address will be the Bon-Air Vanderbilt Hotel, Augusta, Georgia. I am then visiting Europe and I am unlikely to be back in America until June. I shall feel it a great honour to hear from you.

I have the honour to be, Sir, your obedient servant,

A, MacKenzie"

Whether this epistle was ever sent or—if it *was* sent—brought a response, is unknown. There is an air of almost manic enthusiasm to it, suggesting perhaps a burst of mental energy probably running very late into the evening. The dawn may have brought second thoughts about dispatching it. Whether or not it was ever mailed, the draft serves to give us Alister in yet another guise: MacKenzie the Peacemaker. In the prime of his life, closer to its end than he could have known, he felt that the greatest contribution he could make to mankind was through camouflage. Arguably the greatest of his golf design achievements—Augusta National—was being groomed for unveiling, yet Alister's thoughts were far away on what his camouflage ideas might achieve for world peace.

Chapter Five
Golf Architecture—Beyond the Thirteen Points

UNTIL RECENTLY, MACKENZIE'S BOOK *GOLF ARCHITECTURE* WAS THE BASIS FOR MOST OF THE ARTICLES THAT HAVE BEEN WRITTEN ABOUT HIS WORK. IT IS IMPORTANT TO UNDERSTAND THAT THE book was written in 1920, and actually adapted from a series of lectures he had delivered to the North of England Greenkeepers' Association in 1913. Therefore the book does not represent the sum total of MacKenzie's years of experience as a designer, but the ideals and theories of a longtime student of architecture with only a handful of courses under his belt.

Nevertheless, *Golf Architecture* remains the simplest and most profoundly philosophical book ever written on its subject—not to mention the funniest. MacKenzie's sense of humor as a storyteller comes through quite clearly, as one would expect of a book transcribed from a series of lectures. For example, when talking about the value of water hazards, MacKenzie interjects:

A player visiting a Scottish course asked his caddie what the members thought of a stream which was winding in and out between several of the holes. The caddie replied, "Weel, we've got an old Scottish major here who, when he gets ower it says 'Weel ower the bonnie wee burn ma laddie' but when he gets into it he says 'Pick ma ball oot o' thot domned sewer.'

The backbone of *Golf Architecture* was MacKenzie's list of thirteen "Essential Features" of an ideal golf course. Down through the years, golf writers have accepted these points as a veritable "Ten Commandments" of golf course design. This is interesting in light of the fact that MacKenzie

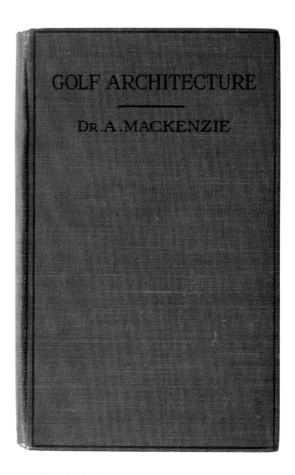

MACKENZIE'S FIRST BOOK ON GOLF COURSE DESIGN WAS PUBLISHED IN 1920. HIS SECOND BOOK WOULD BE PUBLISHED POSTHUMOUSLY 76 YEARS LATER.

broke nearly all of them at some point in his career. Let's take a look at each of the thirteen essential features in order.

1. *The course, where possible, should be arranged in two loops of nine holes.*

MacKenzie, writing 13 years later in *The Spirit of St. Andrews,* explained why:

It is a considerable advantage that a course should be arranged in two loops of nine holes, as on a busy day players can commence at either the first or the tenth tee. On the other hand one can easily sacrifice the best features of good golfing land by being too insistent on this principle.

During recent years in the United States I have had more sleepless nights owing to committees being obsessed by this principle than anything else, and I have often regretted that it had ever been propounded.

In truth, several of his best courses—Alwoodley, Moortown, Cavendish, Cork, Cypress Point, and The Valley Club—do not return to the clubhouse at the ninth. Nor do Lahinch, Kingston Heath, or Royal Adelaide, whose routings he inherited from a previous architect. He preferred that the ninth return — as it does at Royal Melbourne (West), Crystal Downs, The Jockey Club, and Augusta National—but he didn't sacrifice good golf holes in order for it to happen.

2. *There should be a large proportion of good two-shot holes, two or three drive-and-pitch holes, and at least four one-shot holes.*

Note how MacKenzie uses "two-shot holes" instead of "par 4s" or "par 5s." He didn't use the term "par" even once in his book. He also didn't say anything about three-shot holes, though his diagrams of ideal holes include the 14th and 17th at St. Andrews, both usually requiring three shots from the average golfer.

3. *There should be little walking between the greens and tees, and the course should be arranged so that, in the first instance, there is always a slight walk forwards from the green to the next tee; then the holes are sufficiently elastic to be lengthened in the future if necessary.*

Ironically, Dr. MacKenzie's courses have required less lengthening over the years than those of most other architects. Crystal Downs, Pasatiempo, and Cypress Point are virtually the same length as when they opened, but all are still quite testing for today's players. Even Augusta National—visited each year by the world's best players—is less than 250 yards longer than its original form. (Although, no doubt, there are a few members who regret that the doctor left no room to lengthen their short par-5 holes.)

4. *The greens and fairways should be sufficiently undulating, but there should be no hill climbing.*

Undulation was one of the keys to MacKenzie's designs; on many of his courses, there is seldom a level lie to be found in the fairways. Yet, only Augusta National is said to be a difficult walk.

5. *Every hole should have a different character.*

Note that there isn't any mention here about graduating the lengths of holes, as other architects of the day liked to do. The notion that each hole should have character is lost on most architects today.

6. *There should be a minimum of blindness for approach shots.*
As the doctor said later:

On a seaside course there may be a certain amount of pleasurable excitement in running up to the top of a hillock in the hope of seeing your ball near the flag, but this is a kind of thing of which one gets rather tired as one grows older.

Notice that MacKenzie made a distinction between a blind approach and a blind tee shot. He recognized that in hilly country one might have to sacrifice too much in the routing of holes to avoid a blind drive or two. The routing of Royal Melbourne (West) is made by the blind drive at the fourth, which MacKenzie's bunkers at the hilltop transformed into a thrilling shot in its own right.

7. *The course should have beautiful surroundings, and all the artificial features should have so natural an appearance that a stranger is unable to distinguish them from nature itself.*

Here MacKenzie began to really separate himself from the other

architects of his day, most of whom were golf professionals enamored with the playing merits of the course. MacKenzie was the first to recognize that beauty was an important part of the appeal of golf, so he was the first to attempt to create man-made courses as appealing as the natural links of the British Isles.

8. There should be a sufficient number of heroic carries from the tee, but the course should be arranged so that the weaker player with the loss of a stroke or portion of a stroke shall always have an alternative route open to him.

As mentioned previously, Alister's prizewinning design in *Country Life* in 1914 might have been the first hole with an alternate fairway ever drawn. Certainly, his longer par-4 holes are designed with a different, less hazardous route for those content to take three shots to get to the green. Furthermore, instead of designing large, simple greens for such holes, MacKenzie often capped these strong holes with some of his most diabolical greens—for example, the 13th at Crystal Downs, the fifth at Augusta National, and the third at The Valley Club. His reasoning was that the strong player would have to do something more than hit two reasonable shots to assure a four, while the weak player with a canny short game might be able to get close with his third despite the contours.

ABOVE: THE FOURTH HOLE AT ROYAL MELBOURNE. **OPPOSITE PAGE:** TYPICAL MACKENZIE HOLLOWS.

9. There should be infinite variety in the strokes required to play the various holes — viz., interesting brassie shots, iron shots, pitch and run-up shots.

Unfortunately, this is the aspect of MacKenzie's designs that is least preserved today. It's the result of a lack of imagination on the part of greens committees, and the average golfer's preoccupation with green grass. MacKenzie seldom bunkered entirely across the front of a green—like the 11th at St. Andrews, the only golf hole he cited as ideal. He almost always left an opening for the perfectly steered running approach. Sadly, over-watered fairways today stop the low approach from running onto the green; in some cases, golf courses have actually stopped mowing the area in front of the green on his short par 4s as a way of insisting upon an aerial second shot.

Also, because of the improvements in golf balls and equipment—which MacKenzie saw coming—almost no one today carries a brassie (two-wood). Professionals, in fact, easily reach his longest par 4s with mid-irons.

10. There should be a complete absence of the annoyance and irritation caused by the necessity of searching for lost balls.

When MacKenzie began designing, prevailing wisdom was that long grass was a useful partial-stoke penalty for the wayward driver. Alister empathized with the average golfer and advocated the abolition of long grass as a penalty in order to eliminate the annoyance of searching for lost balls. Mackenzie also understood that with wide fairways, a tee shot placed on one side of the fairway offered a different approach problem than a drive placed on the opposite side.

On the other hand, many of MacKenzie's courses featured ragged rough next to the fairways (notably Crystal Downs, Alwoodley, Royal Melbourne, and Kingston Heath), which he felt added texture and beauty to the design and increased the natural appearance of the layout. Apparently, his seventh principle outweighed his tenth.

11. The course should be so interesting that even the plus man is constantly stimulated to improve his game in attempting shots which he has hitherto been unable to play.

This may be the most radical of all the 13 points. Unlike the player/architect who usually designed every hole to reward a particular type of shot, MacKenzie believed that a course should offer shots that even the best player might not yet be able to play—the kind of shot a good player might label "unfair." The doctor was also prepared for the criticism this idea might bring upon him. As he wrote about Cypress Point:

More than half the holes at Cypress Point were of such a nature that I knew by experience that they would at first sight be characterized as unfair. They were so subtle and had such difficult strategic problems that I knew even the best players could not hope to make a good score except after considerable practice. I was not present when the course was opened for play, but my late partner, Robert Hunter, wrote to me and said, 'Everyone without exception thinks that Cypress Point is the best in the United States. There is not a word of hostile criticism.'

My reply was to write back and ask him what was wrong with it. I had been so accustomed to having our best holes torn to pieces that I was actually disturbed at the lack of criticism. I now believe that Cypress Point has escaped criticism simply because it is so incomparably beautiful.

12. The course should be so arranged that the long handicap

player, or even the absolute beginner, should be able to enjoy his round in spite of the fact that he is piling up a big score.

This is exactly the quality that makes the Old Course at St. Andrews beyond compare. MacKenzie, however, did not want the long handicap player to pile up too big of a score. In his later designs—Augusta National and Royal Melbourne in particular—he provided plenty of room for the average player to get around with nothing but bogeys and the occasional six.

13. The course should be equally good during winter and summer, the texture of the greens and fairways should be perfect, and the approaches should have the same consistency as the greens.

In spite of what Alister wrote, he would be aghast at the unnatural effort and expense that many clubs go to today to try and achieve this ideal.

When citing examples of his ideals, MacKenzie almost always referred back to holes on the Old Course at St. Andrews. Indeed, from his drawings it is clear that even his prize-winning design for the Lido course was a more dramatic adaptation of the 14th at St. Andrews.

From a strategic point of view, MacKenzie's genius was in creating holes that used the most prominent features of the ground as an integral part of their design. Previously, all those who called themselves "golf architects" sought natural sites for their greens. MacKenzie was different. His wilder imagination (and his love for St. Andrews far beyond other championship courses) led him to seek out or create more undulating situations than his contemporaries.

Because MacKenzie was not a good golfer himself, his lack of ability profoundly influenced his thinking on the design of greens. While most good players felt that greens should be relatively flat—to reward those who played two good shots home with a birdie try and a relatively certain par—MacKenzie was more concerned about creating *interesting competitive* situations, as opposed to fair ones. (His notion of fairness reverted back to match play: that everything was fair, because both opponents had to deal with the same conditions.)

From this standpoint, a wildly sloped or contoured green that exag-

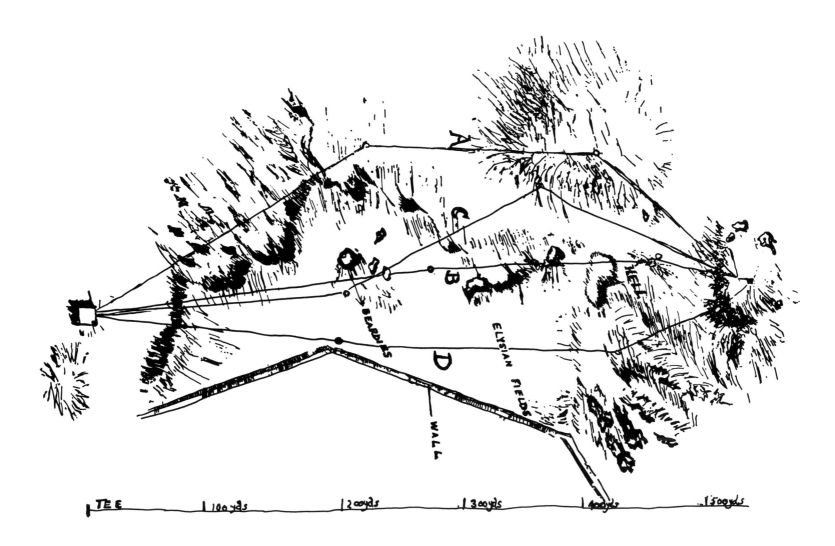

gerated the penalty for playing out of position was ideal. Consequently, the classic MacKenzie green was designed around multiple pin placements on different levels or in different bowls.

MacKenzie was also adept at the placing of wing hazards and at orienting the long axis of a green off center. An orientation like this favored an approach from a particular side of the fairway. In his design drawings of green sites, he usually drew curved lines to the various pin positions to indicate the favored form of approach shot. To simply say "it's a drive and a 7-iron" was not enough to explain the design; depending on the hole, a faded approach from the left edge of the fairway or a *running draw*

off a bank at the right of the green was clearly indicated, whether it was played with a mid-iron or a cleek.

In addition, MacKenzie went further than his contemporaries by seeking interesting ground for the landing areas in the fairways. That way, a drive that landed on a particular spot would be rewarded by an extra kick forward, while another would be carried away to perdition by

FOURTEENTH HOLE AT ST. ANDREWS. A, B, C, D ARE DIFFERENT STRATEGIC LINES FOR PLAYING THE HOLE.

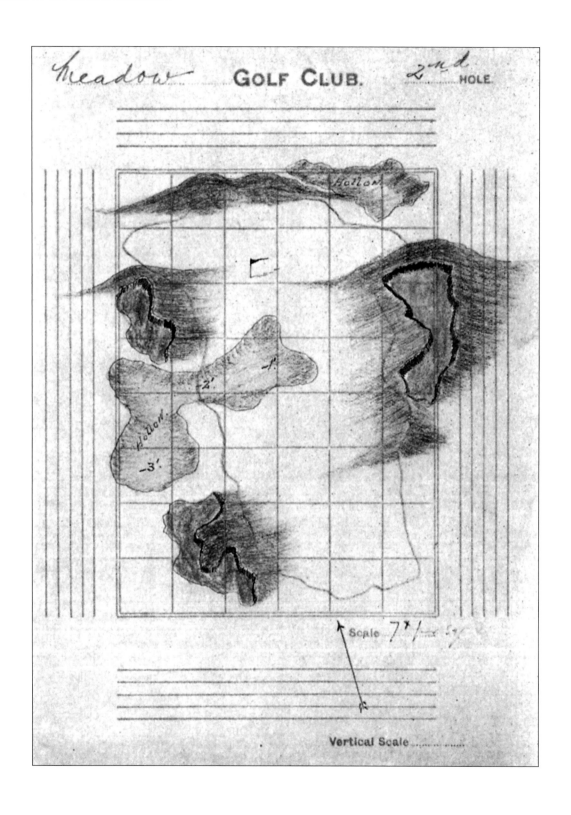

the opposite fold in the ground. Many of the doctor's best holes—the fifth and eighth at Crystal Downs, the ninth at Lahinch, the 16th at Pasatiempo, and the 11th at Royal Melbourne—are made special by the contour of the fairway. Tees were also placed so that existing ridges in the fairway would present bunkers at a useful distance in the driving zone.

But the most telling secret of MacKenzie's designs was the one he never talked about: concentrating his designs on certain ideal lengths of holes.

Alister was clearly against the trend toward longer and longer courses, about which he complained endlessly in *Golf Architecture* in various ways. He didn't believe that length had anything to do with the quality of a hole, so he seldom mentioned yardages or distances (or even

the par) of any hole that he singled out as noteworthy.

Yet, MacKenzie was also adamant about the changing nature of the golf ball, and that the sanctity of the game had to be preserved. Therefore, his belief that length had nothing to do with golf course design is a bit of a contradiction.

OPPOSITE PAGE: SEVERAL OF MACKENZIE'S HOLE DRAWINGS (THIS IS THE SECOND HOLE AT THE MEADOW CLUB IN CALIFORNIA) WERE INCLUDED IN *GOLF ARCHITECTURE IN AMERICA*, A BOOK BY ARCHITECT GEORGE THOMAS, JR. THAT WAS PUBLISHED IN 1927. **ABOVE:** THE PAR-5 EIGHTH HOLE AT CRYSTAL DOWNS IN MICHIGAN.

A close study of MacKenzie's work reveals that he tended to design as many holes as possible *on the edge of par*. The thinking—similar to the design theory of Pete Dye years later—encouraged creating short holes that were short enough to give the shortest hitters hope and long holes that were long enough to make even the longest hitters strain. Quietly, MacKenzie practiced a wisdom that prevailed just after the turn of the century: that there were certain lengths of holes that were more conducive to interesting golf.

MacKenzie's viewpoint on the subject, though, was different from any of his contemporaries. James Braid, J. H. Taylor, and other golfers-turned-architects set down in their books what they felt was the ideal breakdown of hole lengths for any course, supposedly in the name of "variety." But MacKenzie believed that the underlying goal of these player/architects was to see that the target for every hole was proportioned to the scratch golfer—in other words, to reward *themselves*. This conceit lives on today in the work of many golf architects, as well as many more low-handicap green chairmen.

Alister consistently preached that variety in all forms was the key to design success and went out of his way to challenge with (through his work) the leading players' notions of fairness. Instead of a small green for a short approach, he might just as easily design a large green split into many levels, like the eighth at Cypress Point. Additionally, where good players might insist on a large target for a long second shot,

MacKenzie might give them a nasty fall-away green (like the 12th or 13th at Crystal Downs) as a way of insisting that the powerful player also display finesse. Today, these holes capture the souls of even those who see an unfair aspect. MacKenzie built more of them than any architect, before or since, because he wasn't afraid of the hostile criticism they would provoke. Indeed, as he uniquely observed:

Does the average player really know what he likes himself? One often hears the same player expressing totally divergent opinions about the same hole. When he plays it successfully it is everything that is good, and when he is unsuccessful it is everything that is bad. It frequently happens that the best holes give rise to the most bitter controversy.

THE ART OF LANDSCAPING

While MacKenzie was deeply concerned with building golf holes that were interesting in their play, he was also the first golf architect to explicitly recognize the importance of beauty in the design of the course:

I have not the slightest hesitation in saying that beauty means a great deal on a golf course; even the man who emphatically states that he does not care a hang for beauty is subconsciously influenced by his surroundings. A beautiful hole appeals not only to the short but also to the long handicap player, and there are few first rate holes which are not at the same time, either in the grandeur of their undulations and hazards, or the character of their surroundings, things of beauty in themselves.

Certainly, MacKenzie's study of camouflage gave him a unique perspective on artistic golf course construction. He wasn't just concerned with placing bunkers in the right location for golf; if he couldn't make it fit naturally into the appearance of the hole, he'd do without it, and figure out another way to enforce the strategy he intended.

Though he didn't write much about them, MacKenzie inherently understood the principles of art and applied them in his work. For his landscapes to come to life, he knew that he had to build things in the scale of the natural environment. So, though he often pointed out that a small greenside hazard could effectively control the play of a hole, pot

11TH HOLE AT ROYAL MELBOURNE IN AUSTRALIA.

bunkers were not part of MacKenzie's repertoire because he felt they were too puny in appearance. His bunkers are sprawling, to fit the scale of a golf hole. (Pot bunkers on links courses are often invisible from 150 yards away, but are very much human in scale once they have swallowed up a golf ball.)

Even though he was famous for his pronouncements that "rough grass is of little use as a hazard," many of MacKenzie's more famous courses feature fairly large areas of native grasses that give the edges of his bunkers a rugged, natural look.

When working on his routings, MacKenzie was more influenced by potential backgrounds and views than any other architect. This, too, may have come from his appreciation for the Old Course at St. Andrews, where one is constantly lining up on a landmark in town for the tee shots coming home. For example, the back nine at Crystal Downs is laid out in a line, which contradicted the prevailing wisdom that the holes should frequently change directions to make best use of the wind. If he hadn't done this, however, he wouldn't have been able to utilize the site of the short 14th hole, with its distant view of Lake Michigan. Similarly, the fifth hole at New South Wales plays straight out to the point of Cape Banks, while the 13th, on higher ground, plays straight toward Inscription Point on the opposite side of Botany Bay.

It is not surprising that MacKenzie considered nature's beauty on a golf course to be a point of enjoyment on its own merits; as a doctor, he recognized the psychological benefits of being outdoors and playing an interesting game. Equally important, he was the first to define a successful design as one that provided a pleasurable experience for all golfers, rather than one that provided a test to separate the meek from the mighty. He also recognized that by making the holes look more difficult than they really were, the average golfer could gain confidence and enjoyment by overcoming them. This thinking was the opposite of Braid and Macdonald, both of whom located their hazards as part of an elaborate penal system designed to expose the player's weaknesses. Instead, MacKenzie compared his placement of hazards to the fielders in a cricket match, "In both sports many bad shots go unpunished, but in the end the player who has been at the top of his game will come out on top."

ECONOMY AND FINALITY

In *Golf Architecture* and in his consulting reports for clubs all over England, the two words that MacKenzie repeatedly emphasized were "economy" and "finality." In fact, the complete title of his book is *Golf Architecture: Economy in Course Construction and Green-Keeping.* Throughout the text it is clear that Alister was a very practical designer, attempting to get the most out of each piece of land with a minimum of artificial construction. His early budgets for course construction were quite modest (in the range of £2000 to £4000). Even those for Cypress Point and Augusta National were far from extravagant.

Early in his career, MacKenzie stressed economic attributes in order to win over clients. His report for Bury Golf Club said almost nothing about the land, but concentrated on the financial advantages of reforming the club's lost course. When dealing with local authorities, he would postulate that the construction of a course would increase surrounding property values, and therefore the tax receipts of the town. With redesign jobs, he emphasized that reconstruction could save hundreds of pounds in maintenance expenditure per annum (and even, in some cases, pay for the cost of the work itself).

Toward the end of MacKenzie's career, more advanced earthmoving equipment became cost-effective and he didn't hesitate to employ it. His designs for Bayside, The Jockey Club, and Augusta National each required the moving of as much as 100,000 cubic yards of earth (in the first two cases, to create drainage and interest; in the third, to soften slopes). Still, the doctor came up with efficient ways to take utmost advantage of the money that was being spent. He didn't try to build his prize-winning Lido hole on every site.

According to MacKenzie's book, "the truest economy" of course construction "consists in finality." In other words, if a course is poorly designed or constructed, the chances are good that it will have to be redone at some point in time—at considerable inconvenience and expense. A course that is properly designed in the first place, however, could live forever. This was fundamentally a sound message, though it perhaps underestimated the tendency for most humans, including committee chairmen and even golf architects, to believe that anything that

exists can be improved upon. When searching for an example of where true "finality" had been achieved, MacKenzie harped back to the Old Course at St. Andrews. He acknowledged, however, that the Old Course "has been considered too sacred to be touched." Later, in *The Spirit of St. Andrews*, he cited the design work of Max Behr as beyond criticism. This was an ironic example, though, because Behr's Lakeside Country Club in Los Angeles (where Bob Jones filmed his instructional series in the 1930s) has been heavily changed over the past 30 years.

Golf courses are living, growing things that inevitably change, and some of Dr. MacKenzie's more controversial designs—from Sitwell Park to certain holes at Augusta National—have long since been altered by their owners. But Dr. MacKenzie's best work has perhaps achieved "finality" better than that of any of his contemporaries. Donald Ross' most famous courses, for example, include Oak Hill (East) and Oakland Hills (South). Both of them were dramatically lengthened and redesigned by Robert Trent

Jones, Sr. for U.S. Open championships. By contrast, Royal Melbourne, Cypress Point, and Crystal Downs are almost as MacKenzie left them. While it's true that only the first of these three has hosted a major tournament (President's Cup), it's equally true that, MacKenzie would be quick to point out, all three are still enjoyed by their members and guests today.

WEAKNESS

Alister was a brilliant designer and problem-solver. No one in the history of design seems to have made more of the ground offered to him, nor with such apparent ease. Courses such as Crystal Downs, Cypress Point, Royal Melbourne, The Valley Club, and Pasatiempo have endured

A RARITY FOR DR. MACKENZIE: THE ONLY DOUBLE GREEN HE EVER UTILIZED IS THE 18TH/9TH GREEN ON THE BLUE COURSE AT THE JOCKEY CLUB IN BUENOS AIRES, ARGENTINA.

over the years with less need for alteration or added length than the work of any of his contemporaries. Unfortunately, it's also true that many of MacKenzie's designs have been changed beyond recognition, and MacKenzie would not hesitate to say why: because the people who cared for them over the years were fools, unable to understand the point of their design or the true nature of the game of golf.

This was MacKenzie's greatest weakness — his pride and the force of his opinion. He was not afraid to pursue interesting and radical concepts, but it took him many years to understand the unwillingness of others to accept them. It hurt him most during his early years of practice in England, where much of his work was limited to remodeling existing courses. MacKenzie's ideas were so different that it was hard for many people to understand how they would fit into the course that was to be saved. MacKenzie was also penalized to some degree by the conservative nature of the English and their residual distrust of a Scotsman. As a result, most of his early ideas were never allowed to fully bloom.

From a design standpoint, MacKenzie's fondness for exaggerated green contours was his most questioned or criticized feature. It wasn't only the members of Sitwell Park who "refined" things after the architect was finished; "MacKenzie greens" from Lahinch to Pasatiempo to Augusta have been softened over the years.

Ironically, MacKenzie's design work didn't become great until he turned over the construction aspect to those he trusted—people (particularly his brother Charles) who knew when the doctor's ideas needed a bit of toning down. If you looked closely at the elevations marked on MacKenzie's green drawings and compared them to the finished product, you'd learn that few of his greens were built precisely to plan. (The front-to-back rise of the green on his prizewinning Lido hole, for example, was supposed to be 13 feet!) This "quiet assistance" that MacKenzie received from his construction people is an interesting twist to his career. Because where his input went the most unfettered (such as at Sitwell Park and Pasatiempo), the greens are even wilder than on the courses that made him world famous.

Green speeds, of course, have had an enormous effect on our perspective of this issue. If there had been a Stimpmeter in MacKenzie's day, the average speed of a green was probably 5 or 6, a pace at which even his famous green at Sitwell Park might have been fun. Today, anything more than 8 on the Stimpmeter is cause for shame (that speed or faster makes a few of his wildest creations impossible). Unfortunately, though, 10 is the new accepted standard for outstanding courses (which forced revisions at Pasatiempo), and the ever-increasing speeds at The Masters have caused the committees at Augusta National to change some greens two or three different times! Were MacKenzie here with us debating the issue, he would tell us we've lost all perspective—that the slower speeds still provided plenty of putting interest and required great skill, and that maintaining those speeds would have cost us much less in annual upkeep, not to mention the cost savings from not having to rebuild a green.

MacKenzie was unable to anticipate progress in other ways, too. (For example, in the overall growth of the game and in the number of rounds of golf that would eventually be played on his courses.) His practical nature compelled him to try and maximize the use of natural features where few were available, and he often used the same feature as a hazard on two opposing tee shots. His only mention of the subject in *The Spirit of St. Andrews* is a telling one:

One often finds one or more members of a committee obsessed with some pottering detail . . . [such as] the proximity of two adjoining fairways. Danger! Ye gods, when one has given them a hundred and fifty yards in width, and on the Jubilee course at St. Andrews in places there is less than fifty yards for both fairways.

Today, it is not uncommon to find trees planted in key spots to protect golfers from killing one another. The unfortunate result is that neither hole uses the feature on the ground around which it had been laid out.

The explanation for a MacKenzie course not being up to his usual high standard, appears commonly to have been a lack of acreage.

Chapter Six
The Postwar Period—1919-1926

IMMEDIATELY AFTER THE ARMISTICE, MANY OF THE PROJECTS THAT HAD BEEN PUT ON HOLD IN 1914 WERE READY TO COME TO LIFE AGAIN. THE ENGLISH DESIGNER HARRY COLT APPARENTLY felt that the times favored partnerships (that things would proceed much more quickly if they agreed to share the work rather than compete for every single job) because he invited both MacKenzie and Charles Alison to join him as partners. Since Colt had been something of a mentor to the doctor at Alwoodley and he respected him, MacKenzie joined immediately.

When Alister's book, *Golf Architecture*, was published in 1920, it carried an introduction by Colt that referred to the author as "my partner." The same year, Colt and Alison also reproduced as a book a collection of essays that had appeared in *Country Life* under the title "Some Essays on Golf-course Architecture." The book only included one essay by MacKenzie but many of the illustrations were of courses he had designed.

There is a complete account of the Colt-Alison-MacKenzie partnership in Fred Hawtree's 1991 book, *Colt and Co.*, which primarily deals with the life and work of Colt. As Hawtree describes it:

Any partnership [of MacKenzie] *with Colt was probably a tenuous arrangement designed initially to avoid competition and later to apportion the load but not the income. Some contribution to Head Office may have been expected but the style of his* [MacKenzie's] *work and progress suggest that he did not experience any sense of constraint in operating as an independent. One suspects that he was something of a lone ranger all the time.*

From MacKenzie's side, there was never a lack of respect for Colt; his writings right up to his death reveal an admiration for Colt's work, and he was always careful to give full credit for any course that Harry had designed. (The Eden Course at St. Andrews, which was done after Alwoodley but prior to their partnership, is a particular case in point.) Colt was too much of a gentleman to publicly criticize MacKenzie, but it should be noted that when John Morrison succeeded MacKenzie as a partner to Colt and Alison in 1928, Colt went to considerable lengths to ensure they had a watertight legal agreement.

In addition to it being the year that MacKenzie published his book, 1920 was important for another reason: he met Jack Fleming over a game of darts in a pub in Manchester. The Irishman had been trained in Dublin as both a civil engineer and a gardener—two disciplines that MacKenzie prided himself upon. The two men hit it off, and Alister eventually offered Fleming a job on his course construction crew. For both men, it was the start of something bigger than themselves.

In any event, from 1919 to 1923, MacKenzie resumed practice in the north of England with Colt's help in finding leads. He also stretched his net a bit wider in an attempt to snare courses in Ireland, Scotland, and the south of England. Tracing authentic MacKenzie work becomes tricky, however, because of the doctor's habit of crediting all of the partnership's work during this period to the partnership, but then—after the firm's demise—to himself. One prominent example of this is Bob O'Link Golf Club in Chicago: MacKenzie later listed it as one of his designs, but

Charles Alison was definitely responsible for the firm's work in the USA at that time, and it is unlikely that MacKenzie ever visited America before the dissolution of the partnership.

Among the courses that were MacKenzie's responsibility was Malone Golf Club in the southern suburbs of Belfast, which had contracted MacKenzie in 1914 to lay out a new course, though this was not implemented until after the Great War when he was Colt's partner. (The course is also credited to Colt in some circles, but it was clearly MacKenzie's client.) The club had been founded in 1895, but plans were made to move the golf course when the original property was needed to expand a brickworks.

Laid out over a classic parkland estate that was rich in hardwoods, the course was an oasis for its members, with a large central lake figuring prominently on the back nine. Club officials had determined that it would be impossible to route the course in two nine-hole loops, so they were most impressed when MacKenzie devised such a routing on his first day. According to legend, "he walked over the ground one morning, and made a sketch of the proposed new course in the afternoon at a friend's house and from that sketch practically no departure . . . [was] made in the actual construction of the course."

However, there were problems with the finished course, all of which centered on drainage.[1] Like much of Ireland, the ground around Malone

[1] *Interestingly, design efforts in the 1990s by American architects in Ireland were also criticized for drainage problems and for the failure to account for local conditions.*

THE SECOND HOLE AT CLECKHEATON & DISTRICT GOLF CLUB IN WEST YORKSHIRE, ENGLAND, BUILT ON THE SITE OF PIT WORKINGS.

was soggy underfoot, and though much drainage work was done in the construction, it was not enough. The club hired counsel and sent a letter to MacKenzie hoping to submit the matter to arbitration. MacKenzie's response came through someone identified as his "agent," W. J. Quinn, offering to repay £200 (or about two-thirds of his fees for the design). The offer was accepted, but the incident may explain why MacKenzie did not brag much about Malone, which is still regarded as one of the finest courses in Ulster.

Other surviving courses on which MacKenzie worked while in partnership with Colt and Alison include Bramhall Park Golf Club, Stockport; Cleckheaton & District Golf Club, West Yorkshire; Didsbury Golf Club, Manchester; Grange-Over-Sands Golf Club, Lancashire (illustrated in *Golf Architecture*); Shipley Golf Club, West Yorkshire; and Bury Golf Club, Lancashire. Bury is one of the rare projects where it is recorded that more than one of the partners were actually involved on the same project. Both Alison and MacKenzie made site visits there, but perhaps only to reassure one of the investors, a Mr. Duxbury, who exchanged heated letters with MacKenzie throughout the construction asking for more site visits and worrying about the cost and timing of the project. At one point, an exasperated MacKenzie wrote back, "I have been working seven days a week for several months and I cannot do more." Nevertheless, the course was finished promptly and on budget, and it exists today with few changes.

In general, though, Colt, MacKenzie, and Alison were all so busy during this period that there was not much chance to collaborate on design ideas, as they might have done informally in the years before the partnership.

The history of several courses, however, reveals a growing rift between the partners, or at least a growing independence on MacKenzie's part:

SIXTEENTH AT CLECKHEATON.

To win the contract from Blackpool Borough Council for the municipal course at Stanley Park, both Colt and MacKenzie visited the site. But it was MacKenzie who won the contract and signed the report.

MacKenzie also did a course for Hadley Wood Golf Club in Hertfordshire, north of London, which was clearly closer to Colt's territory than MacKenzie's. (The club expanded to 27 holes and then changed back to 18, so only some of MacKenzie's work survives.)

Most pointedly, at Worcestershire Golf Club in Malvern, where Colt himself had learned to play golf, Colt and MacKenzie submitted separate plans *while still partners,* with MacKenzie's design being chosen by the club on the grounds that its implementation would be cheaper. (Near the end of the project, there were some hard feelings that the cost of the project had proved greater than MacKenzie's estimate; Alister replied that the extra cost would not have been incurred if the

Committee had not interfered with his original design!)

In 1923, the partners' split became final, as MacKenzie circulated reprints of his article on "The Growth of Golf in Leeds" from the October issue of *Golfing,* with the following statement printed on the cover:

The four years Agreement of Partnership between Messrs. Colt, MacKenzie & Alison, having terminated, it has been decided that the conditions prevailing before the partnership shall be resumed.

Dr. A. MacKenzie proposes to continue his profession as a Golf Course Architect at Moor Allerton Lodge, Leeds, and also at 222, Strand, London.[2]

[2]*This imposing address was actually the office of the publisher of Golfing, who apparently forwarded inquiries to MacKenzie.*

THE 18TH GREEN AT CLECKHEATON.

Dr. A. MACKENZIE

Golf Course Architect

MOOR ALLERTON LODGE   LEEDS

Scale of Professional Charges and Conditions of Agreement

1—The general supervision which the Architect will give to the work is such periodical inspection by him or his deputy as may be necessary to ensure that the work is being carried out to his intentions, but constant superintendence of the work does not form part of the duties undertaken by him, and is not included for in the following scale of charges.

2—The Architect is empowered to make such deviations, alterations, additions, and omissions as he may reasonably consider desirable in the client's interests, in carrying out the work, provided that no material addition to the cost is caused thereby.

Scale of Charges

1—If the estimated cost exceeds £2,000, the percentage to be 6 per cent. plus all travelling and hotel expenses.

2—If the estimated cost does not exceed £2,000, the percentage to be 10 per cent. in the case of work costing £1,000 graduated to 6 per cent. in the case of work costing £2,000, plus travelling and hotel expenses.

3—For preliminary advice and report on the selection and suitability of a site for a Golf Course, or on the reconstruction of a Golf Course, 10 guineas and expenses a day.

4—In all cases where the material, labour, or carriage, in whole or in part, are provided by the client, the percentage of the estimated cost shall be calculated as if the work had been executed and carried out by a contractor.

NOTE—This scale of professional charges is based on the revised scale 1919 of the Royal Institute of British Architects.

The Architect's remuneration shall be payable by instalments from time to time, as the work proceeds.

MACKENZIE'S "TERMS" FOR COURSE DESIGN WORK.

So Alister was ready to go it alone. At the same time, like all golf architects, he recognized that he required the assistance of an experienced contractor and/or a "deputy" to ensure that the work was carried out to his intentions. As he stretched out his practice to the four corners of the earth, MacKenzie became quick and good at finding talented and like-minded men to help make his ideas a success.

While he was involved with Colt and Alison, Dr. MacKenzie was also developing another "partnership" of sorts with his brother, Major Charles A. MacKenzie, six years his junior. Perhaps in part because of the controversies at Malone and Sitwell Park, it became apparent to Alister that his design ideas could only be successfully realized if implemented by a competent contractor; and also that to act the part of a "professional" architect, it would also be helpful to have someone else handle the grubby necessities of construction. Just prior to the Great War, he recruited Charles to fill the gap.

The fact that they were brothers made things somewhat tricky. In golf design circles, it was considered unprofessional for an architect to hand all of his construction work to one contractor. Since the golf club was his client, the architect was expected to provide options on proceeding with construction so as to keep the contractors' prices honestly competitive. However—then as now—there were few golf course contractors around Britain. Consequently, once Charles's "British Golf Course Construction Company" had a few courses under its belt, it carried out most of Alister's work in Britain after 1921.

He couldn't have realized it at the time, but Charles frequently contributed to Alister's historical record; as the contractor, he made it a point to seek out laudatory letters from clients upon the completion of projects. These letters have helped confirm—in writing—his brother's efforts.

In the late 1920s, the brothers became estranged following Alister's controversial divorce from his first wife, Edith. Their wives were very close friends, and Charles apparently went along with his wife who sided with Edith. This precipitated not only Alister's withdrawal from Alwoodley, where all four had been quite active as golfers and social members, but the end of the MacKenzies' business relationship as well. Perhaps neatly, these tumultuous events coincided with Alister's overseas contracts in Australia and America.

Of all of Dr. MacKenzie's assignments in England after the war, Cavendish Golf Club, in the high midlands at Buxton, Derbyshire, is one of his last and most polished. It has been ignored by many of MacKenzie's disciples because it is only 5,700 yards in length, but the course features several extraordinary holes over an interesting, hilly piece of property.

The first three are laid out in "shooting gallery" fashion across a steep sidehill, but the third, a 281-yard par 4, rises above this setting. The entire hole banks steeply from right to left, and the yardage has strong players thinking about a high drive bounding down to the edge of the putting surface. However, a diagonal line of cross-bunkers beginning 50 yards in front of the green will inflict an awkward punishment on those who pull their drives. On the other hand, playing too far out to the right to skirt the bunkers leaves a straight downhill pitch to a green that slopes away sharply, making it virtually impossible to stop the approach near the hole. For short hitters, it's a straightforward drive up the left and a pitch home—with a sporting chance to win the hole outright if they achieve a good second.

After a tiny drop-shot par 3 along a stream, the course heads out into a broad meadow and then down toward another valley at the turn. The ninth is another difficult par 3 to a small green. The classiest hole on the course is the 422-yard par-4 10th, a stout one for any layout. The drive must be solid to reach a plateau fairway that runs away to the left; the more the tee shot bears to the left along the brink of a drop-off, the better the angle into the green so that the approach does not have to be played back toward the cliff edge. Ninety yards short of the green, the fairway stops abruptly at a deep valley with a stream. The fairway resumes on a high bank 60 yards further, requiring a small pitch to a green that's well bunkered on both sides. The 10th is equal to any of MacKenzie's best designs, and proof by itself that Cavendish is anything but a pushover.

Two other holes at Cavendish worthy of mention are the 11th and 15th. The par-4 11th features a drive along a bluff, followed by a diagonal, downhill second over the stream. The short 15th is also very nice, with its green set into a hillside guarded by Eden-like bunkers at left- and right-center.

Dr. MacKenzie also had chances to do design work in Scotland dur-

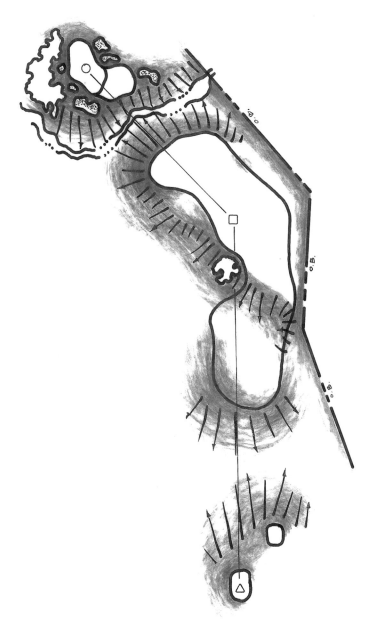

TENTH AT CAVENDISH. (COURTESY OF DON PLACEK, RENAISSANCE GOLF DESIGN, INC.)

ing this period, but the courses he did were far removed from the linksland he had studied. In 1922, he designed the Pitreavie Golf Club in Dunfermline, just a few miles inland from St. Andrews. That same year he remodeled the Pollok Golf Club in Glasgow and the Duff House Royal Golf Club in Banff on the northeast coast of Scotland. However, none of these courses have distinguished themselves enough to compete for tourist attention with the great links of Ayrshire or East Lothian.

Two other well-known Scottish venues are credited to MacKenzie, but there were growing pains for each. The doctor was originally commissioned to design the 18-hole Rosemount course at Blairgowrie Golf Club in Perthshire in 1914, but for various reasons it was not completed until 1934, and even then it was said that "the MacKenzie extension was far too restricted and did not play as well as anticipated." (Several architects, including James Braid, have tinkered with the highly regarded Rosemount course over the years.)

MacKenzie's other noteworthy Scottish commission, Hazlehead Municipal Golf Club in Aberdeen, was beset with problems during construction that caused a fierce public controversy. As the Aberdeen Press and Journal reported at the time of Alister's death:

Dr. MacKenzie was widely criticised in respect of his estimating (later events showed that the cost was about £18,000 rather than an estimate of £8,000), his drainage plans for the moss and his general layout. But despite all the criticism the present course at Hazlehead is practically identical with the scheme prepared by the architect.

MacKenzie's rebuttal-from-the-grave is interred in the pages of *The Spirit of St. Andrews*, where he referred to the project while discussing the subject of construction:

At Aberdeen, Scotland, we had [rocks and roots] with which to contend. We found that we could tell the size of a rock by the character of the sound when we tapped it with a hammer. If it were a small one we removed it, but if it were a large, we covered it with topsoil and seeded it. By this means also we made delightful undulating fairways.

Unfortunately all our hard thinking was wasted. The authorities who took over the course thought they knew more about golf courses than we did. They considered that these fairways should be flat and not undulating, and then proceeded to flatten them out by exploding the rock and then covering the

fragments. They have been troubled ever since by these fragments of hard rock working through the surface. . . .

We were rather proud of our course in Aberdeen and thought we had given them the best inland course in Scotland. It was an amazingly difficult course to construct, as it consisted entirely of pine trees, rocks, bog and heather.

We also had bad luck with the construction work. We anticipated we should be able to cart all the trees away over frozen ground in the winter, but for the first time for twenty years there was not frost and so we had to make expensive roads over bogs. We saved a tremendous amount of labour and avoided the removal of tree roots and rocks by covering them with soil and using them to make undulating ground like the marvelous links land they have in Aberdeenshire. It was particularly galling to find that our efforts were not appreciated.

Ironically, though, one of the most significant commissions of Dr. MacKenzie's career was to come from Scotland—on a course he did not alter!

FAMOUS LINKS

In addition to his new-course work, the doctor provided consultation to existing clubs that sought to modify their courses. Two of his proudest associations were with clubs that did not need much in the way of modification.

In his later brochures, Alister proudly listed the Royal St. George's Club, Sandwich, among his clients. This involvement is unconfirmed, however, because the club's minutes for 1913-28 were lost after being removed by the War Department during their World War II use of the clubhouse. Having played the course, though, we are confident that the wildly undulating ninth green is a MacKenzie original. It was relocated from its original position sometime after 1910, when Bernard Darwin described the hole in his opus, *The Golf Courses of the British Isles*. The green at the par-4 17th may also be MacKenzie's work. Originally a punchbowl, it was moved further back and redesigned with even more undulation by someone in the 1920s (probably Alister). Approach shots that land short now gather in the natural punchbowl/hollow area in front of the putting surface.

A more important feather in MacKenzie's cap was his 1924 appointment as "Consulting Architect" to the Royal and Ancient Golf Club, St. Andrews. He didn't make any changes to the course—if anything, he *discouraged* them from making the changes that they were suggesting—but he did draw the famous map of the course that hangs in pro shops, 19th holes and golfers' homes around the world; among other details, the map documents the Old Course's famous bunkers and their names. He also helped the club determine a selection of cup locations on the greens of the Old Course, a list that is used to this day for the Fall Meeting competitions and for major championships.

MacKenzie's knowledge of the subtle contours of the Old Course was probably more complete than any golf architect since Old Tom Morris himself, and his reverent references to the ancient layout undoubtedly helped him gain admirers from all over the world (including the great Bobby Jones). More tangibly, his position as "Consulting Architect" to the Royal & Ancient Golf Club provided connections that ultimately led to his first important commission overseas. It came about when the R & A recommended him to Dr. William Mackinnon, the visiting president of Royal Melbourne Golf Club.

Unfortunately, MacKenzie's visits to the west of Scotland were less productive. He did lay out the Portland course at Troon, on which Gene Sarazen failed to qualify for the 1923 Open Championship on Troon's Old Course, but MacKenzie had nothing to do with the famous Royal Troon. Meanwhile, he also advised Prestwick Golf Club on the extension of their course in the 1920s, but his comments in *The Spirit of St. Andrews* make it unclear whether his advice was badly followed or ignored:

Some years ago I advised the Prestwick Club, who owned a magnificent piece of links land and had one of the most famous of the British Championship courses, regarding new 7th, 8th, 9th, 10th, 11th, and 12th holes. The committee decided to carry out the work themselves. The general opinion of the club is that the changes have been a great improvement on the old holes, but I know, and, doubtless other golf architects know, that they have made a complete mess of some marvelous natural golfing country. . .

When a green committee carries out an architect's plans, the result is rarely even a partial success, and in any case the committee takes the credit for any improvement and the architect gets the blame for any failure.

A LAST HURRAH IN LEEDS

Possibly Alister's last important commission in England, and certainly his last work around Leeds, was for Sand Moor Golf Club, located adjacent to Moortown. The designer of record for the course is one Noel Barnes, who was actually the club's greenkeeper. But Alister and Charles MacKenzie were both founders/members and served on the green committee there, so it is impossible to believe that they did not dominate the design process when they were present. It is also entirely possible that because of their close association with other clubs nearby and the positions they held at Sand Moor, it was better to disclaim credit for the design than be accused of nepotism or of being traitors to their earlier clubs.

Four of the holes at Sand Moor were changed years ago to make way for a land sale that would be profitable to the club. The rest of the course, however, features many dramatic bunkers and two-tiered greens that make it highly likely that Dr. MacKenzie was heavily involved in the design. Its one-shot holes are some of Dr. MacKenzie's best.

From 1929 on, following the rift that occurred with his divorce, Alister returned to Leeds only to spend time in the summer with his sister Marion and her family. While there, it was his custom to stay in an opulent suite in the Grand Hotel, Harrogate. Another of his extravagances during these trips was to bring his DeSoto automobile on the trans-Atlantic liner with him.

IRELAND—STEPPING STONE TO AN INTERNATIONAL CAREER

Prior to his intercontinental travels, MacKenzie had already done several courses in Ireland in the early 1920s. Included among these are Malone Golf Club and Knock Golf Club in Belfast—both built just after World War I—and three clubs near the southern city of Cork: Muskerry, Monkstown, and Douglas.

Doctor MacKenzie's one-day visit to Muskerry in 1920 was documented in the club's history:

The Doctor, after a march over that then gorse-grown ground, returned to the Pavilion and, whilst awaiting lunch, sat apart with paper and pencil. In that short interval he 'roughed out' our new 11 holes and astonished members present by placing before them his still crude but perfect design.

His revisions at Monkstown in 1925 were less thorough (only costing £520), but a year later Douglas Golf Club hired the British Golf Course Construction Company (brother Charles again) to reconstruct their course according to Alister's plans.

Also in 1926, the board of governors of Lahinch Golf Club in southwest Ireland voted to invite Dr. MacKenzie to suggest alterations to their course. This opportunity was a watershed moment in MacKenzie's career, not only because it was one of his first noteworthy international commissions but because it was really the first time he was given a dramatic canvas on which to perform his work.

At the time, Lahinch was one of the most famous courses in Ireland, the home of the South of Ireland championship. It was originally laid out by Old Tom Morris in 1891 and revised by Charles Gibson (the professional at Westward Ho!) in 1910. Because the original layout straddled Ennistymon Road between some huge sand dunes to the west and an estuary, the club's goal was to get all eighteen holes on the west side of the road. To do so meant venturing into the large dunes to create several holes.

As it turned out, MacKenzie was the perfect man for the task. His flair for the dramatic came to life in the dunes, and his economical use of natural features also enabled him to crowd the last six holes into a confined area along the roadway. Only four of the original holes were preserved intact, including Morris's famous "Dell" (now the sixth), a blind par 3, and Gibson's "Klondyke," a blind par 5 that precedes it. The chances are good that MacKenzie—who was not at all fond of blind approaches—was instructed to keep these already famous holes intact. Hopefully, though, he also recognized them as natural wonders with their own golfing value. In any case, the need to keep the four old holes did not deter his confidence in the new scheme: he wrote that if implemented, "Lahinch will make the finest and most popular golf course that I or, I believe, anyone else, ever constructed." The committee accepted his report and the project was completed over the winter of 1927, at a cost of £2,000.

The genius of MacKenzie's work at Lahinch is that it satisfied two entirely different sets of users. First of all, he managed to maintain and extend its reputation as a fitting championship test (in fact, the amateur career of Lahinch native John Burke blossomed after he won the first

South of Ireland Championship over the revised course in 1928). At the same time, though, the importance of the golf club to the community could not be overstated: it was, and remains, the centerpiece of the town's identity as a summer resort. MacKenzie understood that the course also had to appeal to resort visitors, good and bad golfers alike, and he accomplished this goal.

None of Ireland's other championship courses are as playable for all levels of golfer as Lahinch. Ballybunion, County Down, and Portmarnock are great championship tests: the first two are also among the game's most scenic venues, but they are intimidating and frustrating for the average player. Not so Lahinch. For sure, the contours of MacKenzie's greens made it difficult to get up and down for par. But because half of the greens were located in natural hollows, it was not so difficult for the less accomplished player to chip onto the green and two-putt for his bogeys. Ironically, though, the course has been changed considerably from MacKenzie's design. Two of his green sites (the present eighth and 12th holes) were set close to the beach and were frequently buried with sand by coastal gales and had to be abandoned in 1936. Other trademark MacKenzie greens (tiered), including that of the par-4 13th, were flattened by John Burke and club professional/greenkeeper Bill McCavery because they became too keen during the summer months without irrigation. In all, MacKenzie built a dozen new greens in 1927. Only two remain intact, the ninth and 11th, though the club is currently at work on a plan to restore several other greens to their original form.

The short par-4 ninth hole is a wonderful creation. The narrow, rippling shelf of a green is set against a steep drop-off to the left and guarded by a bunkered knob at the right-front. By far the best angle from which to hold the green is straight in, from the left edge of the fairway. This, however, requires that either the tee shot carry a deep hollow on the left or that the second shot be played from well below the green. The par-3 eleventh, played through a slot in the dunes to a small green half-hidden behind a pot bunker and a dune at the front-left, is one of the best short holes anywhere.

The only other true MacKenzie touch remaining at Lahinch is the short par-4 13th, a dogleg to the right of just 274 yards. There is an overwhelming temptation to try and drive the green, but any miss to the

THE 381-YARD PAR-4 NINTH AT LAHINCH GOLF CLUB IN IRELAND. FROM THE BACK
TEE, HIGH ATOP A DUNE, THE DRIVE IS DOWNHILL TO A PLATEAU OF FAIRWAY WITH A
SEVERE DIP ON THE LEFT SIDE. EVEN IF ONE TRIES AND FAILS TO MAKE THE CARRY,
LEAVING A HALF-BLIND SECOND SHOT, THE ANGLE TO THE LONG AND NARROW
GREEN IS A DISTINCT ADVANTAGE. "SAFE" ROUTES TO THE RIGHT LEAVE AN ALMOST
IMPOSSIBLE SECOND SHOT PAST A STIFF BUNKER AT THE RIGHT FRONT OF THE GREEN.
MOST SHOTS THAT CLEAR THE BUNKER WILL THEN CARRY OVER THE SHELF OF THE
GREEN DOWN TOWARD THE TENTH TEE FAR BELOW. **RIGHT:** THE ELEVENTH AT LAHINCH.

right is gathered into a grassy abyss next to the fairway. From here, a four is very unlikely. A few years ago, in conjunction with lengthening the 12th hole, a new back tee was built on the 13th so players wouldn't have to walk so far to reach the old teeing ground. The new tee was soon abandoned, however, when players finally realized that the original, awkward length of the 13th was its greatest asset. The walk to the old tee was worth it.

Lahinch is a village that's steeped in golf, very proud of its MacKenzie heritage. More than any of his other clients, perhaps, the residents of Lahinch—practically from cradle to grave—enjoy and appreciate the "pleasurable excitement" that the doctor provided.

At the same time that Lahinch was being developed, Alister was also contracted to expand the Cork Golf Club at Little Island from nine holes to eighteen. It was the last of the "four Cork courses" (after Muskerry, Monkstown and Douglas) to use his services. Little Island was another site that required ingenuity because the land for the expansion, though

close by to the edge of the sea, was mostly in the bowels of an old stone quarry. (It would be a full 60 years before Tom Fazio's Black Diamond Ranch made "quarry golf" popular.)

At Cork, MacKenzie again captured the full drama of the terrain in his golf holes. After three pedestrian parkland holes, remnants of the original nine, the long par-4 fourth requires a dramatic drive across the edge of the sea on the right to a pinched fairway. The 330-yard sixth is the first of the quarry holes: after driving from the rim of the quarry down into its bowels, with the elevated tee encouraging an overswing, one must play a very precise pitch to a small, skinny plateau green. Two

MANY PLAYERS ARE VERY TEMPTED TO TRY AND DRIVE THE 274-YARD 13TH AT LAHINCH. BUT TROUBLE AWAITS THE ERRANT TEE SHOT. **OPPOSITE PAGE, TOP:** THE NINTH GREEN AT IRELAND'S CORK GOLF CLUB. **OPPOSITE PAGE, BELOW:** THE SECOND SHOT ON THE PAR-5 11TH AT CORK MUST FLIRT WITH A DEEP AND DANGEROUS QUARRY.

dramatic short holes, the seventh and ninth, also play within the excavations; and after exiting on the long par-4 tenth, the second shot on the par-5 11th skirts the rim of the quarry on the right to a green perched on the cliff edge. At 495 yards, the length tempts long hitters to go for the green, but there is no recovery of errant shots to the right. Unfortunately, after this, the parkland finishing holes are a distinct letdown.

Little Island was also the right place and time to be working in golf course construction, for as the job was being finished by Jack Fleming, Dr. MacKenzie returned from America with contracts for several new design jobs. MacKenzie asked Fleming to accompany him overseas—and to bring along any of the crew who might be interested. Before the year was out, they were in California, the Irish backbone of Robert Hunter's American Golf Course Construction Company.

Chapter Seven
MacKenzie the Golfer

MANY—IN FACT, NEARLY ALL—FAMOUS GOLF ARCHITECTS TOOK UP THE PROFESSION BECAUSE OF THEIR REPUTATION AS OUT-STANDING PLAYERS. THE COMMON THOUGHT WAS THAT A PERSON who played the game well must understand it, and, therefore, must understand golf courses, too. And how to design them.

Professional golfers have always played a major role in course architecture: From Jack Nicklaus and others today, back to James Braid and Willie Park, Jr., even as far back as Old Tom Morris, the St. Andrews professional (and early Open champion) who was really the first to be commissioned to lay out new courses. Many architects, in fact, whose playing careers are mostly unknown, were excellent golfers. Harry Colt was the captain of the Cambridge University team, as was Charles Alison, his partner. George Fazio was the longtime professional at Pine Valley who lost in an 18-hole playoff with Ben Hogan for the 1950 U.S. Open. A.W. Tillinghast played in numerous U.S. Amateur championships, as did Pete Dye two generations later, and, of course, Charles Blair Macdonald was the winner of the first Amateur championship in 1895.

The one noteworthy exception to the rule is MacKenzie. He rarely played at all until the age of 28, and until near the end of his life, he was never more than a social player with only middle-handicap talent. His

ALISTER PLAYED LITTLE GOLF UNTIL LATE IN LIFE, AND HE WAS NEVER MUCH MORE THAN A SOCIAL PLAYER AND A MIDDLE HANDICAPPER.

relative inability at golf had a profound effect on the early progress of his career and also upon his perspective of the ideals of golf course design.

There is little documentation of Alister's early interest in golf. Though a Scotsman by heritage, nearly all of the MacKenzie family's time in Scotland was spent in Lochinver in the west Highlands. The community was more than 50 miles from the nearest course at Dornoch. He first played the game in Scotland at about the age of 18, but soon after injured his wrist playing rugby and avoided the game for several years.

MacKenzie's name does appear in the first book of minutes of Leeds Golf Club around 1900, but it isn't proof that he was playing much, if at all. Neither is it revealing that he was also a member of Headingley Golf Club, as were many of the founders of Alwoodley Golf Club in 1907.

Eventually, however, Alister *did* begin playing on something of a regular basis, although there is even less of a record of his abilities as a golfer. He had modest success at Alwoodley—shooting scores in the mid-80s in monthly medal competition—and he and his first wife, Edith, along with Alister's younger brother Charles and his wife, made up a regular foursome at Alwoodley until Alister's divorce. But until the mid-1920s, his career was hampered by the fact that he was a mediocre golfer.

Years later, in *The Spirit of St. Andrews*, he made light of his golfing difficulties:

I am as keen as ever on golf, but will always remain an indifferent player. Some years ago I was playing in the final of the Yorkshire Medical Cup [1926]. In the first eighteen holes I was up on my opponent, and at the eighth hole of the second round he put two shots out of bounds whilst I was nearly on the green with my second shot. I socketed my third to the right of the green, my fourth to the back and my fifth back again nearly to where I had started from. I ultimately lost the hole I seemed certain to win. I continued shanking my shots and lost the match by a heavy margin.

Several friends of mine were looking on, and after the game was over one of them, in a very mysterious and confidential way, buttonholed me and said, 'Mackenzie, do you mind me giving you a bit of advice? You are just off to Australia to lay out golf courses. For God's sake don't let them see you play golf or you will never get another job.

Through the wisdom of hindsight, MacKenzie seems to have recognized that his career took off after he left England. What's for certain is that his new clients were less aware of his own difficulties in hitting a golf ball.

Early in his career, MacKenzie had vocal disagreements with several professional golfers. These players had complained about the severity and "unfairness" of his courses in general, and his tiered putting greens in particular. This was the easiest way for his competitors in the golf architecture business to criticize MacKenzie, since frequently the committee chairmen and golf developers of the day were among the better players at a club. The fact that they were also much better golfers than Dr. MacKenzie allowed them to feel that maybe their opinions were justified.

Perhaps MacKenzie invited this criticism. Privately, he seethed at the idea that an uneducated golf professional would make a better golf architect than a more educated man like himself. *Golf Architecture* contains at least one thinly veiled attack on golf professionals-turned-architects. It occurs with the very first quality that he cites as a requirement for the making of a successful golf architect:

In any case the possession of a vivid imagination, which is an absolute essential in obtaining success [in golf architecture], may prevent him attaining a position among the higher ranks of players. Everyone knows how fatal the imagination is in playing the game. Let the fear of socketing once enter your head and you promptly socket every shot afterwards.

In *The Spirit of St. Andrews*, he took his argument even further:

Although I know scores of excellent golf courses designed by amateur golfers, I do not know of a single outstanding one by a professional golfer. Not that there are not plenty of professionals who are men of considerable education, but the fact that they are constantly playing competitive golf makes them view with resentment anything that is likely to disturb their sequence of threes and fours.

He was well aware, however, that most of the criticism that his golf courses were "unfair" were coming from the narrow perspective of low-handicap players, and that the fairway hazards they complained the most about were the ones that bothered only them, because the average player could not reach them from the tee. Whereas most of the good players who designed courses were caught up in making the course "fair" for the scratch man—that is, placing hazards that magnified the difference in ability between good players and poor ones—MacKenzie sought to make the game more interesting by locating his hazards in places that

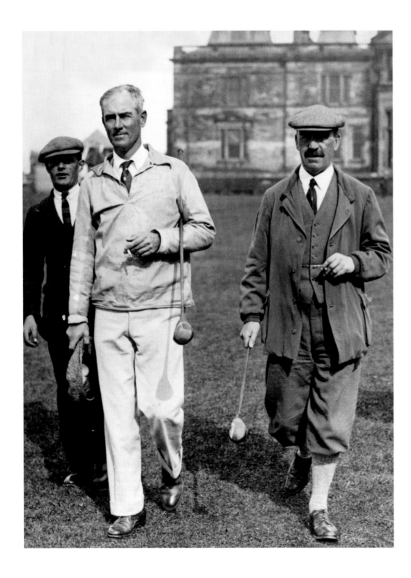

also universally regarded as "great." In discussions of this kind, Alister's brimming self-confidence and occasional short temper worked against him. Also hampering his career in England before 1920 was his eagerness to goad the professionals by his designs, notably at Sitwell Park where his most radical ideas were not embraced.

Yet MacKenzie definitely knew the game and understood how it was played at the highest level. He spoke with affection of the great players of the day—everyone from Andrew Kirkaldy to Ted Blackwell to Joyce Wethered—and with admiration for the variety of strokes they could play. He befriended the more thoughtful of the good players, including John Low and Max Behr, and gained insight from what they felt were the merits of great courses, particularly the Old Course at St. Andrews. He attended some of the great events of the day, too, such as the 1926 Walker Cup and 1927 Open Championships at St. Andrews, where he walked with O.B. Keeler following Bobby Jones. Throughout the latter half of his career, MacKenzie also developed associations with many people who had played the game at the highest level (from Harry Colt to Marion Hollins to Alex Russell to Bob Jones, national champions all) golfers from whom he could continue to learn the subtleties of the game.

Through these discussions, MacKenzie tested the experts' views against his experiences as a mediocre golfer and against his steadfast belief that courses should be built "to give the greatest good to the greatest number of players." In that respect he was truly an original thinker. Yet, it was only after he headed overseas—with impressive credentials and a much smaller "establishment" to challenge his views—that his ideas were given the respect they were due.

After Alister turned 60 (when there were few golf courses to build), he suddenly developed into a fairly good golfer, capable of breaking 80 on occasion. In *The Spirit of St. Andrews* he credits his later-in-life success to his friendships with Bobby Jones and the great English teaching professional Ernest Jones. Ernest had become the wintertime professional at Pasatiempo, where MacKenzie was living, and the doctor's comments implied that his biggest hurdle had been a mental block:

forced the better player to think his way around. He positively reveled in placing holes along the edge of severe natural hazards, daring the good player into possibly making a mistake. At the very same time, though, he endeavored to make the course "look more difficult than it really was" for the average player, thereby boosting his confidence. He also rightly pointed out that golfers do not know what they really want. An example of this was the green at the Road Hole on the Old Course at St. Andrews. Generally accepted as the most difficult green in all of Scotland, it was

MAX BEHR AND MACKENZIE AT THE OLD COURSE AT ST. ANDREWS.

When [Ernest] Jones first gave me a lesson, I told him I would never be able to swing a club because during my football days I had broken a bone in my left wrist which had never united. He replied, "I've only one leg but that does not prevent my swinging one."

Apparently empowered because of some success at the game, MacKenzie went on to devote a whole chapter to golf instruction!

Within it, he acknowledged that "during the thirty years when the rest of my golf was rotten I was a consistently good putter," which was undoubtedly the other reason he was fond of severe greens. Every golf architect—consciously or unconsciously—tends to design for the part of the game that he or she can comfortably visualize. Not even Dr. MacKenzie was immune to this form of self-gratification.

MACKENZIE PREPARES TO DRIVE ON THE TENTH HOLE AT CYPRESS POINT.

ALISTER PUTTS ON THE 13TH GREEN AT CYPRESS POINT.

～ R E C O R D   A T   A L W O O D L E Y ～

MacKenzie played in many competitons at The Alwoodley Golf Club from the very early days in 1907 until his resignation from the club in 1928. The lowest handicap he recorded was 5 in 1921 when he won the April Medal.

Alister was a graduate of Cambridge University but did not appear to be a member of the Oxford and Cambridge Golfing Society. He certainly was not a golfer of the caliber of Harry Colt and Bernard Darwin, both Cambridge graduates of the same period.

The first Monthly Medal at Alwoodley was played in July of 1907 and won by Mr. T. Tannett. Alister, however, won the next two Medals in August and September. He repeated this feat in 1908. Listed below are his appearances and achievements.

Monthly Medals
August, 1907: 89 (11) = 78
September, 1907: 85 (9) = 76
August, 1908: 89 (9) = 80
September, 1908: 84 (7) = 77
April, 1921: 81 (5) = 76

1909: Captains Prize. MacKenzie (7) won in the first round (2 up) vs Mr. G. Garland but lost in the second round to Mr. R.D. Kitson (1 down)
1911: Scratch Medal. MacKenzie was 4th with 94 + 90 = 184
1913: Captains Prize. MacKenzie was the winner (competition format was not recorded).
1914-1918: War years.
1920: Scratch Medal (Sept 18). MacKenzie was 4th (out of 8) with 92 + 89 = 181.
1920: Ladies vs Gents (May 15). The Ladies were in receipt of "a half and 4 biscs."
Mrs. E. MacKenzie lost to Mr. C.H. Badeley
Dr. A. MacKenzie lost to Mrs. Harland
1920: Mixed Foursomes (July 13).
Mrs. E. MacKenzie and Mr. J.H. Brand placed 5th (out of 14).
Mrs. H.D. Middleton and Dr. A. MacKenzie placed 6th.
1920: Moynihan Cup. MacKenzie won the trophy (still played for today). It is open only to players from the medical profession in Leeds.
1921: Ladies vs Gents (June 29).
Dr. A. MacKenzie won 4 & 2 vs Mrs. H.D. Middleton
Mr. R.D. Chorley won 8 & 6 vs Mrs. E. MacKenzie

Mr. C. MacKenzie won 6 & 4 vs. Mrs. W. Harland
1921: Mixed Foursomes Flag Competition (Aug 7). Thirteen couples entered for the prizes presented by Dr. & Mrs. MacKenzie. The first prize was 2 boxes of the well known Silver King "Blue Dot" golf balls.
1922: Scratch Medal (July 15). MacKenzie 4th out of 12 (8 no returns) with 86 + 89 + 175.
1925: Harwood Cup (June 20). MacKenzie 8th with 91 + 88 (-16) = 163.
1925: Remainder vs West Riding Club Members (Wed/July 1). MacKenzie lost 5 & 4 to Mr. H. Ives. In the evening, the West Riding Club dined their opponents at the West Riding Club and a very happy evening was spent.
1925: Match vs Ilkley (Wed/July 15). MacKenzie won 5 & 3 vs Mr. C.P. Holiday.
1926: Match vs Ilkley (Wed/May 15). MacKenzie won 1 up vs Mr.R.E. Wainwright.
1927: Remainder vs West Riding Club Members (Wed/June 16). MacKenzie won 1 up vs Mr. S. Wilson. In the evening, the Remainder dined their opponents at the Leeds Club and a very jolly evening was spent.
1927: Match vs Ilkley (Wed/June 15). MacKenzie lost 4 & 2 to Mr. D. Fletcher.
1927: Match vs The Army GS (Sat, Sun/ May 28, 29). MacKenzie played all four games with Mr. G. Hirst and won 2, halved 1 and lost 1.

There is no further mention of Dr. Alister MacKenzie in the competition records of The Alwoodley Golf Club. (Nick Leefe, Alwoodley Golf Club, Leeds)

Chapter Eight
Two Months that Changed A Continent

THE PEAK OF ALISTER'S CAREER WAS APPROACHING WHEN HE SET SAIL FOR AUSTRALIA IN 1926. HE HAD BEEN INVITED BY THE PRESIDENT OF ROYAL MELBOURNE GC (AT THE RECOMMENDATION OF the Royal & Ancient Golf Club) to make design suggestions for a new course. The result—in no more time than it took MacKenzie to get there from England—forever altered Australia's place in the golf world.

Before Alister's arrival, a committee of Royal Melbourne members had already put many of the plan's pieces into place. At the doctor's suggestion, his contract with the prestigious club offered it 50 percent of any consulting fees that he obtained from other clubs in Australia. The clever proposition gave Royal Melbourne a reason to trumpet MacKenzie's arrival to clubs all over the continent. This was good publicity for Royal Melbourne. MacKenzie, then not widely known in Australia, benefited and received good "consultation" income from clubs elsewhere in Australia. Even though he had written *Golf Architecture* six years earlier and was consulting architect to the Royal & Ancient, his credit list at the time was limited to Alwoodley, Moortown, and 50 or so lesser known English courses where he had provided a consultation. MacKenzie's connection with Royal Melbourne was an instant boost to his credibility.

Not long after arriving, MacKenzie met two men already in the service of Royal Melbourne: club member Alex Russell, the amateur Australian Open champion of 1924, and superintendent Michael "Mick" Morcom, the greenkeeper at the existing Royal Melbourne course in nearby Black Rock. MacKenzie hit it off famously with both men.

In Russell, he found a kindred spirit who understood the architect's noble aim to provide enjoyment for the average player. Alex was also a champion golfer whose support precluded any objections by the committee. The two got on so well that MacKenzie named Russell his design partner, responsible for following up on his designs and any future contracts that might result from their work together.

In Morcom, the doctor found a naturalist who not only quickly grasped the principles of camouflage but could apply them beautifully in his construction work. Mick's son Vernon assisted him in the construction work. (Vernon later completed the work at Kingston Heath and eventually became a golf architect.)

This new "triumvirate" worked so well that MacKenzie modeled future cooperative ventures on it. Unlike his partnership with Colt and Alison, where each was responsible for following through on his own jobs, Russell and Morcom were placed in very important but clearly subordinate roles: MacKenzie did the routings and instructed them on the finer points of quality construction; his partners then followed up and finished the project while "the master" set sail. It was the perfect

AFTER MACKENZIE ARRIVED IN AUSTRALIA IN 1926, HE MADE AN ARRANGEMENT WITH THE OFFICERS OF ROYAL MELBOURNE GC: IF THEY HELPED HIM OBTAIN CONSULTING WORK WITH OTHER CLUBS, HE'D SPLIT THE FEE 50-50.

ROYAL MELBOURNE GOLF CLUB,
SANDRINGHAM.

27th. October, 1926.

The Secretary,
Royal Sydney Golf Club
Rose Bay   NSW

Dear Sir,

     Dr. A. Mackenzie arrived here on the 25th inst. and is now engaged in planning out alterations and additions to our present course. He expects to remain in Australia for some five or six weeks and will be prepared to undertake work for other Clubs if time permits.

     His fee would be, if required to report fully, and to plan alterations to a course £250 but if only a small amount of work were required of him a reduction would be made. His permanent address is care of this Club.

                Yours faithfully,

                <u>Secretary</u>.

arrangement for MacKenzie, a quick thinker who often lacked the patience for dealing with committees. Also, he would soon be moving so quickly around the world looking for new commissions that he wouldn't have time to wait and see each course completed. He was already in the process of lining up Robert Hunter, Perry Maxwell, and Jack Fleming as future associates in America. In addition, his successful relationship with Russell would encourage MacKenzie to accept the design advice of future clients Marion Hollins and Bob Jones instead of fretting over their interference.

As for Mick Morcom, he had to grasp MacKenzie's ideas quickly because the doctor was not to be around for very long. On November 18, 1926—just 23 days after he arrived—MacKenzie presented Royal Melbourne with his plans for the new West course. During that time he had also spent five days in Adelaide and had visited the sites of five other courses around Melbourne to offer his expertise.

ROYAL MELBOURNE

Ask devotees of MacKenzie's work to nominate his best single course and many would be inclined to say the West course at Royal Melbourne. Many of its characteristics are features we now associate with the doctor's design style: the wide fairways, which limit the need to search for lost balls; the bold bunkering, which offers many optional carries and makes the course look harder than it plays; the wild growth within and around the bunkers, which gives the course a rugged, natural look; and the slick, tilting greens, which ultimately penalize those who have played too conservatively. It's hard to find anyone who has seen Royal Melbourne who doesn't consider it to be one of the world's great courses.

And yet MacKenzie, who was as enamored with his own work as any architect, did not boast of Royal Melbourne as one of his greatest efforts. In fact, he failed to mention it even once in *The Spirit of St. Andrews*. The reason for this is quite simple: after leaving Australia in 1926, he never returned to see the fruits of his ideas. Much of the course's brilliance, therefore, has to be credited to Russell and Morcom, even if all they did was follow MacKenzie's instructions as exactly as they could.

Indeed, it is a phenomenon of many of MacKenzie's best known cre-

ations that they seem to have come to fruition in his absence. How? We know it's not because he left exacting plans to be carried out to the letter; his surviving sketch plans for greens are quite exaggerated and were seldom built precisely to scale. In truth, MacKenzie relied heavily on finding a construction supervisor who understood his style and intent. That meant either bringing one along, or getting to know the man onsite, as he did with Morcom.

What should not be underestimated, however, is the power of MacKenzie's routings for his courses. By making the holes at certain lengths and by skirting fairways along the very brink of trouble—usually a sharp drop-off into which dramatic bunkers could be cut—many holes on each course were destined to be exciting as soon as their centerlines had been committed to paper. All that was left for the construction crew was to build hazards and greens in the same spirit as the land that MacKenzie had assigned to them.

The first nine holes of Royal Melbourne's West course are brilliant examples of MacKenzie's genius for routing. After two long and relatively straightforward holes to start the round, the next seven holes are all influenced by one or both of the two large hills in the center of the property: The short par-4 third plays along the base of the larger hill; the brilliant fourth up over the hilltop; the fifth back into the side of the larger hill; the par-4 sixth down off the larger hill from the tee and into the side of the smaller hill on the approach; the par-3 seventh from one hill to the other; the eighth off the lower hill to a wooded corner; the ninth back to a green site in the side of the hill; and the short par-4 tenth, from the second hill to a third. (MacKenzie would have especially enjoyed the play at the West 10th—the "composite 12th"—in the 1999 President's Cup Matches. While he would have been astounded that players like Tiger Woods and Ernie Els could reach the green with a 3-wood in the four-ball matches, he would have been pleased to see that securing a win or a half required either a daring tee shot executed to perfection, a patient iron followed by a perfect pitch, or a great scrambling play from around the small green.)

After the tenth, the next six holes of the West course are borrowed from the previous Royal Melbourne layout, though Dr. MacKenzie did place new tees and bunkers to add strategy to the lines of play. The only

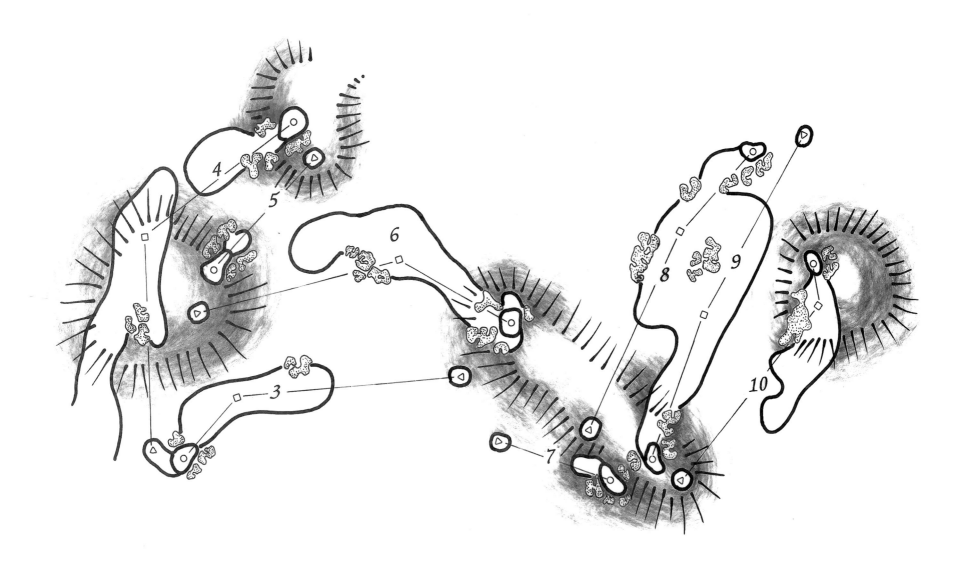

THE THIRD THROUGH TENTH HOLES ON MACKENZIE'S WEST COURSE PLAY AROUND TWO LARGE HILLS AND TWO SMALLER ONES. (COURTESY OF DON PLACEK, RENAISSANCE GOLF DESIGN, INC.)

THE THIRD AT ROYAL MELBOURNE'S WEST COURSE IS A 365-YARD PAR 4. THE TEE SHOT ON THIS DOGLEG LEFT APPEARS STRAIGHTAWAY, AND THERE IS A NATURAL TEMPTATION TO HUG THE LEFT SIDE OF THE FAIRWAY AND SHORTEN THE HOLE. HOWEVER, THE GREEN IS RAISED AT ITS LEFT, FRONT CORNER AND TILTED TOWARD THE BACK, MAKING IT DIFFICULT TO STOP APPROACHES QUICKLY. A SHARP SWALE ALONG THE RIGHT FLANK OF THE GREEN WILL COLLECT ANY PUSHED APPROACH. THE BEST TEE SHOT IS IN FACT LONG AND RIGHT, SO THAT THE APPROACH IS PLAYED PERPENDICULAR TO THE SWALE AT THE FRONT OF THE GREEN. **OPPOSITE PAGE, TOP:** ROYAL MELBOURNE'S (WEST) FIFTH HOLE. **OPPOSITE PAGE, BOTTOM:** THE SIXTH AT ROYAL MELBOURNE'S WEST COURSE.

THE 470-YARD PAR-4 FOURTH AT ROYAL MELBOURNE'S WEST COURSE. THE TEE SHOT IS BLIND BUT WELL DEFINED, UP OVER BUNKERS AT THE CREST OF A HILL, 30 FEET ABOVE THE TEE. A LONG AND STRAIGHT TEE BALL WILL GAIN CONSIDERABLE RUN ON THE BACK SIDE OF THE HILL, WHILE ANY SHOT HEDGED TO THE LEFT WILL RUN WELL AWAY TO THE LEFT, LEAVING A MUCH LONGER SHOT ON THIS DOGLEG RIGHT. TO GET HOME IN TWO, THE LONG APPROACH MUST FLIRT WITH BUNKERS SET ALONG THE EDGE OF THE FAIRWAY ON THE RIGHT, WHERE THE GROUND FALLS AWAY INTO TREES. SECOND SHOTS PLAYED AWAY FROM THE TROUBLE ON THE RIGHT LEAVE THIRD SHOTS THAT ARE STYMIED BY A LARGE BUNKER AT THE LEFT-FRONT OF THE GREEN. **OPPOSITE PAGE:** SKETCH COURTESY OF DON PLACEK, RENAISSANCE GOLF DESIGN, INC.

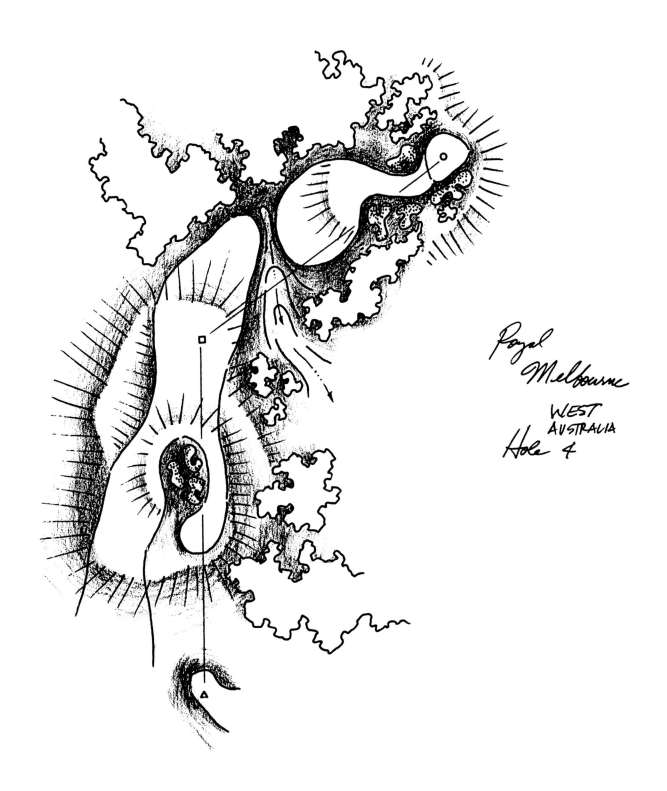

Royal
Melbourne
WEST
AUSTRALIA
Hole 4

hole he left intact was the par-5 15th and its cross bunkers, "to show future generations how silly golf course architecture used to be." The last two holes are MacKenzie originals—back-to-back bruisers, with the approach to the 17th always singled out as the most dramatic on the course.

The expansiveness and broad sweep of the Black Rock property are the essence of Royal Melbourne—the scope of it led MacKenzie to design the course and its hazards on a huge scale. Of all the holes, the West's fourth best embodies the course's spirit. Though MacKenzie was very much against blind holes in principle, the routing of the entire front nine hinged on his break from form on the tee shot at the fourth, which must be played up over yawning bunkers at the highest point on the property. There is fairway around to the left of those bunkers (now shared with the East 17th) but because it is sloped, it will kick a drive further to the left and leave the green clearly out of range for the second. Even a slight pull from the tee results in a frightening approach; a large bunker with an overhanging lip covers the left side of the green. The approach from the right appears daunting, too; the green hangs off the side of the hill, with scrub-filled bunkers below it on the right. However, the fairway in front of the green from this angle does allow a long approach to bounce short and run home.

The East Course at Royal Melbourne was not completed until 1932, so clearly most of the credit for it belongs to Russell and with Morcom, whose magnificent bunkers bring this much flatter terrain to life. Eleven holes are on property acquired years after MacKenzie's visit, but the first three holes are part of the additional nine which MacKenzie and Russell laid out before the doctor's departure. These three, along with Russell's East fourth, 17th and 18th, are part of the club's Composite course, devised so that tournaments could be played without crossing Cheltenham Road. Today, it is the Composite course that is world-famous—further tribute to Russell and Morcom for building golf holes that were good enough to improve on MacKenzie's West course.

THE SAND BELT

Royal Melbourne lies in the southwestern corner of what is known in Melbourne as the "Sand Belt." Along with the Sand Belt of Berkshire and Surrey near London, the Monterey Peninsula, and Long Island (New York), it has one of the highest concentrations of outstanding golf courses in the world. The underlying reason for all of these great courses is the same for each location: perfect sandy soil that facilitated easy construction, and which supported the fine-textured grasses, bracken fern, and shrubbery that is reminiscent of the great links courses.

During the time he resided at Royal Melbourne, MacKenzie is credited with having designed or redesigned four other prominent Sand Belt courses—Kingston Heath, Victoria, Metropolitan, and Yarra Yarra. (Three fine courses in the area that are not MacKenzie designs are Commonwealth and Woodlands, whose committees imitated the beautiful features that MacKenzie and his collaborators left behind, and Huntingdale, laid out in 1941 by MacKenzie's onetime partner C. H. Alison.)

Today, Kingston Heath is generally considered to be the second best course in Australia. It was designed by Australian golf professional Dan Soutar and opened in 1925, just prior to Alister's arrival in Australia. In those days, it was commonly agreed that bunkers be kept to a minimum on a new course and then added (or not) after observing play over a period of time. When MacKenzie arrived in Melbourne, he was a natu-

THE 16TH AT ROYAL MELBOURNE'S EAST COURSE.

ral choice to consult on bunker placement at Kingston Heath.

The doctor's report went further, suggesting a change in the routing to eliminate one blind hole and to create a new par 3. His report was adopted, and Morcom and son were contracted to carry out the work. Mick took the job, however, on the condition that he was allowed to deviate from the plans when he felt it was necessary. Whether this was just following MacKenzie's advice, or because Morcom realized that MacKenzie's plans could sometimes be extreme, is not certain.

In the end, MacKenzie's and Morcom's bunkers transformed Kingston Heath's 130 acres into a great test of golf. Through bold placement of the hazards, short and flat holes such as the 296-yard third and the 370-yard ninth were given character. And though Kingston Heath is visually similar to its big sister, Royal Melbourne, it is completely different in personality and scale. Kingston Heath's bunkers are as intricate as Royal Melbourne's are sweeping and expansive.

(Some of the credit for Kingston Heath's current acclaim must be given to its curator of recent times, Graeme Grant. With great care, he re-contoured a handful of greens, rebuilt all of the tees and many of the

IN 1926, ALISTER WAS HIRED TO OFFER SUGGESTIONS ABOUT BUNKER PLACEMENT ON THE NEWLY-OPENED KINGSTON HEATH COURSE IN THE SAND BELT AREA OF AUSTRALIA. HIS BOLD BUNKERING ENLIVENED BLAND HOLES LIKE THE 370-YARD PAR-4 NINTH.

THE MUCH ADMIRED 155-YARD PAR-3 15TH AT KINGSTON HEATH. **BELOW:** KINGSTON HEATH'S 370-YARD PAR-4 13TH. TAKING A RELATIVELY STRAIGHTAWAY PAR 4 LAID OUT BY DAN SOUTAR, MACKENZIE ADDED DEEP BUNKERS ALONG THE LEFT SIDE OF THE FAIRWAY AND MORE BUNKERS AT THE RIGHT FRONT OF THE GREEN. THIS FORCED PLAYERS TO EITHER FLIRT WITH BUNKERS OFF THE TEE OR CARRY THE OTHER CLUSTER ON THEIR APPROACH.

bunkers, and brought the course into championship condition.)

Kingston Heath's most memorable holes are its three short ones, and of these the 155-yard 15th—MacKenzie's new hole—has become world famous. A nest of bunkers run from the foot of the tee along to the right side of the elevated green. The green is shaped like an inverted "L", and it wraps around a deep and sinister bunker at the left front. The putting surface itself (the only one at Kingston Heath that MacKenzie built) is full of contour, so that a "safe" play to the back or the right results in a breakneck putt across its slopes. Like it is at another MacKenzie par 3, the famous 16th at Cypress Point, no medal score is safe until one has found the green here.

The doctor was also invited to consult on the bunkering at Victoria Golf Club, which lies adjacent to Royal Melbourne's East Course. The club had just completed its new course, but it had yet to open when MacKenzie visited.

There are many who consider Victoria to be the number three course in Australia, or at least in Melbourne. But this is probably a carryover from the magic year of 1954 when the Open and Amateur championship trophies of Britain were on display at the club after victories by Victoria members Peter Thomson and Doug Bachli. Its status is due in part to the MacKenzie pedigree but not because of his actual bunker work, most of which has been lost through the years. Indeed, the routing of the course is very un-MacKenzie-like, failing to make dramatic use of topography that is quite similar to Royal Melbourne's. In addition, most of the bunkers at Victoria are roughly oval in shape and no match for the beauties across the street. MacKenzie's handiwork is evident in a 1930s aerial photograph in the men's bar. What it reveals is that Morcom and his son definitely built some dramatic bunkers here. Why they were allowed to relapse is unclear.

There has been some movement in recent years toward restoring some of the bunkering, and perhaps the best hole on the course today is one of the few that has been restored. At the short par-4 15th, a dogleg left, the green is driveable if the tee shot is perfectly placed through the neck of the fairway. A miss to either side, though, will leave an awkward 50-yard bunker shot that may result in a four or a five. (Alex Russell built an almost mirror-image replica of this hole for the 15th on the East Course

at Royal Melbourne, but added an intriguing bend in the fairway.) Properly restored, Victoria would boast many other fine par-4 holes.

On the other flank of Royal Melbourne lies Sandringham, a public course which indirectly received the MacKenzie touch: Mick Morcom built some of its bunkers in an imitation of Royal Melbourne. Though it touches Royal Melbourne's West Course, none of the Sandringham course was ever part of Royal Melbourne. The starting and finishing holes of the original Royal Melbourne layout lay to the west of the present course, while Sandringham is all to the north.

Doctor MacKenzie also did a report for the Metropolitan Golf Club, which is a prominent course in the Australian championship rota, but it is not clear how many of his suggestions were actually implemented. In 1959, the course was remodeled significantly by American architect Dick Wilson. Only a few traces of MacKenzie's work remain, mostly on the front nine.

South of Melbourne, two outlying clubs also paid for Dr. MacKenzie's advice. The linksy Barwon Heads Golf Club was the first; though the club has never trumpeted MacKenzie's involvement, and may not have followed his advice, he is documented to have stayed at the club on November 11-14, 1926. The small Flinders Golf Club, on the south-eastern Mornington Peninsula, also retained Dr. MacKenzie to make recommendations on the layout during his visit to Royal Melbourne. Ironically, according to correspondence unearthed by Royal Melbourne member Bill Whitton, MacKenzie was already familiar with the location.[2] He had stayed there with his cousin Mrs. David Maxwell during a previous trip to Australia in 1902, when her husband (a St. Andrews native) was planning the original Flinders course on the family farm. If MacKenzie had been involved in the discussions and any of his ideas implemented on the original course, it would predate by five years his first work at Alwoodley. However, it was years before the club had any funds available to carry out part of MacKenzie's 1926 suggestions.

[2] Alister had probably traveled to Australia as a ship's surgeon, a frequent practice at that time among young doctors keen to see the world.

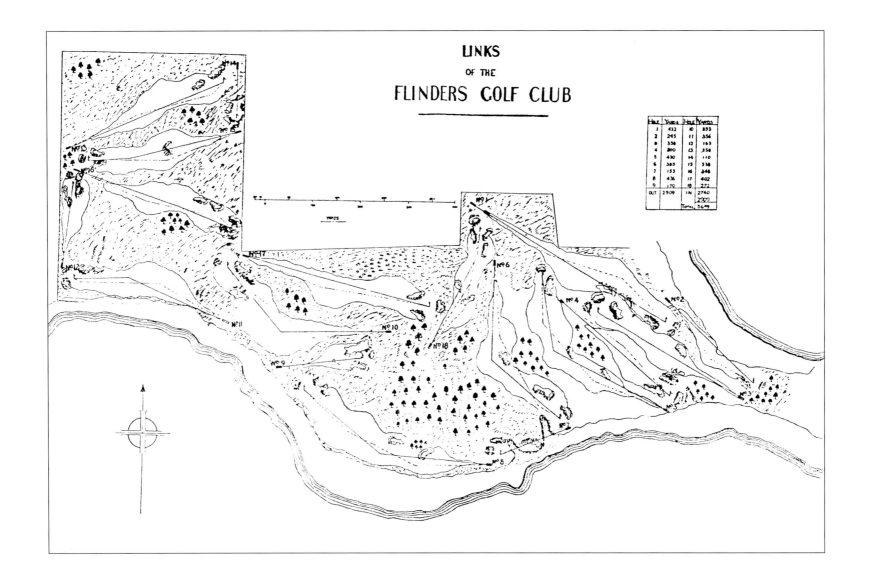

DURING HIS TRIP TO AUSTRALIA, MACKENZIE WAS ALSO RETAINED BY FLINDERS GOLF CLUB TO MAKE IMPROVEMENT SUGGESTIONS. HOWEVER, IT WAS YEARS BEFORE RECOMMENDATIONS WERE IMPLEMENTED.

YARRA YARRA

The only other original "MacKenzie" layout in Melbourne is Yarra Yarra Golf Club, which the partnership of MacKenzie and Russell announced in January of 1927, six weeks after the doctor's departure from Australia. This was another older club that followed Victoria and Metropolitan to the growing Sand Belt suburbs.

The Yarra Yarra property is between Royal Melbourne and Kingston Heath, both in location and topography; it is gently rolling, with the clubhouse sited along a broad, 30-foot high ridge that runs across the midsection of the property.

While not as difficult as some of MacKenzie's other famous courses, Yarra Yarra does offer several outstanding holes. The most renowned of these are the quartet of short holes, considered by Dick Wilson to be the best set of par 3s in Australia. They start out with a bang: the 220-yard first hole plays slightly downhill behind the pro shop to a well-bunkered green. It makes Yarra Yarra the only MacKenzie course in our experience to start with a par 3. The short fourth is harrowing, with yawning bunkers to the left waiting to catch a pulled eight-iron. At the equally short 15th, deep bunkers sit at both sides of a sharply two-tiered green. Most famous of all is the 173-yard 11th, with a cascading green guarded by two huge bunkers across the front and the right side of the putting

surface, and another bunker set into the slope at back left. This is a classic MacKenzie green—so severely contoured that no other architect would have dared build it. He must have had a role here, although it is hard to document because there isn't any surviving correspondence between MacKenzie and Russell.

Yarra Yarra also features some very strong two-shot holes. The slight dogleg right par-4 13th is somewhat reminiscent in strategy of the Road Hole at St. Andrews. It's well bunkered at the inside of the bend and severely so at the left front of the green. Though MacKenzie disdained the idea of copying famous holes, he had nominated the Road Hole many times as one of the few ideal holes in golf. If he had mentioned that belief to Russell (who was also familiar with St. Andrews), it is not surprising that the hole was given more than a passing resemblance.

Even more dramatic is the 438-yard fifth, one of the best par 4s in Australia. The tee shot is fairly innocent; the hole doglegs to the right over a small crest with a fairway bunker in the corner, no more than 200 yards off the tee. Only when you have reached the corner, however, is the importance of carrying the fairway bunker made clear. The second shot must be played from a slightly downhill lie back up to the green. About 50 yards before the green, in the left-center of the fairway, there's a rough knob with terrifying bunkers cut into it.

With a solid drive to the right, it is possible to carry past the frightening hazard and onto the green. The more the drive goes to the left, though, the tougher the approach becomes. For the short hitter, there are many options for the second shot. Should one attempt to carry the bunkers? Lay up and face a half-blind third shot? Or skirt by the right side of the bunkers? (But not too far right or else the bunkers to the right of the green come into play for the third shot.) Even for those who can carry the hazard easily, its left-center location induces many a subconscious push out to the right, where greenside bunkers await.

ROYAL ADELAIDE

In the middle of his Melbourne visit, MacKenzie traveled by train to the South Australian capital of Adelaide for four days to consult on the

ONE OF THE BEST PAR 4s IN AUSTRALIA: THE FIFTH AT YARRA YARRA.

ALISTER RE-WORKED THE ROUTING AT ROYAL ADELAIDE IN ORDER TO BRING AN AREA OF DUNES MORE INTO PLAY. PHOTOGRAPHED FROM THE REAR, THIS IS THE 301-YARD PAR-4 THIRD. **BELOW:** THE 14TH AT ROYAL ADELAIDE. THE HOLLOWS GUARDING THE RIGHT SIDE OF THE FAIRWAY LOOK NATURAL BUT WERE CREATED BY DR. MACKENZIE.

Royal Adelaide Golf Club, which had existed on its present location since 1904. The club was anxious to have MacKenzie re-route several holes in order to avoid crossing the Grange-to-Adelaide tram line, which was about to be electrified.

Situated about a mile inland from the Gulf of St. Vincent, the property is mostly flat with an area of forested dunes at the center of the square. Prior to MacKenzie's visit, the golf course largely avoided the dunes area by working around its perimeter. MacKenzie changed the routing so that the holes are constantly working back into the center of the property where the action is. Nearly all of the best holes interact with the dunes in some way.

The first hole on which the dunes are encountered is the 301-yard third, an apparent pushover that has been the undoing of several players in championship play. Along the right side of the hole from tee to green are the dunes, covered with native grasses and lichens; a narrow ridge blanketed by thick rough is at the front left of the green. The fairway goes over a slight crest at about 180 yards from the tee. This crest obscures the green and introduces a bit of uncertainty for the strong player. Though the hole is quite straightforward beyond the rise, only the straightest of drives will do; a loss of concentration can result in major trouble.

The tee on the dogleg fourth is located within the dune country, and it takes a solid hit to carry back into the parkland. A drive to the left, close to fairway bunkers inside the bend of the dogleg, improves the angle for the second shot significantly.

The green setting of the long par-4 sixth is elevated into the side of the dunes, so that a pulled second shot winds up well below the green. The par-3 seventh is just tee and green among the dunes, with a line of small and nasty pot bunkers across the green's flank. The next three holes circumnavigate the north end of the dunes, and then the par-4 11th dives back in, for a heroic second shot across sand and scrub into an amphitheater green. The long par-3 12th requires a final carry to exit the dunes.

There are some strong holes at the finish (particularly the long par-4 14th) that feature another brilliant MacKenzie touch. Essentially a flat hole at birth, what really makes the 14th is a nest of fairway bunkers on the right that guard the shortest line to the green. These bunkers are built into the face of what appear to be natural depressions. But everything here is MacKenzie's work. By excavating large hollows and then only making part of them into sand, he created the impression that the hollows were natural—camouflage at its finest.

The tram line, ironically—Royal Adelaide's principal reason for inviting MacKenzie—was never electrified. Ten years after his visit, the trams were converted from steam to diesel.

SYDNEY

No visit to Australia would have been complete without a visit to the state of New South Wales and its capital city of Sydney. But Dr. MacKenzie almost didn't make it, thanks to the intense rivalry between Royal Sydney and Royal Melbourne. What happened was that the former club's preliminary attempts to contact the doctor were not passed on by Royal Melbourne, even though their arrangement with MacKenzie would have given them a share of the fees. (When Dr. MacKenzie was paid for his consulting work on December 16, he made no arrangement to give Royal Melbourne its commission.) Eventually, though, a letter addressed to MacKenzie in care of Royal Melbourne did get through. He left Melbourne in early December and headed straight for the Royal Sydney clubhouse in the posh suburb of Rose Bay, with its yacht basin immediately across the street.

Despite the luxury accommodations, MacKenzie was less than tactful in detailing what he perceived to be the deficiencies of the Royal Sydney course. Repeatedly, he described the profusion of bunkers that were not to his liking as representing "the penal philosophy" underlying Australian course design. He believed Royal Sydney was "far too difficult for the average golfer but not a sufficiently high test for the scratch man and has little effect in stimulating him to improve his game." Most of his suggestions went towards reducing the number of bunkers, and the implementation of his ideas was left in the hands of the Secretary, Colonel Bertram, whom MacKenzie noted "has had the advantage of learning his golf at St. Andrews!"

While in Sydney, MacKenzie also consulted at The Australian and Manly golf clubs. The Australian Golf Club is still one of the continent's premier golf clubs and championship venues, but today's course owes

3rd   November   1926

Dr. A. Mackenzie
  c/o Royal Melbourne Golf Club.
      Sandringham.

Dear Sir,

        I have been advised that you are at present engaged
in planning out alterations and additions to the Royal
Melbourne Golf Course, and that possibly you may have a
little time to spare on the completion of that work.

        My Committee hope that you will be able to visit
us and give us the benefit of your advice as to any
improvements which you could suggest. I understand that your
fee depends on the amount of work which is neccessary, and
can hardly be determined.beforehand.

        If you come to Sydney, I think that I can arrange
accomodation for you at this Club, and in this case I should
be glad to hear from you as early as possible so that a
room could be reserved.

                        Yours faithfully,

                             Secretary.

ONCE WORD GOT OUT, OTHER GOLF CLUBS IN SYDNEY WERE ALSO INTERESTED IN OBTAINING MACKENZIE'S SERVICES.

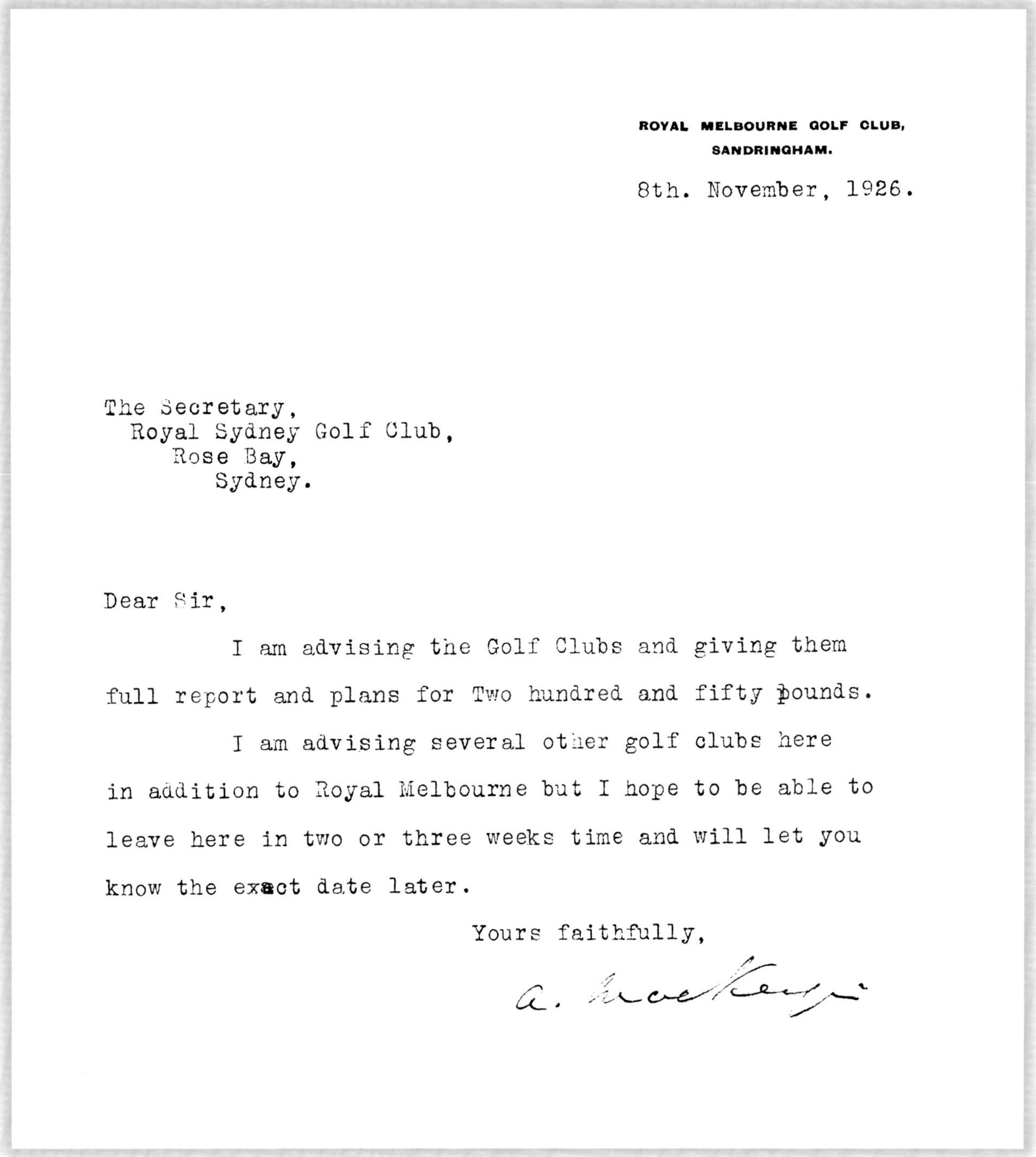

ROYAL MELBOURNE GOLF CLUB,
SANDRINGHAM.

8th. November, 1926.

The Secretary,
  Royal Sydney Golf Club,
    Rose Bay,
      Sydney.

Dear Sir,

        I am advising the Golf Clubs and giving them
full report and plans for Two hundred and fifty pounds.

        I am advising several other golf clubs here
in addition to Royal Melbourne but I hope to be able to
leave here in two or three weeks time and will let you
know the exact date later.

                    Yours faithfully,

                    A. MacKenzie

ALISTER WAS MORE THAN HAPPY TO TAKE ADVANTAGE OF HIS NEW POPULARITY.

New South Wales Golf Club does have an historic and prominent setting: the furthest point from the clubhouse (the sixth tee) is located on the end of Cape Banks, the rocky point that forms the northern end of Botany Bay. It was around Cape Banks that James Cook sailed *Endeavor* in 1770, landing across the bay to make the European discovery of Australia.

It is a wild property, intersected by several sharp ridges and completely exposed to gales off the ocean. Out-of-play areas are covered with native "bottle brush," a dense shrub that must have reminded MacKenzie of the whins of Scotland.

MacKenzie's routing did not shelter in the valleys; it attacks the dramatic contours of the property boldly and head-on, making for some memorable holes and golf shots. The par-5 fifth plays up and over a humpbacked ridge that few players can carry from the tee. It leaves a blind second over the top of the hill, a shot that is hard to keep down into the stiff headwind. Once players clear the summit, though, they are rewarded with a jaw-dropping view down the fairway to a green near land's end. (Another golfing descent that may be as breathtaking is also MacKenzie's: the tenth fairway at Augusta.) The dogleg par-4 13th, with its approach played toward Inscription Point on the far side of Botany Bay, and the short par-4 14th with its dramatic tee shot across the edge of a chasm down to the shore, also remain as classic MacKenzie holes.

Although the New South Wales course is justifiably rated among the top fifty in the world, in this instance too much of the credit may have gone to MacKenzie. In the early 1930s, the requisition of some land for coastal fortifications precipitated a substantial revision of the layout by Eric Apperly, the fine amateur player who had helped to complete MacKenzie's bunker scheme. Several of the course's most famous holes are Apperly's designs, including all the par 3s. Surprisingly to many, the "signature" par-3 sixth—with its tee on the rocks of Cape Banks and often compared

little to MacKenzie. A parkland course on gently undulating ground, MacKenzie's suggestions in 1926 were to grass over many superfluous bunkers and add a few in strategic spots. Fifty years later, the club had another crisis of confidence: the course was considered too short for championship play. In 1976, businessman Kerry Packer convinced the club to reorganize and finance a total redesign of the course by Jack Nicklaus (only his third commission as a designer). Nicklaus's primary change was in adding several water hazards around the course, but he also modified the routing of the holes and rebuilt all the greens and bunkers.

NEW SOUTH WALES GOLF CLUB

MacKenzie's one new project in Sydney was south of the city at La Perouse, on the shores of Botany Bay. Colonel Bertram of Royal Sydney accompanied MacKenzie on his visits to the site and after finishing the layout, MacKenzie suggested that Bertram be retained at a "nominal fee" to supervise the work. This arrangement suggests just how quickly MacKenzie recruited his partners and how tenuous the relationships were (Alex Russell, his new Australian partner, had no role at New South Wales). It may also explain why New South Wales, in contrast to MacKenzie's Melbourne courses, has more functional but less beautiful bunkers.

THE18TH HOLE AND CLUBHOUSE AT ROYAL SYDNEY GOLF CLUB. **OPPOSITE PAGE, TOP:** VIEW FROM THE FAIRWAY AT THE PAR-5 FIFTH AT NEW SOUTH WALES GOLF CLUB. **OPPOSITE PAGE, BOTTOM:** THE APPROACH INTO THE 13TH AT NEW SOUTH WALES. INSCRIPTION POINT IS IN THE BACKGROUND ON THE FAR SIDE OF BOTANY BAY.

IN THE EARLY 1930S, SEVERAL HOLES AT NEW SOUTH WALES WERE REVISED. THE PAR-3 SIXTH—SIMILAR IN SOME WAYS TO MACKENZIE'S 16TH AT CYPRESS POINT—WAS DESIGNED BY ERIC APPERLY, NOT ALISTER. **BELOW:** THE 14TH AT NEW SOUTH WALES IS A "CAPE"-TYPE PAR 4 OF 355 YARDS. THE TEE SHOT IS ACROSS THE CORNER OF BOTANY BAY TO A SEVERELY TILTED FAIRWAY, AND THE SECOND SHOT IS UPHILL TO A VERY SMALL GREEN. MACKENZIE'S ORIGINAL GREEN WAS IN THE VALLEY, 30 YARDS SHORT OF THE PRESENT PUTTING SURFACE, BUT THE HEROIC NATURE OF THE TEE SHOT IS STILL THE ESSENCE OF THE HOLE.

to the 16th at Cypress Point—is not MacKenzie's design. Apperly added a short hole between the current fifth and seventh (both MacKenzie holes) to make up for the original short fourth — sacrificed for the defense of the nation. The famous tee out on the rocks was added in the 1950s. Holes 1, 2, 8, 11, and 17 are also Apperly's. Still, one cannot discount Dr. MacKenzie's role in establishing the seed of golf on this dramatic headland.

OTHER AUSTRALIAN CONTRACTS

Doctor MacKenzie is sometimes credited with two courses in other parts of Australia, but our research confirms only one. His voyage from England in 1926 made landfall at Fremantle before going on to Melbourne, and it led some to believe that he may have seen the site for Lake Karrinyup Golf Club in Perth at that time. MacKenzie, however, never saw the site. Lake Karrinyup is entirely Alex Russell's work, though MacKenzie may have helped with the routing plan. The lake for which it is named is an excellent watering hole, and the expansive property gives the wallabies plenty of room to roam. Few of the holes here, though, have the wild MacKenzie spirit.

Dr. MacKenzie did, however, spend a full week in December in Brisbane, and consulted on three courses there. Royal Queensland Golf Club embraces it association with MacKenzie; their par-3 eighth hole is regarded as the best surviving example of his work there. In contrast, Brisbane Golf Club disagreed with many of the doctor's suggestions and did not follow through on them. As for the third course, MacKenzie wrote after his trip that he had laid out an entirely new course for Indooroopilly Golf Club (now St. Lucia C.C.), but it is not known if his redesign was put into action.

NEW ZEALAND

On his way from Australia to America by steamship, Dr. MacKenzie did stop for several days at Auckland, New Zealand and made a consulting visit to the Titirangi Golf Club, where he made plans for the expansion of a course opened in 1921. The doctor's original plan for the new course still hangs proudly in the Titirangi clubhouse.

The doctor's plan called for several new holes at the far end of the course to be hacked from the subtropical jungle. A deep ravine formed by the Whau stream runs out the lower end of the property, and holes 11 through 15 all make use of it. The short 11th plays alongside the ravine to a green set on a ridge, somewhat reminiscent of the famous Redan (but set completely sideways to the line of play requiring a carry). The long 12th and 13th run down and back on either side of the ravine, a spur of which intrudes from the left short of the 13th green. The short 14th must carry the ravine to a heavily contoured green. MacKenzie also sandwiched a new short 7th hole in among the holes adapted from the previous layout.

Titirangi appears to be MacKenzie's only design contract in New Zealand. Heretaunga in Wellington and Queenstown Golf Club on South Island have also been listed as having been designed or redesigned by MacKenzie at various times, but this has not been confirmed. In addition, the dates of the courses' development do not fit with his only visit to New Zealand. Alex Russell might possibly have had something to do with these, and it may have been inferred that MacKenzie was his partner.

MacKenzie did visit other parts of New Zealand before leaving, notably Rotorua in the volcanic central region of North Island. The thermal activity fascinated him: when he stuck his walking stick into the ground, the tip came out charred. He also liked the story—and added it to his repertoire—of the cockney founder of the local golf club who was given to claim, "This is the only course in the world that 'as 'ot 'oles as 'azards."

At the end of his visit to New Zealand, MacKenzie boarded a steamer and was off to America to follow up on the jobs for which he had laid the groundwork just prior to his Australian sojourn. On the month-long voyage to California, visions of Cypress Point were undoubtedly dancing in his head.

LAKE KARRINYUP GC IN PERTH WAS DESIGNED BY ONE OF MACKENZIE'S COLLABORATORS, ALEX RUSSELL, ALTHOUGH ALISTER MAY HAVE ASSISTED WITH THE ROUTING PLAN. THIS IS THE 2ND HOLE. **OPPOSITE PAGE, TOP:** AS FAR AS IS KNOWN, TITIRANGI GOLF CLUB IS THE ONLY COURSE MACKENZIE CONSULTED ON IN NEW ZEALAND ON HIS WAY BACK TO AMERICA. THE 11TH HOLE IS ONE OF FIVE AT TITIRANGI THAT UTILIZES A DEEP RAVINE ON THE PROPERTY. **OPPOSITE PAGE, BOTTOM:** THE SHORT SEVENTH AT TITIRANGI GC.

~ MACKENZIE'S CHANGES AT TITIRANGI ~

On his way back to America from Australia, Alister stopped in New Zealand and did some consulting work on an existing layout called Maungakiekie Golf Course. It was later re-named Titirangi Golf Club. MacKenzie's report on what he wanted to change was typed on his letterhead:

The ground on which the Maungakiekie Golf Course is situated is exceptionally well adapted for golf. It is undulating without being hilly and has many fine natural features such as ravines of a bold and impressive nature, intersecting the course in many places.

The subsoil consists largely of clay, but the turf is good and appears to be improving yearly and the improvement is largely due to the judicious drainage, and particularly the mole draining that has been done on the course.

The course on the whole has been well designed, and with slight alterations and a scheme of bunkering it can be made not only most interesting and pleasurable for all classes of players, but will stimulate golfers to improve their game and be a test of golf which will be quite good enough for any Championship.

At the present time the fairways are far too narrow and there is too much long grass about, and the first essential is to make the course so that hunting for balls is entirely eliminated.

Golf is played for pleasure and can be made quite difficult enough with bunkers and other features, and there should be no continuous stretches of rough between the Tees or Greens or dividing parallel holes. Irregular islands of attractive vegetation should be quite sufficient. I believe the unpopularity of golf during the summer months in New Zealand is due to similar defects being almost universal there. I would strongly advise the Club to obtain a Pattinson's Tractor and Quintuplemowing machine so

that the whole of the rough can be kept constantly mown. I would also advise that all the open drains be covered so that the bottom of all the valleys can be kept mown. The trees in the ravine should be thinned out in irregular groups so that there is no risk of losing balls and this should be completed before play is allowed on the new holes.

The alterations I suggest are as follows:

1st. HOLE — Present 1st. Bunker as on the plan.[?] up the back of the green by means of a large sand faced hummock.

2nd. HOLE — The tee should be placed to the right and the hole bunkered so as to give a big advantage to the player who takes the long carry over the ravines. The back of the green should be made more conspicuous.

3rd. HOLE — Bunker similarly to the famous 16th hole at St. Andrews, so as to give a narrow route to the right and broad one to the left. Raise the sides of the green by Bunkers and hollows.

4th. HOLE — This can be made a much finer hole by enlarging the Bunkers and making them of a more impressive appearance.

5th. HOLE — A hole played back near the road.

6th. HOLE — This should be a vastly superior hole to the present 14th.

7th. HOLE — A new one shot hole played to near present 18th Green. This should not only make a fine hole but it will also give alternative staring off place near the Club house.

8th. HOLE — Played to existing 15th green from near the Club house.

9th. HOLE — Existing 16th lengthened and played dog-legged.

10th. HOLE — Existing 10th lengthened.

11th. HOLE — New short hole constructed so that the surface of the green is absolutely visible. This should make a famous hole.

12th. HOLE — Present 5th. Played dog-legged from the opposite side.

13th. HOLE — Present 7th. With Tee shot over the Ravine.

14th. HOLE — This should make an excellent one shot hole somewhat similar to the famous Eden hole at St. Andrews.

15th. Hole — Present 8th. Played over the Ravine. Note: It is essential that before play is commenced on this and preceding holes that the ravine be cleaned out so that no balls will be lost.

16th. Hole — Present 9th — with green placed in plateau beyond existing green. The green might be made in two levels so that the front is in a punch bowl.

17th. Hole — Existing 17th with Tee lengthened and preferably the green shortened.

18th. Hole — From lengthened Tee played dog-legged to avoid the evening sun to a new green.

FURTHER SUGGESTIONS: I would suggest that at least 12 new men with scoops, ploughs, etc. be employed at once to get the new greens ready for seeding in the Autumn and the remainder of the bunkers and alterations to existing greens in the winter. The course should be fit for play next Spring.

My experience is that work of this kind cannot be done by a Committee and that it is essential that it should be left entirely in the hands of one man. He is certain to make a few mistakes, we all do, but he will learn by these mistakes and the work should be left entirely in his hands until it is completed.

If there is any difference of opinion in the interpretation of my ideas, it should be borne in mind that the standard of golf is rapidly improving, and what may appear very difficult to-day may not be so to-morrow, so that the tendency should be to place bunkers further from the Tees provided there is always an alternative route open to the weaker player. There is no reason, for instance, why on occasions there should not be a voluntary carry of 250 yards in the direct line to this hole, this will have the effect of stimulating players to lengthen their drives and is absolutely fair as weaker players have alternate routes to the right or left or short, and if they get trapped it is clearly an error in judgment on their part.

On the other hand the fairways and greens should be large but the bunkers should be immediately on the edge of the greens so that the man who is wide of them has such a difficult pitch that he frequently worse off than if he is in them.

It is difficult to estimate the cost of construction as this depends on the weather, unexpected drainage problems, etc., but I would suggest that at least £2,000 be allocated for the construction work.

A. MacKenzie.

Chapter Nine
The Land of Opportunity

DR. MACKENZIE FIRST RECEIVED EXPOSURE IN AMERICA AS EARLY AS 1914, THANKS TO HIS PRIZE IN THE *COUNTRY LIFE* COMPETITION. *COUNTRY LIFE* WAS READ BY HIGH SOCIETY IN BOTH COUNTRIES, and Bernard Darwin's writing on golf was read by all who loved the game. When The Lido was finally erected after the war, Macdonald did employ MacKenzie's design, though the final product was a mirror-image of the hole with one less alternate route and the green significantly toned down. It is unrecorded if Dr. MacKenzie ever saw his design as a work in progress, but it is unlikely, as he did not mention the changes in his writings.

After the war, the partnership of Colt, MacKenzie and Alison pursued several American contracts, including Bob O'Link in Chicago, the Country Club of Detroit, and Timber Point on the south shore of Long Island. Alison was the representative for the firm in America, so it is doubtful that MacKenzie made his own trip during that period. If so, it would have provided a fortuitous contact because the Timber Point course was developed by members of Westbrook Golf Club, one of whom was the father of the young U.S. Women's Amateur champion, Marion Hollins.

After he published *Golf Architecture* in 1920, MacKenzie was sought out by Americans interested in the subject. In 1926, a few months before his trip to Australia, MacKenzie traveled through the United States to visit two of these new acquaintances—men who were to help lay the groundwork for his American operations.

The first was Perry Maxwell, an Oklahoma banker turned golf architect who had met MacKenzie when he made his own tour of British links in 1923. Maxwell had suggested upon their meeting that MacKenzie would find much work in America and that he was welcome to visit him. The doctor remembered the offer and used it to take a break from his cross-country train trip after arriving on the east coast. Maxwell then quickly arranged for MacKenzie to be brought on as a paid consultant on the design of his newfound contract at Melrose Country Club in Philadelphia.

The second man was Robert Hunter, one of the more interesting characters to become involved in the golf business. Married to an heiress, Hunter established his fame with his 1904 book, *Poverty*, hailed as one of the key books in the growing Socialist movement in the United States. His heartfelt look at the plight of the masses attracted the attention of

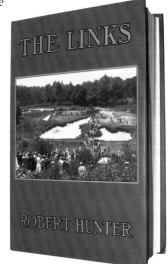

MACKENZIE COLLABORATOR ROBERT HUNTER BECAME INTERESTED IN GOLF COURSE ARCHITECTURE AFTER VISITING GREAT BRITAIN IN 1912.

∾ MacKenzie in America ∾

Famous British Golf Architect Will Plan Melrose C.C. Links

Dr. Allister Mackenzie, Builder of More Than 400
Courses, Is Designing Layout for New
Club at Elkins Park

By TED HOYT

DR. ALLISTER MACKENZIE, of Leeds, England, famous golf architect, who has designed more than 400 courses during his long career which began in 1906, and who is planning the links for the new Melrose Country Club of Elkins Park, has some very interesting ideas as to how a course should be laid out.

He insists that tees and greens, traps, bunkers, fairway and rough should so fit into the surrounding landscape as to look perfectly natural and not be obviously the work of man, as is the case at many links.

And he firmly believes that while each hole should be so constructed as to test the ability of the stars to the limit yet there should be more than one way of playing the hole so that the dubs, the older men and the short but accurate hitters will have a chance to reach the green in a reasonable number of shots.

Seen yesterday at the office of Wayne Herkness, a member of the Construction Committee of the Melrose Country Club, in the Land Title Building, Dr. Mackenzie said that he always used natural hazards whenever possible and tried to make those he added look natural.

In designing holes, he continued, he always sought to put a premium on brains as well as brawn. The drive must be placed for the second shot at the par four holes and at the long ones, unless the tee shot and the brassie were deadly accurate it would be impossible to reach and hold the carpet with the third.

Dr. Mackenzie does not believe it's "golf" to have every green banked at the rear and facing the ball so that most any old pitch shot will stick. He slopes his green to right or left or even toward the rear, depending on the nature of the terrain and the effect he is striving for, and the only way a player can hold the ball on one of their carpets is to approach it from just the proper point on the fairway.

"It's the strategy of the game that makes it so fascinating," according to Dr. Mackenzie. "On a course I have designed a man must play each shot so as to make it possible to get the desired results with the next one. This holds good until the ball is in the cup. You cannot stand on the tee and hammer the ball in the general direction of the green and expect to make low scores. Distance yes, but right along the line."

First Invasion of Eastern Territory

While Mackenzie-made courses are scattered through the British Isles, in Australia, New Zealand, California and other sections of the West, this is his first effort in Eastern territory and he is, quite naturally, anxious to give the Melrose C.C. a layout both he and the club can be proud of.

And, of course, local linksmen are keen to see what the man who is known in England as the "dean of golf architects" will produce as his initial contribution along the Atlantic seaboard.

Speaking of the terrain of the Melrose C.C., which was formerly the Curtis Country Club, Dr. Mackenzie said it had every natural advantage and he believed he and his partner, P.B. Maxwell, would be able to plan and build a course there that would attract golfers from far and near.

Mr. Maxwell has already drawn some tentative plans, and he and Dr. Mackenzie will spend several days going over the property. Then they will decide on the final plan—and work will begin at once. Already a sawmill has been installed and the task of cleaning out some of the thick clumps of woods that dot the terrain has been started.

The actual construction of the course will be in charge of Dean Woods, chief engineer of the Mackenzie-Maxwell organization, but Mr. Maxwell will pay frequent visits here to supervise the job.

An interesting point is that there will be only one steep climb on the course, though the ground is hilly and has a valley through the central part, where gently ambles the Tacony Creek. This stream will be utilized as a water hazard at a number of holes.

Dr. Mackenzie is a graduate of Cambridge University, both from the collegiate department and the medical school. After the usual period of hospital duty, he hung out his shingle in Leeds and settled down to be a regular medico. Then came the Boer War and he went into the Medical Corps of the British Army.

It was during his service in Africa that he evolved the thought of camouflage as applied to men, trenches, guns and so on and which proved so useful during the World War. He frankly confesses that he got the idea from the Boers and that he first applied the principle to golf courses when he went in for that line of work around 1906.

wealthy do-gooders in New York and elsewhere, and he became the center of a group of "millionaire Socialists" who pleaded for better treatment of the poor while enjoying the fruits of inherited wealth.

After traveling to Britain in 1912, Hunter became fascinated with golf architecture and its influence on how the game is played. In 1926 he published *The Links*, a scholarly look at the art of golf design. His book differed from all the others simply because he was not a designer and thus not someone trying to attract commissions. Therefore, he used the best examples he could find from all the leading architects of the day as well as the ancient links. In compiling drawings and photographs for his book he was particularly indebted to Dr. MacKenzie, who contributed not only greens sketches and photos of his own work, but helped Hunter find some good pictures of the famous British links.

By fortunate coincidence, Hunter had moved his home to Pebble Beach in the early 1920s and had invited MacKenzie to visit him in California, where there was much work. In fact, *The Links* caused several

would-be golf course developers to seek out Hunter's advice. Consequently, MacKenzie's help with the book would be repaid on a much grander scale.

THE MEADOW CLUB

Hunter and MacKenzie's first design collaboration in California was at The Meadow Club, sited atop a high meadow in the hills of Marin County, north of San Francisco. The long, twisting drive to the club on the side of Mount Tamalpais is so difficult even today that it is hard to imagine the impetus for founding the club here in the mid 1920s. Nevertheless, when MacKenzie arrived in California he was almost immediately ushered north to see the property. He quickly devised an

OPPOSITE PAGE: MACKENZIE'S DRAWING OF THE FOURTH HOLE AT THE MEADOW CLUB THAT APPEARED IN GEORGE THOMAS'S *GOLF ARCHITECTURE IN AMERICA*.

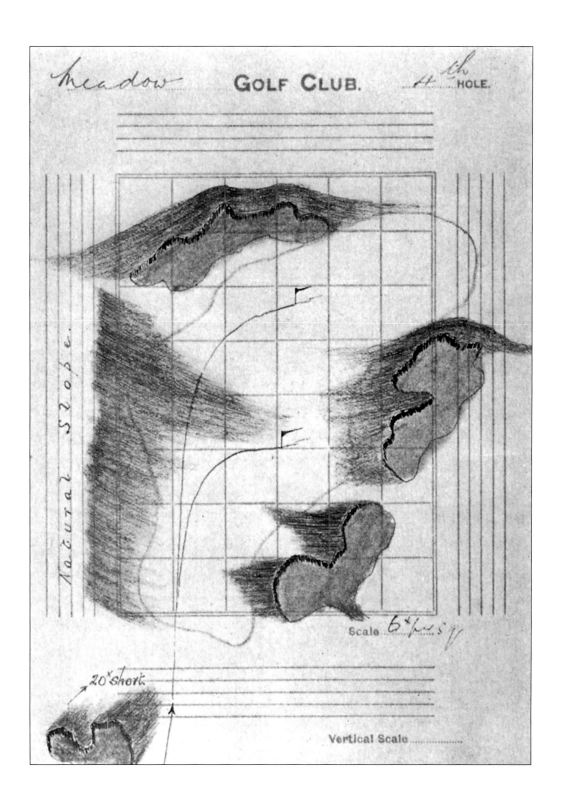

18-hole routing plan and individual greens sketches for Hunter to implement. [Two of these were illustrated in George Thomas's *Golf Architecture in America* in 1927, coinciding with the opening of the club.] Judging from the dates of the opening, however, most of the work to the course must have been completed while MacKenzie was en route back to England and then on to Australia, with the finishing touches applied upon his return.

Unfortunately, though the location of the site is quite dramatic, the undulations of the property were meager and its rocky subsoil proved difficult. The result was that Dr. MacKenzie's first finished project in America was not quite the showpiece it was intended to be. Today, all of its bunkers and greens have been rebuilt from the original. Though the club is proud of its MacKenzie heritage, in truth the design is not well preserved. Serious efforts at restoration are now underway.

CYPRESS POINT

The real impetus for Dr. MacKenzie's trip to America in 1926 was Robert Hunter's interest in the land that would become Cypress Point Club. In 1922, after founding the Women's National Golf & Tennis Club on Long Island, Marion Hollins traveled west to settle on the Monterey Peninsula. She quickly became the leading salesperson and promoter for Samuel Morse's Del Monte Properties Company to develop the penin-

sula. Acting upon a suggestion from Hollins, Morse decided that, with her background in golf, she was the perfect fit for organizing the development of a private club at Cypress Point, christened in 1774 by the Spaniard, Father Tomas de la Pena.

Marion and Roger Lapham (director of the California Golf Association and one of the most influential men in San Francisco) hired Seth Raynor to design the new course. He was the design protégé of C. B. Macdonald who had assisted in the development of the Women's National. At the time, Raynor was already working on the Dunes Course for the Monterey Peninsula Country Club. But before construction could begin, Raynor died unexpectedly in 1926. Robert Hunter, Jr., from Marion's polo-playing circle of friends, then suggested that Marion talk to Dr. MacKenzie, a friend of his father's who would be visiting soon.

MacKenzie and the elder Hunter surveyed the dunes and forest at the terminus of 17-Mile Drive (the end was a traffic circle just past the now-famous 16th green) and were enthralled. For once, probably, there was no hint of exaggeration in MacKenzie's report for the club prospectus:

ABOVE: MEADOW CLUB. **OPPOSITE PAGE:** LEFT TO RIGHT, ROBERT HUNTER, JR., ROBERT HUNTER, SR., H.J. WIGHAM, AND ALISTER MACKENZIE.

It would be difficult to over-estimate the great possibilities of a golf course at Cypress Point. I am fully acquainted with the world's greatest golf courses and have no hesitation in saying that in the beauty of its surroundings, the magnificence of its sand dunes, its spectacular sea views, its glorious Cypress trees — there is an opportunity of making [a golf course] which should be superior to any other.

Cypress Point has interested me more than any land I have ever had to deal with. For the sake of my reputation I should like to make you the best golf links in existence.

The partners also supplied a revised routing plan for the golf course that Raynor had begun to lay out.

After a triumphant return from Australia and a quick visit back to Ireland and Britain to be on hand for the Open Championship at St. Andrews, MacKenzie returned to California in the summer of 1927 to begin work on what many consider to be his masterpiece. The project was also to be one of his most fruitful collaborations. Robert Hunter, Jr.'s American Golf Course Construction Company did the construction work, with Hunter frequently on hand to answer questions. Jack Fleming, over from Ireland, was also involved in the construction—although

THE DUNES OF CYPRESS POINT PRIOR TO CONSTRUCTION.

～ MARION HOLLINS ～

The second Marion in Alister's life was Marion Hollins, his great supporter in California. Several times larger and more extraordinary than life, this Marion was born in 1891, the rich child of very wealthy parents. Marion Hollins was something of a "tomboy." At an early age she excelled at a wide range of sports, including tennis, golf, motor racing and equestrianism, especially polo. Her parents encouraged her to focus upon golf—with dramatic results. In 1913, at age 22, she was the runner-up in the U.S. Women's Amateur Championship. She won the event in 1921. In 1932, after being named "Outstanding Woman Athlete of the 1920s," she was named captain of the first United States Curtis Cup team.

Like the other Marion (Alister's sister), she was an active suffragette—although she was certainly not deprived of opportunities because she was a woman. But being active in sports was not the only string in her bow. In a biography of Hollins, *Champion In A Man's World* by David Outerbridge, she is described as a tall handsome woman. "Large," according to Outerbridge, "with a deep, throaty voice." She cared little about what she wore. She held her own with males not only in sport but in business matters as well. In the mid-1920s she was hired by the Pebble Beach Company and encountered MacKenzie in relation to Cypress Point. At the time of

Alister's upheavals, they were working together on completion of the Pasatiempo development, a site that provided a magnificent view of Monterey Bay. A small investment on possible California oil less than a year earlier had suddenly yielded her $2.5 million.

Alister had given much time and effort to the Pasatiempo project, which included a number of exclusive home sites around the golf course. Marion had booked one of the finest for herself (33 Hollins Drive) and she arranged for another (70 Hollins Drive) to be available for Alister and Hilda when they came across the Atlantic to live in California. She then introduced them to a whole range of rich, important, and/or interesting people that they would never have met otherwise. They remained good friends until Hilda returned to Europe following Alister's death.

On occasion, over the years it has been implied that Marion and Alister may have once had an affair, but there doesn't seem to be any evidence to support this suggestion. It would not match at all with MacKenzie's contented years at Pasatiempo with Marion as a good neighbor to himself and his new bride and family.

Unfortunately, the once rich and famous Marion Hollins died alone and destitute in a nursing home in Pacific Grove, California in 1944. She was 52 years old.

Hunter later credited Dan Gormley as being the construction fore-man—and "a young man named Paddy Coll must be given credit for much of the finishing touches to the beautiful (if damned) bunkers."

Years later, Jack Fleming's son John, superintendent of The Olympic Club in San Francisco, described MacKenzie's operation in the context that his father was the construction man and Hunter was "The Suit," given the task of keeping the members and founders at bay. Hunter's skill at this impressed even MacKenzie, who had had his share of run-ins with clients early in his career. Prior to construction, Hunter drew up a ten-page memorandum as to methods—an early forerunner of the "Specifications" golf course architects use today. It delegated issues of drainage, soils, and grasses to experts from the University of California and described the establishment of turf plots to determine the best combination for the fairways and greens. His thorough approach was the perfect contrast to MacKenzie's impressionistic design style and lack of precise plans.

Roger Lapham's son, Lewis, was then about to head off to Yale University to play on its golf team. Because he was a strong young player, he was enlisted by MacKenzie to help determine the position of some of the back tees. Recalled Lapham:

I specifically remember numbers two, eight, sixteen and seventeen. . . . We spent the better part of four or five mornings more or less in the vicinity of the present tees on those holes. The Doctor had a small portable mat for me to hit from and two men out yonder to measure my drives. He would put the mat down, seat himself on a shooting stick, and tell me to 'Hit away, laddie.'

"My first three or four tee shots were generally in the spinach, but as I say, the Doctor was a patient man. When I finally flushed one, he'd move the mat five, ten, fifteen yards right, left, up, back or whatever, and we'd go at it again, seventy or eighty balls a morning. We spent a lot of time on seventeen, moving way out to the right of the present tee. And I think, but cannot be sure, that he tried a couple of possible tee positions up the dunes above the present tees for holes twelve and thirteen.

Without question, though, MacKenzie's most influential collabora-tor at Cypress Point was his client, Marion Hollins. Marion was beside MacKenzie whenever he was on site and not only as a sounding board for his ideas. She was also unafraid to make suggestions of her own. It was Marion who put to rest the decision on whether the famous 16th

was to be a par 3 or a short par 4. When Seth Raynor had lamented that it was a pity that the carry over the ocean was too long to enable a hole to be designed on the site, she teed up a ball and drove to the middle of what is now the green, commenting that if she could do it, she was sure that there were some men who could make the carry, too. This story is verified by MacKenzie in *The Spirit of St. Andrews*.

While the 16th and its two oceanside counterparts are rightly world famous, they have unfairly overshadowed the rest of the course. MacKenzie's routing for the course wanders among the dunes, into the cypress forest, back up into the dunes, into the forest again, and back through some links country before coming to the point at the short 15th—like a wonderful story that takes its time arriving at a climax.

The hole-by-hole progression of the course makes it clear how much MacKenzie's designs were driven by the landscape, instead of from an established idea of where certain types of holes should fall in the round. Much has been made of the back-to-back par-5 holes on the front nine, and the back-to-back par 3s near the end, but MacKenzie was so occu-pied with other thoughts he may not even have noticed this rarity until late in the process.

The giveaway to his thought process is found in the variety of back-drops on the course and the way that no two holes repeat themselves, regardless of their length. For example, there is a huge sand dune in the center of the property that MacKenzie connived to use as a feature on eight different holes. It is a background for the third, sixth, ninth, and 11th holes, an elevated tee location for the seventh, 10th, and 12th, and a defining shoulder for the tee shot on the eighth. Interestingly, one of the few field changes MacKenzie made from his original plan was to com-bine two shorter holes into the long sixth and then reverse field for a new short seventh, thereby squeezing yet another hole out of the central dune.

On the four holes where the central dune serves as backdrop, it is set up slightly different for each one. At the third, the tee and green are posi-tioned so that the line of play extends past the right side of the dune,

THE 219-YARD PAR-3 16TH AT CYPRESS POINT. THE MOST DRAMATIC HOLE IN GOLF, PLAYING DIAGONALLY ACROSS A COVE OF THE PACIFIC OCEAN OUT TO A GREEN SET ON A POINT. IN SOME CONDITIONS, EVEN A FULL DRIVE WOULD NOT BE ABLE TO REACH THE GREEN. WITH THIS IN MIND, PLAYERS ARE OFFERED THE OPTION OF A SAFE TEE SHOT OVER 120 YARDS OF WATER TO A BASE OF THE PENINSULA, WHERE A DOWNSLOPE WILL SCOOT THE BALL AHEAD INTO THE NARROWEST PART OF THE FAIRWAY. FROM THERE, THEY HAVE THE CHANCE TO PLAY A 50-YARD PITCH AND GET UP AND DOWN FOR A THREE. IN STROKE PLAY, DISCRETION IS USUALLY CALLED FOR. IN MATCH PLAY, HOWEVER, THE FIRST PLAYER TO DARE AND SUCCEED SEIZES THE ADVANTAGE. AND IN NON-COMPETITIVE SITUATIONS, THE THRILL OF TRYING FOR THE GREEN IS ALMOST IRRESISTIBLE.

ANOTHER ANGLE OF THE STUNNING 16TH AT CYPRESS POINT DURING THE 1952 CROSBY NATIONAL PRO-AM.

OPPOSITE PAGE: VIEW FROM BEHIND THE 16TH GREEN, LOOKING BACK TO THE TEE.
RIGHT: A LARGE DUNE IN THE CENTER OF CYPRESS POINT SERVES AS THE BACK-
DROP FOR SEVERAL HOLES, INCLUDING THE SIXTH. **BELOW:** THE 291-YARD NINTH
AT CYPRESS POINT IS A SHORT BUT DRAMATIC PAR 4 BUILT ATOP A RIDGE OF DUNES.
THE LONG AND NARROW GREEN ANGLES WELL OFF TO THE LEFT, REWARDING A
LONG TEE SHOT DOWN THE RIGHT THAT FLIRTS WITH A STEEP DROP INTO SAND. IT
IS POSSIBLE TO REACH THE ENTRANCE OF THE GREEN FROM THE TEE, BUT TO MISS
WITH A DRIVER LEAVES A VERY AWKWARD HALF-SHOT APPROACH, OFTEN FROM A
SANDY LIE. MANY PLAYERS LAY BACK FROM THE TEE WITH MEDIUM IRONS TO GIVE
THEMSELVES A FULL WEDGE SECOND SHOT. BUT EVEN THEN, THE TEE SHOT MUST
LAND ALONG A NARROW ISTHMUS OF FAIRWAY.

LEFT: THE LARGE DUNE APPEARS AGAIN AT THE LONG PAR-FOUR 11TH. **OPPOSITE PAGE:** THE THIRD AT CYPRESS POINT PLAYS TOWARD THE TOE OF THE SAME DUNE, WITH THE 11TH FAIRWAY VISIBLE BEYOND. **BELOW:** AT ONLY 365 YARDS, CYPRESS POINT'S 13TH IS AN EXCELLENT DRIVE-AND-A-PITCH HOLE TO A SMALL GREEN SET AMONG DUNES. THE TEE SHOT CROSSES A LOW DUNE ON THE DIAGONAL, WITH LONGER DRIVES TO THE RIGHT REWARDED BY A HEAD-ON SHOT TO THE GREEN.

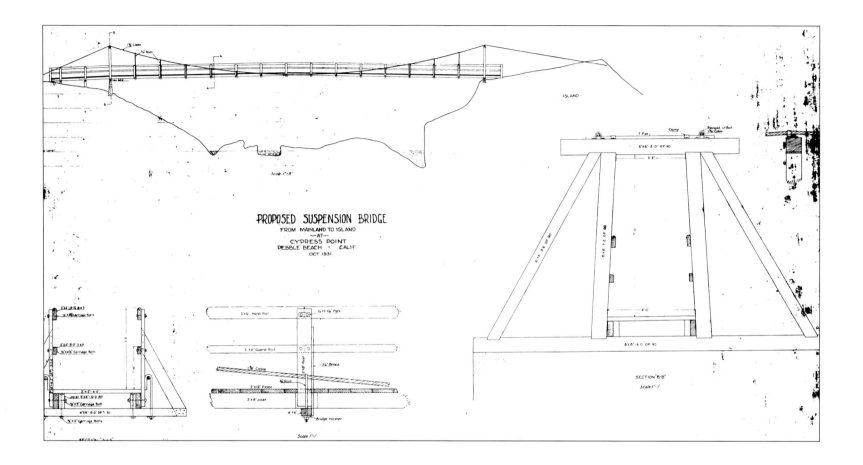

exactly through a saddle formed by a smaller dune, between which players on the tee see a "window" to the tenth fairway. At the sixth, the approach is to the base of a ridge that spurs off the dune, aligned directly at the seventh tee above. At the ninth, the big dune dominates behind the green as one stands on the tee. The line of play up the right side, however, leaves a pitch aligned so that the peak is beside the approach to the right. Finally, at the 11th—the one of the four that features the greatest potential elevation change—the long par 4 plays directly to the base of the looming sand dune.

From there inward, the backgrounds lead the player home. At the long 12th, a good drive lets the player look straight through the green at a flag set against the blue Pacific—even though it is actually several hundred yards away. MacKenzie was careful here not to build any mounds

behind the green that would block the view. At the 13th, in contrast, the approach plays right into a dune, with the green set halfway up. At the 14th, the approach is between huge groves of cypress trees and uphill to a flag set against the sky. At the 15th, the approach is played directly into a dark background of gnarled cypress trees. At the 16th, the background is the point itself. For the approach at the 17th, the golfer looks down the coastline past the green toward Big Sur.

MACKENZIE WAS SERIOUS ABOUT BUILDING A TEE FOR CYPRESS POINT'S 18TH ON AN ISLAND OUT IN THE PACIFIC. PLAYERS WOULD GET THERE VIA THIS BRIDGE. HOWEVER, IT WAS FINALLY DECIDED THAT THE BRIDGE COULD NOT WITHSTAND WINTER STORMS SO THE IDEA WAS DISCARDED.

The short par-4 18th is really the only hole that has been criticized (Jimmy Demaret described Cypress as "the best 17-hole course in the world"), but because of the way the 16th and 17th holes and the clubhouse are positioned, number 18 pretty much had to be as it is. For MacKenzie, whose mind worked in match-play circles, if there was going to be a weak hole it ought to be the 18th, since many matches never reached the last. Clearly, he agreed with Bernard Darwin's view that "it is the duty of any great course to have a great 17th hole."

But a close look at the original Cypress Point routing plan reveals an interesting fact: MacKenzie had a much more dramatic 18th in mind. Fifty yards out in the sea, beyond and to the right of the 17th green, there is a rock upon which the doctor wanted to place a back tee! He was serious enough about this to draw up a plan for the suspension bridge that would be used to access it. Unfortunately, the idea had to be discarded. Even though Morse was willing to pay for the bridge, if needed, he believed that the force of the ocean would quickly destroy it, and he did not want to remove a large cypress tree near the present tee for a tee that would turn out to be useless.

The overwhelming artistic success of Cypress Point made MacKenzie and Hunter much in demand in California. So much so that MacKenzie made California his full-time home the year after it opened. This move also coincided with his divorce from his first wife, Edith, his virtual exile from Alwoodley mentioned earlier, and his remarriage to Hilda Sykes Haddock, the daughter of his collaborator at Alwoodley, Arthur Sykes.

Several California contracts were immediately laid upon MacKenzie's doorstep, including a course for the Union League Club in San Francisco (now Green Hills Country Club), Stockton Golf & Country Club, Claremont Country Club in Oakland (a revision), The Valley Club in Santa Barbara, and Pasatiempo. All of these remain authentic examples of MacKenzie's design. However, with Hunter in Santa Barbara and MacKenzie working at Pasatiempo, one suspects that the others were given less of the doctor's attention during his hectic 1928-1929 schedule. When asked about Green Hills, John Fleming quickly remembered that though the design credit goes to "MacKenzie, Hunter and Egan," one of his father's Irish friends and drinking buddies, Paddy Coll, was in fact

responsible for building the whole course. In any event, it is highly likely that the crew that built Cypress Point was spread thin to cover all these simultaneous projects.

MacKenzie's timing was impeccable in landing the Cypress Point contract. It was also fortuitous in attracting attention to his work across the nation. Marion Hollins was keenly aware of the value of promotion and was anxious to have the course fully mature by the summer of 1929. By doing so, the American golf establishment could see it while in California for the U.S. Amateur Championship to be held at Pebble Beach.

Prior to the championship, MacKenzie's friend and leading amateur H. Chandler Egan was asked to make some significant design changes to the Pebble Beach course, which included changing the ninth and tenth to their present form. When MacKenzie and Egan later became partners, MacKenzie claimed responsibility for the course. But in the illustrations for George Thomas's 1927 book, *Golf Architecture in America*, it appears that one of the most famous of Pebble Beach's greens was

BEFORE LEAVING FOR AUSTRALIA IN 1926, MACKENZIE MADE IMPROVEMENTS ON TWO OF THE GREENS AT PEBBLE BEACH GOLF LINKS IN CALIFORNIA: THE EIGHTH (SHOWN) AND THE THIRTEENTH.

MacKenzie's idea. The photo of the "new eighth green" at Pebble Beach is credited in parentheses as being Dr. MacKenzie's work. This was very unlikely to be an error because Thomas was meticulous in assigning these credits correctly, even deferring the credit for holes on his own courses where there was a hole left over from an earlier designer's work.

The championship was thrown into quite a stir when the great Bobby Jones was beaten in the first round of match play by unknown Johnny Goodman. Instead of sulking away home, though, Jones remained in the area and played golf at year-old Cypress Point. A few days later, he went up to Santa Cruz with Marion Hollins to play an opening exhibition at her other new course, Pasatiempo, where Dr. MacKenzie was part of the gallery. After playing the two MacKenzie masterpieces, Jones recruited MacKenzie to help with the creation of his own developing project in Augusta, Georgia.

THE VALLEY CLUB

In the spring of 1928, Dr. MacKenzie traveled south to Los Angeles to meet architect George Thomas on the site of his Riviera Country Club course. Thomas had recently published *Golf Architecture in America*. The two men spent a day together chatting amiably. Afterwards, however, MacKenzie took a backhanded swipe at the par-3 course that Thomas had built there, exaggerating that "almost every hole was a monotonous pitch on to a small green completely surrounded by bunkers." Some believe that MacKenzie arrived disappointed to find that he was not being hired to consult on the design of the course.

On his way back north MacKenzie stopped at Robert Hunter's new home in Santa Barbara and helped inspect potential sites for a private golf club there. When the founders of The Valley Club of Montecito published their membership prospectus in June of 1928, it included a routing by MacKenzie and Hunter for eighteen holes set in a valley one mile back from the Pacific Ocean. The founders of The Valley Club were extremely well organized. By November 1928 they had enough members signed up to enter into a contract with MacKenzie and Hunter to design the golf course. They also contracted with Hunter's American Golf Course Construction Company to construct the course. The new course opened for play on December 30, 1929.

As at Cypress Point, MacKenzie made repeated use of a handful of features: two creeks plunging down from the surrounding mountains, and two small hills on the far side of the road that divides the course in two. The first and larger of the two hills is the background for the third green, the elevated tee for the 4th hole beside the seventh green, the elevated tee for the eighth, the backdrop for the tenth green, and the elevated tee for the eleventh. The second, smaller hill is beside the seventh fairway, the green site for the eighth, and the tee for the ninth.

It is probable that Hunter spent more time on The Valley Club than on any of his other collaborations with MacKenzie, and perhaps this is why their bunkering in Santa Barbara featured such elaborate patterns. While working to restore bunkers on the fifth hole from old photographs, Tom Doak's associate Jim Urbina began to notice that the capes and bays that they were restoring fit together like the pieces of a jigsaw puzzle from different viewpoints along the hole. From the tee, the first

ABOVE: THE THIRD GREEN AT THE VALLEY CLUB IN SOUTHERN CALIFORNIA.
OPPOSITE PAGE: FIFTEENTH GREEN AND CLUBHOUSE AT THE VALLEY CLUB OF MONTECITO. (COURTESY THE VALLEY CLUB)

LEFT: RECOGNIZABLE MACKENZIE BUNKERING AROUND THE VALLEY CLUB'S THIRD GREEN. (COURTESY THE VALLEY CLUB)

BELOW: VIEW OF THE VALLEY CLUB'S THIRD GREEN FROM THE SIDE. (COURTESY THE VALLEY CLUB)

OPPOSITE PAGE, TOP: NUMBER EIGHT AT THE VALLEY CLUB. (COURTESY THE VALLEY CLUB)

OPPOSITE PAGE, BOTTOM: FOURTEENTH GREEN AND 15TH FAIRWAY (BACKGROUND) AT THE VALLEY CLUB. (COURTESY THE VALLEY CLUB)

THE ORIGINAL ROUTING PLAN FOR THE VALLEY CLUB WAS UNUSUAL IN THAT
GOLFERS FACED BACK-TO-BACK PAR 5s TWICE OVER THE 18 HOLES. THREE PAR 5s ON
THE BACK NINE WAS ALSO UNUSUAL. NOTE THE PLAN HAS THE NINTH GREEN AT THE
FURTHEST POINT FROM THE CLUBHOUSE. (COURTESY THE VALLEY CLUB)

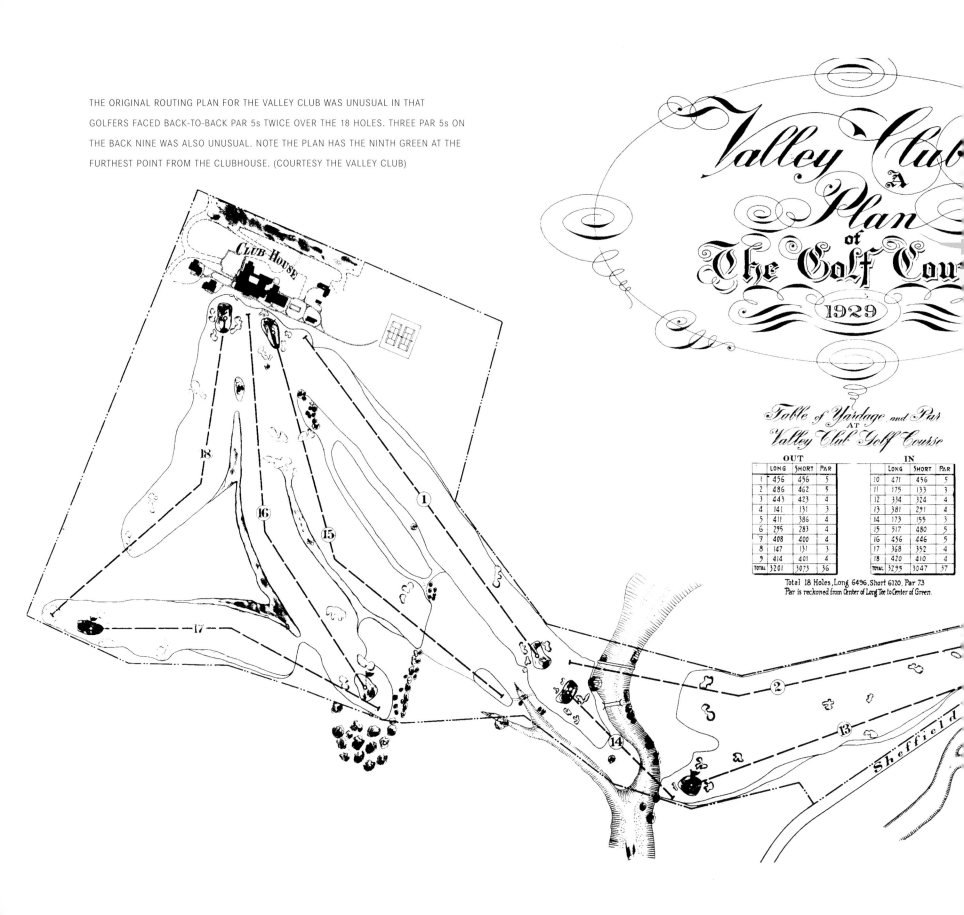

Valley Club

A

Plan

of

The Golf Course

1929

Table of Yardage and Par
AT
Valley Club Golf Course

	OUT				IN		
	LONG	SHORT	PAR		LONG	SHORT	PAR
1	456	456	5	10	471	456	5
2	486	462	5	11	175	133	3
3	443	423	4	12	334	324	4
4	141	131	3	13	381	291	4
5	411	386	4	14	173	155	3
6	295	283	4	15	517	480	5
7	408	400	4	16	456	446	5
8	147	131	3	17	368	352	4
9	414	401	4	18	420	410	4
TOTAL	3201	3073	36	TOTAL	3295	3047	37

Total 18 Holes, Long 6496, Short 6120, Par 73
Par is reckoned from Center of Long Tee to Center of Green.

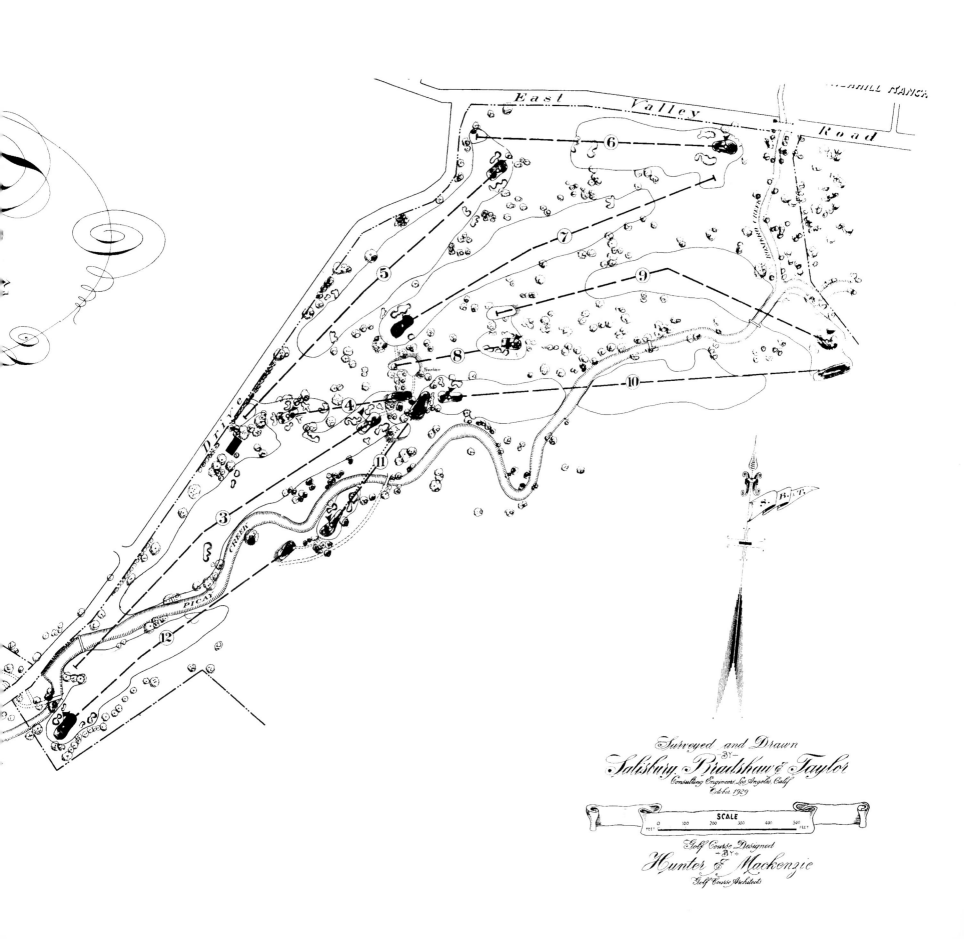

East Valley Road

6

7

5

9

8

10

4

11

3

12

Drive

CREEK

PICAY

S. B. T.

Surveyed and Drawn
-BY-
Salisbury, Bradshaw & Taylor
Consulting Engineers, Los Angeles, Calif.
October 1929

SCALE

0   100   200   300   400   500
FEET   FEET

Golf Course Designed
-BY-
Hunter & Mackenzie
Golf Course Architects

fairway bunker on the right overlaps the greenside bunkering to create a receding diagonal line. The left-hand fairway bunkers formed the third point of a triangle. From the ideal driving zone in the fairway, a similar triangle is formed by the short fairway bunker and the greenside bunkers to the right and left. Furthermore, the capes of grass that extend into the bunkers formed overlapping patterns when viewed from different spots.

While the long par-4 third is generally singled out by low-handicap players to be the best hole at The Valley Club, its quartet of par 3s must also rank among MacKenzie's most outstanding work. The eighth hole leaps from hilltop to hillside, with a sharp fall to the right; the 11th is dominated by an elaborate bunker short-left and the barranca on the right; and the 14th is a magnificent picture, across a deep valley to an Eden-type green guarded by a huge bunker at right front and with the fifteenth fairway, the clubhouse and the Santa Barbara mountains forming the backdrop. But the one truly original hole at The Valley Club is the short fourth (just 140 yards) with its tiny green set in the midst of a grove of huge sycamores. Most golf architects of the day (and most of The Valley Club's subsequent superintendents) would have scoffed at such a location for a green. But MacKenzie was among the first designers (along with George Thomas) who realized that trees could make both an interesting and beautiful hazard.

Robert Hunter became one of the early members of The Valley Club.

With demand for golf architects almost nonexistent, he happily directed his efforts to being chairman of the Green Committee on his own most personal design. He continued to live in Santa Barbara until his death in 1942.

A PARALLEL TRACK EAST OF THE ROCKIES

While all this was going on out West, MacKenzie's new friend Perry Maxwell was also quite busy on the doctor's behalf. After their whistle stop visit in 1926, Maxwell suggested that MacKenzie be brought on as a consultant to the design of his new Melrose Country Club course in Philadelphia. So, on MacKenzie's way back from Australia through America to England, Maxwell arranged for him to spend a day on the site making suggestions. He also arranged for the doctor to visit Pine Valley and Merion's East Course. In addition, Maxwell made sure that the Philadelphia press covered MacKenzie's visit. This coverage raised the stature of both the partnership and the project, and it played to MacKenzie's healthy ego.

ABOVE, LEFT: MACKENZIE'S AND HUNTER'S BUNKER WORK ON THE FIFTH HOLE AT THE VALLEY CLUB. ABOVE, RIGHT: THE LONG PAR -4 THIRD IS CONSIDERED BY MANY TO BE THE VALLEY CLUB'S MOST CHALLENGING HOLE. OPPOSITE PAGE: THE FOURTH GREEN IS SET IN A GROVE OF SYCAMORES.

C   O   P   Y

DR. A. MACKENZIE

Golf Course Architect
Expert in Landscape Work

American Partners

West of Rocky Mountains
Robert Hunter
   Pebble Beach
      California

East of Rocky Mountains
Perry D. Maxwell
   Ardmore
      Oklahoma

Moor Allerton Lodge
   Leeds   England
   Telephone 61990

February 18, 1928

My dear Maxwell:

When I originally asked you to come
into partnership with me, I did so because I thought
your work more closely harmonized with nature than
any other American Golf Course Architect. The
design and construction of the Melrose Golf Course
has confirmed my previous impression.

I feel that I cannot leave America
without expressing my admiration for the excellence
of your work and the extremely low cost compared with
the results obtained. As I stated to you verbally,
the work is so good that you may not get the credit
you deserve.

Few if any golfers will realize that
Melrose has been constructed by the hand of man and
not by nature. This is the greatest tribute that can
be paid to the work of a Golf Course Architect.

Yours very sincerely,

(Signed)   Alister MacKenzie

CRYSTAL DOWNS

In 1926, a small group of men began to develop property on the shores of Crystal Lake in northwestern lower Michigan. Two years later, with a rough nine-hole golf layout complete, Frederick Baird, one of the developers, wrote to Robert Hunter (because he was the author of *The Links*) for his advice on the project. Magnanimously (and without mentioning that they were partners), Hunter suggested MacKenzie for the design job, offering his opinion that Alister was the "greatest of them all." The timing, he went on to say, would be ideal because MacKenzie had just finished both the building of Cypress Point and a remodeling of Pebble Beach and was about to cross the country to return to England.

After the arrangements were made, a man named Walkley Ewing met MacKenzie and Maxwell at the train station in Grand Rapids, Michigan, and drove them northward. The doctor was reported to be "coldly courteous" about the interruption in his long trip. Once Ewing swung over to the Lake Michigan shoreline on the way north, however, the two architects became captivated by the constantly changing landscape of hardwoods and sand dunes. A couple of hours later, they arrived in the town of Frankfort to survey the site.

"In England we would call this kind of land 'downs land,'" offered MacKenzie. Consequently, the development was named Crystal Downs.

MacKenzie and Maxwell stayed on for several days to establish a routing plan for the course and to begin the design of the greens. At one point, finding themselves stuck on a final solution to the beautifully undulating but rather tight front nine, MacKenzie sent Maxwell into town for provisions. When Maxwell returned an hour or two later, he found the doctor sitting on the hill where the pro shop is now located, bottle at his side. "I have the front nine finished," declared MacKenzie. "Come and see what you think." After studying the plan, Maxwell's reply

Even though MacKenzie only saw the Melrose course once more during construction and once at the end, he was most impressed with Maxwell's work and quickly appointed him as his partner "East of the Rocky Mountains." Their collaboration at Melrose is still there, though not intact. Over the years the property has been encroached upon by building development and roads, which have reduced the original layout down to today's sporty 5,800 yards, a length that resulted in the course being generally overlooked in the golf-rich Philadelphia area. Several dramatic holes and wildly contoured greens remain, but it is difficult to imagine now that when it opened, it was declared to "resemble more the famous Pine Valley than any other Philadelphia course."

After the completion of Melrose Country Club, Maxwell returned to Oklahoma. Once back home, Maxwell received a commission for him and MacKenzie to design 36 holes for Dr. G. A. Nichols of Oklahoma City. (What's left of the course today is part of the Oklahoma City Golf & Country Club.) Even more noteworthy, however, was their next contract, obtained with an assist from Robert Hunter — the now-famous Crystal Downs Country Club in Michigan.

OPPOSITE PAGE: AFTER MACKENZIE RETURNED FROM AUSTRALIA, PERRY MAXWELL ASKED HIM TO MAKE SUGGESTIONS ON A COURSE MAXWELL WAS DESIGNING IN PHILADELPHIA: MELROSE COUNTRY CLUB. ALISTER WAS SO IMPRESSED WITH MAXWELL'S WORK THAT HE ASKED HIM TO BECOME A PARTNER IN HIS DESIGN FIRM.
ABOVE LEFT: FIRST HOLE AT CRYSTAL DOWNS CC IN FRANKFORT, MICHIGAN.

LEFT: THE PAR-4 FIFTH AT CRYSTAL DOWNS. **BELOW:** THE SEVENTH AT "THE DOWNS" IS A 335-YARD PAR 4. PLAYERS MUST CHOOSE ON THE TEE WHETHER TO DRIVE INTO A DEEP VALLEY (LEAVING A HALF-BLIND APPROACH) OR LAY UP TO THE EDGE OF THE DROP-OFF AT 190 YARDS (BUT WITH A CLEAR VIEW OF THE GREEN). A POOR LAY-UP WILL MISS THE NARROW PLATEAU OF FAIRWAY AND LEAVE AN AWK-WARD STANCE AND SOMETIMES A LONG SECOND SHOT. THE PUNCHBOWL GREEN IS BOOMERANG-SHAPED, WRAPPED AROUND A LARGE BUNKER AT RIGHT-CENTER. PUTTS FROM FRONT TO BACK CAN BE BANKED OFF THE SIDESLOPE AT THE ELBOW OF THE GREEN.

was that it was wonderful, but there were only eight holes. MacKenzie promptly added a short hole along the ridge on which they sat: today's celebrated and deadly par-3 ninth.

Once all the plans were approved, Maxwell returned as the construction foreman to carry out the doctor's design. He rebuilt the existing nine holes into today's front nine in 1929, and then added nine more a year later that climbed to the even higher plateau that ran parallel to Lake Michigan. Fortunately, the golf course did not become as cramped by homes as Pasatiempo. The main reason was that the principal attraction of the property was not the golf course. Due to the spectacular view of Lake Michigan from the bluff, all but a couple of the homes at Crystal

THE 175-YARD NINTH AT CRYSTAL DOWNS IS THE HOLE THAT MACKENZIE "FORGOT" TO PUT INTO THE PLANS. THE TEE AND FAIRWAY PLAY ALONG THE CROWN OF A SHARP RIDGE, UPHILL TO A GREEN SET AT THE BRINK OF A DROP-OFF TO THE LEFT. WITH THE STEEP BACK-TO-FRONT TILT OF THE PUTTING SURFACE AND TROUBLE ON BOTH SIDES, THE ONLY SAFE PLAY IS JUST IN FRONT OF THE GREEN. PLAYERS WHO TAKE THIS OPTION WILL BE REWARDED WITH A RELATIVELY STRAIGHTFORWARD UPHILL CHIP.

cap stance and lie for the long second shot at the 550-yard 8th hole—one of MacKenzie's best three-shotters anywhere.

The native rough, full of fescues, switchgrass, and bluestem, give the Crystal Downs course a texture more akin to Alwoodley or Melbourne than to any of MacKenzie's other American courses. Yet, this same rough also raises a question of playability. What, one might easily ask, about MacKenzie's decree that "the course should be free of looking for lost balls"? It's a fair question. In this case, though, Crystal Downs didn't have such high rough at its inception; originally, the entire through-the-green area was gang-mowed. Only since the 1980s has the rough been established by the superintendent. MacKenzie would certainly have approved, however, because he would have been the last to let one of his own thirteen points get in the way of his founding principle—to make the course as beautiful and natural in appearance as possible.

MacKenzie, of course, was too busy with Pasatiempo and The Valley Club—not to mention attending the Ryder Cup at Moortown and the U.S. Amateur at Pebble Beach—to spend much time in Michigan in 1929. But he did visit Crystal Downs long enough to participate in building some of the greens on the front nine, and some of these—particularly the multi-tiered first, third and sixth look more like MacKenzie's drawings than any we have seen elsewhere. Ron Haswell, the long-time superintendent of the course who also worked on the original construction crew, years later remembered Maxwell's instructions to build the tiers in the greens razor-sharp in the dirt because he didn't want them to become too soft over time. In fact, MacKenzie must have liked the horseshoe-shaped seventh green immensely because, after Crystal Downs, he built several (although inferior) versions: at Claremont CC in Oakland, at the University of Michigan GC in Ann Arbor, and even the original eighteenth green (now the ninth) at Augusta National.

However, it is clear from its lack of mention in *The Spirit of St. Andrews* that MacKenzie never saw the finished course and probably never knew what Maxwell did with it. Starting at the eighth—although

Downs are literally across the street from the course.

Because of its remote setting, Crystal Downs never attracted the attention of other MacKenzie courses until interest in golf architecture soared in the 1980s and people began to seek out the rest of his designs. Thankfully, due to its relaxed summer-club atmosphere and low membership fees, the club never contemplated making major changes to the course. Amazingly, only two back tees have been added to the doctor's original plan. Therefore, when it was "rediscovered" in the 1980s, Crystal Downs quickly ascended to prominence as one of MacKenzie's best and best-preserved works.

What makes the course truly special are the abrupt undulations of the property—particularly on the front nine—which no doubt offered to MacKenzie's eye some strikingly original golf holes that he had not seen anywhere else. In addition, these holes provided the perfect setting for the doctor's brand of roller coaster putting greens. Every hole on the golf course is special, but particularly in the stretch from the fifth through the ninth; they are unlike any other holes in the game. A deep undulating valley through this part of the course presents a diagonal driving hazard at the short par-4 fifth; a heroic carry at the 390-yard sixth, a choice of whether to lay up from the tee at the seventh before approaching a boomerang-shaped green set in a punchbowl, and a mad-

THE PAR-3 11TH AT CRYSTAL DOWNS. **OPPOSITE PAGE:** THE SCABS AT CRYSTAL DOWNS.

THE SPECTACULAR PAR-4 17TH AT CRYSTAL DOWNS. FROM THE GREEN, PLAYERS
CAN SEE BOTH CRYSTAL LAKE AND LAKE MICHIGAN.

it's still a wild putting experience—the greens seem more tilted and crowned than the earlier ones, a feature of Maxwell's later work at Prairie Dunes Country Club in Kansas. The fall-away putting surfaces at the twelfth and thirteenth, though not out of character for MacKenzie, are particularly reminiscent of Maxwell's Old Town Club in North Carolina. And we can only wonder what Dr. MacKenzie would have said about the two finishing holes, which Maxwell moved from their planned locations.

After the completion of Crystal Downs, Maxwell also served as the construction foreman on Dr. MacKenzie's layout for the University of Michigan, recently restored by Arthur Hills after it suffered over the years from the wear and tear of double-duty as a parking lot for U of M football games. Following MacKenzie's death, Maxwell assisted Augusta National Golf Club in constructing a couple of remodeled greens. He was not, however, on site during the original construction of that course.

A footnote on Maxwell: In 1936, officials at Ohio State University began a search to find the right person to build the two golf courses that MacKenzie had designed for the institution before his death. Both

Maxwell and Robert Trent Jones (then a fledgling 30-year-old architect) were recommended. When the professional at Augusta National was queried about Maxwell, he reported that Bobby Jones was not familiar with the man.

OPPOSITE PAGE, TOP: THE 550-YARD PAR-5 EIGHTH AT CRYSTAL DOWNS. A WON-DERFUL NATURAL HOLE WITH NO NEED FOR FAIRWAY BUNKERS. SHORT DRIVES LAND IN AN UNDULATING BOWL OF A FAIRWAY AND LEAVE A DIFFICULT STANCE FOR THE LONG SECOND SHOT, WHERE PLACEMENT IS KEY. THE SECOND SHOT IS UPHILL OVER A VALLEY, WITH A NARROW SHELF OF FAIRWAY ON THE RIGHT BEING THE PREFERRED LANDING ZONE. ALL OTHER SPOTS WILL LEAVE A SHARPLY UPHILL AND SIDEHILL LIE. THIS MAKES IT DIFFICULT TO PICK THE CORRECT CLUB FOR THE APPROACH TO A VERY SMALL GREEN THAT IS GUARDED BY A DEEP HOLLOW AT THE LEFT-FRONT AND A BUNKER TO THE RIGHT. **OPPOSITE PAGE, BOTTOM:** DOGLEG RIGHT PAR-4 18TH AT CRYSTAL DOWNS. **ABOVE, LEFT:** THE 18TH AT CRYSTAL DOWNS IN THE EARLY DAYS. **ABOVE, RIGHT:** THE 18TH AT CRYSTAL DOWNS TODAY.

THE DEVILISH THIRD GREEN AT THE UNIVERSITY OF MICHIGAN GOLF COURSE. EVEN A SHORT IRON REQUIRES PRECISION ON THIS MASTERFUL 535-YARD, PAR 5. (COURTESY UNIVERSITY OF MICHIGAN GOLF COURSE)

THE UNIVERSITY OF MICHIGAN GOLF COURSE DURING CONSTRUCTION. (COURTESY UNIVERSITY OF MICHIGAN GOLF COURSE)

FOR YEARS, THE COURSE MACKENZIE DESIGNED FOR THE UNIVERSITY OF MICHIGAN WAS USED TO PARK CARS DURING WOLVERINE FOOTBALL GAMES. **OPPOSITE PAGE:** ORIGINAL DRAWING OF THE UNIVERSITY OF MICHIGAN GOLF COURSE RECENTLY DISCOVERED BY THE UNIVERSITY'S OFFICE OF FACILITIES, PLANNING AND DESIGN. NOTE THE SPELLING OF (MCKENZIE) ON THE DESIGN MAP AND A RARE SIGNATURE BY PERRY MAXWELL.

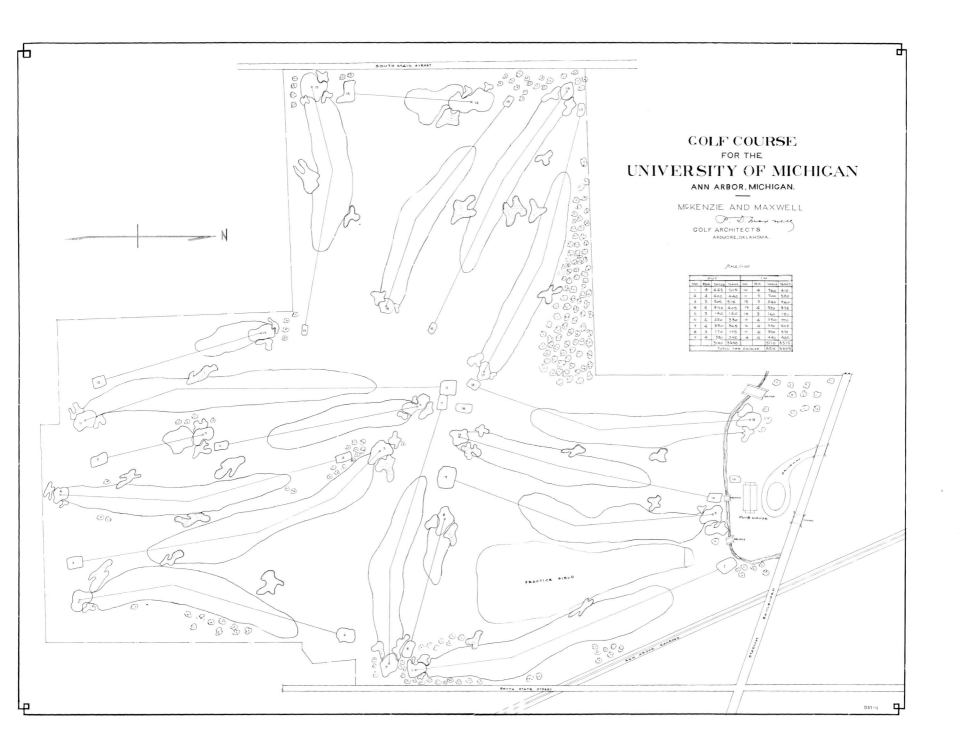

GOLF COURSE
FOR THE
UNIVERSITY OF MICHIGAN
ANN ARBOR, MICHIGAN.

McKENZIE AND MAXWELL

GOLF ARCHITECTS
ARDMORE, OKLAHOMA.

SCALE 1"=100'

	OUT				IN		
NO.	PAR	YARDS	YARDS	NO.	PAR	YARDS	YARDS
1	4	445	505	10	4	360	410
2	4	400	440	11	5	500	520
3	5	505	515	12	3	240	260
4	4	390	405	13	4	320	335
5	3	140	160	14	3	160	180
6	4	370	330	15	4	350	370
7	4	350	365	16	4	390	405
8	3	170	175	17	4	350	375
9	4	380	345	18	4	440	465
		3100	3240			3110	3315
		TOTAL FOR COURSE				6210	6605

WESTERN UNION

CLASS OF SERVICE

This is a full-rate Telegram or Cablegram unless its deferred character is indicated by a suitable sign above or preceding the address.

SIGNS

DL = Day Letter
NM = Night Message
NL = Night Letter
LCO = Deferred Cable
CLT = Cable Letter
WLT = Week-End Letter

NEWCOMB CARLTON, PRESIDENT   J. C. WILLEVER, FIRST VICE-PRESIDENT

The filing time as shown in the date line on full-rate telegrams and day letters, and the time of receipt at destination as shown on all messages, is STANDARD TIME

Received at 33 East Gay St., Columbus, Ohio Always Open

1929 AUG 12 PM 3 45

CB660 40 DL=SANTACRUZ CALIF 12 1142A

L W STJOHN=

    OHIO STATE UNIVERSITY COLUMBUS OHIO=

REFERENCE TO YOUR LETTER RECEIVED TODAY AM MOST SATISFIED
WITH CYPRESS POINT AND SANTACRUZ COURSES DOCTOR MACKENZIE
DESIGNED FOR ME CONSIDER ALL HIS WORK EXCELLENT AND MOST
REASONABLE CAN HIGHLY RECOMMEND HIM AS A GREAT GOLF
ARCHITECT AND RELIABLE PERSON=
    MARION HOLLINS.

THE QUICKEST, SUREST AND SAFEST WAY TO SEND MONEY IS BY TELEGRAPH OR CABLE

IN 1929, THE ATHLETIC DIRECTOR AT OHIO STATE UNIVERSITY WAS ALSO INTERESTED IN HIRING DR. MACKENZIE TO DESIGN A GOLF COURSE FOR THE CAMPUS. TWO OF THE PEOPLE HE CONTACTED WERE MARION HOLLINS AND THE PRESIDENT OF CYPRESS POINT CLUB.

OFFICE OF THE
PRESIDENT
AND
ASSISTANT SECRETARY
ROOM 627
215 MARKET STREET
SAN FRANCISCO, CALIFORNIA

CYPRESS POINT CLUB

LINKS AND CLUB AT
CYPRESS POINT
MONTEREY COUNTY, CALIFORNIA
——
P. O. ADDRESS
PEBBLE BEACH, CAL.

August 12 1929.

Mr. L. W. St. John,
    Director of Athletics,
        The Ohio State University,
            Columbus.

Dear Mr. St. John:

I have your letter of August eighth, asking my opinion of Dr. McKenzie.

As a Director and later as President of the Cypress Point Club, I had an excellent opportunity to judge Dr. McKenzie as a man and in his professional capacity as golf architect. The Cypress Point Club turned over to Dr. McKenzie and his associate at that time, Mr. Robert Hunter, the job of constructing an eighteen-hole golf course over what looked to be very unusual terrain including woods, sand dunes and ocean. We gave the architects a free hand, and were more than pleased with the job when it was done, as well as with the way in which it was done. The course was constructed and ready for play in about nine months and the final cost was less than what most of us guessed it would be.

Dr. McKenzie seems to have the art of making everything look natural, and I consider him one of the most reasonable and practical golf architects with whom it has been my pleasure to deal.

You will take it from what I have said that I have no hesitation whatever in recommending Dr. McKenzie as a man and as a golf architect.

Sincerely,

President.

RDL:HW

GEORGE SARGENT

EAST LAKE COUNTRY CLUB

LESSONS BY APPOINTMENT   ATLANTA, GEORGIA

Mr L W St John,
 Ohio State University,
 Cols,Ohio.   5- 25-36

    Dear Saint
               Talked to Bob Jones about your situation;
He gave me the names of two men that were familiar with Dr
McKenzie's idea's;

               They are Robert Trent Jones of New York;
and Bob Hunter Jr of Santa Barbara,Calif.

                              He did not know their
addresses,but if you would beinterested in either of these men
I can get our P G A representatives to look them up for us without much delay.

               Bob thought that either of these men would be
quite capable of taking a set of McKenzie plans and properly
carry out the Doctor's idea's.

                         Also asked Bob about Maxwell,but
he was not familiar with any of his work;so do not believe it would
be well to consider him.

                    Let me know if I can help you with either
of the men mentioned,will be glad to help.

                         Kind Regards
                         Yours Sincerely   George Sargent

PASATIEMPO

Even while she was working on the formation of Cypress Point, Marion Hollins had begun to look for property to develop on her own. She found it in California on the high ground overlooking Santa Cruz and Monterey Bay. She named the property Pasatiempo, Spanish for "pastime." And it was here that she fulfilled all her ambitious dreams for a single community, providing the best of everything for residents and her many famous visitors. Golf, tennis, and polo were all part of the sporting equation. In addition, the residential plan was developed by the famous Olmsted Brothers of Boston (though few of the lots were to be sold for many years). Marion's sense of taste was further confirmed by her choice of other collaborators. The then-unknown architect William Wurster was selected to design the "Pasatiempo style" of homes, and landscape architect Thomas Church was commissioned to do the gardens and landscape of the homes, starting with Marion's own.

Alister MacKenzie, not surprisingly, was again commissioned to design the golf course. For this project, MacKenzie received even more encouragement from Marion to spare no expense and to try to make it the greatest of all courses. Consequently, MacKenzie not only spent more time on site here than at Cypress Point, he made Pasatiempo his residence after it was completed in 1929. As he wrote in *The Spirit of St. Andrews*, he had always wanted "to have a home where I can practice golf in my pyjamas in the morning."

THE HIGHLIGHT OF PASATIEMPO'S OPENING DAY FESTIVITIES WAS AN EXHIBITION THAT FEATURED CYRIL TOLLEY, MARION HOLLINS, BOBBY JONES AND GLENNA COLLETT.

~ THE CLIMACTIC YEARS ~

Alister's life had been far from humdrum over its first 60 years. But in 1929 and 1930, it was struck by major convulsions of intercontinental dimensions. Actions in America were to produce quite disproportionate reactions in Britain. These happenings were to affect his friends, his golf clubs, and all but destroy his family. Under great distress, he was to learn, often bitterly, who were his true friends and who were of the fair-weather variety. Amidst all of this turmoil, Alister revealed himself more clearly than ever before as the brave and bold character he was, ready to face adversity courageously.

The story of these turbulent years has become clear only recently, but earlier investigations of Alister's life at Leeds and Lochinver had raised suspicion that there was a part over which a veil had been drawn. At Alwoodley Golf Club in Leeds, the late Ralph Middleton—who had long been the Honorary Secretary and was highly knowledgeable on the club's early days when Alister was involved—once gave a long interview with a wealth of detail. He then abruptly concluded it by saying, "Don't ask me any more questions! I've told you all I know about the man!" The language and its tone sent a strong message that there was something more to be told.

It was around this period that Alister's portrait, that had hung on the wall of the Alwoodley clubhouse, seems to have mysteriously disappeared. Rather more sinister, there had been an attempt, apparently willful, to obliterate from the club any and all memory of MacKenzie. This was akin to the rewriting of history often indulged in by totalitarian rulers. The analogy is not too far fetched. While "Honorary Secretary" was the benign title given to the person in control of Alwoodley at that time, the office was by appointment, without any question of election by the members, and the tenure of office was for life. "Dictator" gives a better impression of the extent of authority the post held. The situation was, no doubt, a conse-

quence of Alister's influence on the drawing-up of the club's constitution. His abhorrence for the petty democracy of golf club committees knew no bounds, so he arranged that all authority at Alwoodley was placed beyond the interference of any democratic committee.

Partial explanation of this gap in MacKenzie's life came from Mary Bowman, his favorite niece. Conversation with her brought Alister alive and it revealed that he had, in his early days, courted a girl named Hilda, a student of music at Leeds. MacKenzie, however, had a strong rival for Hilda's hand—Edgar August Haddock. Not only was he one of Hilda's teachers, he was "Principal" of the Leeds College of Music and, presumably, in receipt of a comfortable income. Not surprisingly, Haddock won the day. They married and started a family.

HILDA S. H. MACKENZIE.

In 1907, Alister married Edith Wedderburn, who would later become a founding member of Alwoodley. Beyond creating a partnership for rounds of golf and tables of bridge, the marriage was apparently not an outstanding success. There were no children and, perhaps more significant, the trial adoption of a child was terminated by Edith after only six weeks. Evidently the demands and disruptions created by a baby did not match with her ideas of conjugal bliss.

From 1914 onward, Alister was never at home for long, and home was probably a pretty joyless place to return to. After leaving the army in 1918 his expanding golf course commitments around Britain and, later, abroad, took him away ever more frequently.

Eventually, most of his time was spent in California. With these lengthy, long distance separations, the marital bonds were no doubt coming close to breaking. In 1929, Alister obtained a divorce from Edith. Significant to the way things developed, this was filed in Reno, Nevada. Even more significant was that, in the meantime, Edgar Haddock had died, leaving Hilda an eligible widow. In 1930, Alister married her and acquired a step-son and two step-grand-sons—all a joy to him because he had previously been denied the children he very much wanted. Alister, Hilda, and family set up home in California in the delightful surroundings of Pasatiempo Golf Club, the course designed by Alister in the development organized by Marion Hollins.

These events in California provoked eruptions amongst MacKenzie's family and friends back in Leeds and Lochinver to a degree that is incomprehensible today and surely surprised Alister then. In Yorkshire and Scottish society of the early twentieth century, divorce was certainly not unknown, but was very rare in the professional class of the MacKenzies where a puritanical ethos dominated.

However, even making the most liberal allowance for the change in ethos over the intervening seven decades, the extent of outcry was hard to comprehend. It ultimately became clear that the real sticking point was the site of the divorce. Just as at that time Gretna Green in Scotland, close to the English border, was then the place to which elopers could escape and go through a "no questions asked" form of marriage at the local blacksmith's anvil, Reno, across the Nevada border, was the choice of Californians wishing a quick and easy divorce. The crux was that there was no acceptance in Yorkshire or Scotland of the validity of Reno divorces. Thus, when Alister married Hilda, the rigid citizens of Yorkshire and Scotland regarded it as bigamy. Hence the outcry.

In the close circle of Alwoodley Golf Club members, the overwhelming majority sided firmly with Edith in the belief that she was seriously wronged. Edith, along with her brother-in-law Charles MacKenzie and his wife (who had for so long "made-up-a-four" with Alister and Edith), remained at Alwoodley and were given succour as if bereaved. Alister was regarded as being "quite beyond the pale" and the uncanny effort of collective willpower to erase all recollection of the dastardly man came into play.

Seventy years later, his niece Mary Bowman, who had been only in her early teens at the time, was still exquisitely conscious of the impact of these events on the life of herself and her family—ostracized from the society in which they had mixed. Such had been her distress that she placed an embargo on using her reminiscences in her lifetime. Otherwise, she was sure that it would resurrect the unhappiness of those days.

The close family, not surprisingly, was torn asunder. Charles's branch never re-established contact with his sister Marion's family. As the only supporter of Alister, Marion bore the brunt of the antagonism. When other friends and relatives gave her older brother the cold shoulder, and he became estranged from his beloved Alwoodley Golf Club, she remained a staunch supporter.

Like Alister, Marion had inherited the robust, extrovert personality that was dominant in the MacKenzie line. In her day, few women became established in medicine. Marion did, as one of the early female graduates of Edinburgh University. Her doughty constitution was put to the most exacting of tests on her wedding day—which actually didn't occur. Although all the essential parties for the ceremony turned up, the marriage was not solemnized due to the highly unusual reason that the Registrar who was to officiate was too drunk to perform his duties. Family history records that Marion and her "husband" spent the night in separate bedrooms in the Scarborough Hotel, just down the corridor from the empty bridal suite that had been reserved for them. A very subdued Registrar managed to stumble through his lines the following morning.

After Alwoodley, then, Pasatiempo is certainly the most personal of MacKenzie's designs. It is also the one where he spent the most time, making refinements to the holes himself. Compared to the doctor's overall body of work, it is a bold and untempered design, and it causes one to suspect that his construction foremen deliberately toned down some of the more radical slopes in the doctor's sketches for other courses. Without MacKenzie around, Dan Gormley and Jack Fleming wouldn't likely have built five greens with seven feet of fall from back to front, as MacKenzie did at Pasatiempo—even Crystal Downs and Augusta National, two of the most severe putting tests in golf, don't have a green that severe.

Then again, MacKenzie's bold design is entirely in keeping with the Pasatiempo property, probably the most rugged the doctor had ever been given. From the top of the course to the bottom there is more than 250 feet of elevation change, as the property cascades toward Monterey Bay, one mile and 800 feet of elevation below. The first tee shot was originally directed straight toward the end of the Monterey Peninsula, visible on a clear day 35 miles across the bay. Today, the tee has been pushed to the right to accommodate a practice range.

The upper end of the property, which contains the back nine, is cut up by deep ravines known locally as "barrancas." A barranca must be crossed on six of the holes on the inward nine and skirted at two others. MacKenzie was brilliant in using this natural feature as many times as possible, but differently at each hole. A solid strike is required to carry the ravine on the 10th tee; there's a diagonal carry on the uphill second shot to the 11th (with only the boldest players going for the green); the shot across the barranca at the 12th is a short downhill pitch; two more forced-carry tee shots are called for at the 15th and 18th; and there are diagonal carries on both the drive and second at the 16th. MacKenzie told Marion Hollins that the 16th at Pasatiempo was his personal favorite of all his designs.

ABOVE, LEFT: DOCTOR AND MRS. MACKENZIE ON THEIR VERANDA AT THE SIXTH FAIRWAY AT PASATIEMPO. **ABOVE, RIGHT:** PASATIEMPO'S 13TH.

Rather amazingly, even the holes that don't require a crossing use the barranca in their strategy. The best of these is the par-4 14th, where the drive must flirt with a valley on the left (which leads into the barranca along the left side of the hole) to open up the green for the second shot.

Unfortunately, the front nine had somewhat less natural features to work with. Consequently, in attempting to make the most of it, MacKenzie crammed its holes together too tightly. In later years, as the course became busy, it also became dangerous for the players. To resolve this problem, trees were planted between some of the fairways. Unfortunately, they straitjacketed some shots and spoiled the open views from the holes above. To be fair, there was originally plenty of room between the first and ninth holes until the addition of a practice range shifted the first hole to the right. Now the dramatic sweep down toward the Pacific is through a tunnel of trees. A back tee at the second also had to be abandoned because it created a tee shot across the entrance road. This change turned a short par 5 into a long (but still excellent) par 4. Originally, the very long par-3 third had a line of cross-bunkers off the tee. After choosing to skirt these bunkers, players frequently found themselves in front of the fourth tee or down on the second fairway. Trees were planted to eliminate this option, but they blocked the alternate routes that MacKenzie had allowed. Eventually, the cross-bunkers had to be filled in.

The most dangerous of all the holes, though—in terms of golfers being hit by balls—are the parallel sixth, seventh and eighth. The short par-4 seventh plays along a hog-backed ridge southward toward the bay. On

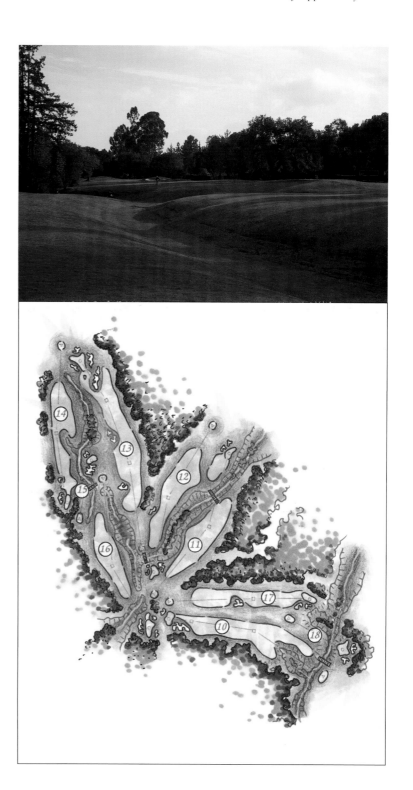

ABOVE, RIGHT: THE 440-YARD PAR-4 14TH AT PASATIEMPO. A DEEP SWALE IN THE LANDING AREA ON THE RIGHT SIDE OF THE FAIRWAY FORCES A DECISION ON THE TEE. SHORTER HITTERS MAY PLAY UP THE SAFER LEFT SIDE, BUT LONG HITTERS MUST RISK BEING TRAPPED IN THE DEPRESSION UNLESS THEY PLAY WELL OUT TO THE RIGHT. THE GREEN ANGLES FROM LEFT-TO-RIGHT BEHIND A SINGLE LONG BUNKER, COMPOUND-ING THE DIFFICULTY OF THE APPROACH FROM THE RIGHT OF THE FAIRWAY. AS WITH MOST OF MACKENZIE'S BETTER LONG HOLES, HOWEVER, THE SHORT HITTER WHO PLAYS THE HOLE AS A THREE-SHOT DOUBLE DOGLEG CAN EASILY AVOID MOST OF THE FAIRWAY HAZARDS. BOTTOM, RIGHT: DRAWING OF BACK NINE AT PASATIEMPO.

PASATIEMPO'S 385-YARD PAR-4 16TH. BEFORE HE DIED MACKENZIE NAMED THIS HIS FAVORITE HOLE, AND IT IS CERTAINLY AMONG HIS MOST DRAMATIC AND CHALLENGING

TESTS. BOTH THE DRIVE AND THE APPROACH MUST CARRY A DEEP BARRANCA THAT RUNS ACROSS IN FRONT OF THE TEE, CONTINUES DOWN THE LEFT OF THE FAIRWAY, THEN

CROSSES AGAIN CLOSE BESIDE THE GREEN ON THE RIGHT. THE CROWNED FAIRWAY OFFERS A BIT OF A ROLL TO WEAKER DRIVERS BUT FORCES LONGER HITTERS TO PLAY PER-

ILOUSLY CLOSE TO THE TROUBLE ON THE LEFT, OR RISK GOING THROUGH THE FAIRWAY INTO TREES. THE THREE-TIERED GREEN IS ONE OF THE MOST SEVERE MACKENZIE

GREENS STILL IN EXISTENCE, WITH MORE THAN SEVEN FEET OF RISE FROM FRONT TO BACK.

PASATIEMPO GOLF CLUB, THE FIRST AND NINTH FAIRWAYS.

the right is the long sixth; on the left is the short eighth. In total, the width of these three holes is only 500 feet—a measurement barely considered enough for two holes today. After a player on the eighth green was killed by a pulled drive from the seventh, heavy plantings were installed on both sides of the seventh hole. Sadly, this eliminated its strategic fairway bunkering and turned it into a bowling alley between the trees. Due to today's liability laws, it is impossible to restore the hole so that players can appreciate the openness of the original design and the view that used to be available from the clubhouse.

The narrow corridor that is now the sixth hole forces players hitting their second shot to run a gauntlet between the trees and a row of homes to the left. Ironically, a pulled second shot is quite likely to clear a screen fence and land in the backyard of 70 Hollins Drive. This was the residence of MacKenzie and his second wife, Hilda Sykes Haddock, from 1930 until the doctor's death there in January of 1934.

The fairly modest MacKenzie home was just down the street from the much more glamorous home of Marion Hollins. The MacKenzies enjoyed socializing with Hollins's friends from the sports world, high society, and the entertainment industry—everyone from Helen Wills to Mary Pickford—at Marion's lavish parties. Marion's successful investments supported a full social calendar during the dark days of the Depression until 1938, when the wear and tear of the good life (and an injury in an automobile accident) caught up with her and she was forced to sell out.

Unfortunately for MacKenzie, he had altogether too much time to enjoy home life between 1930 and 1934; the Depression had brought a grinding halt to the development of new courses—both in America and elsewhere around the world. The doctor did have a few great successes during that period (more than others in the business; many were virtually without work) but he would also spend many hours fruitlessly corresponding with potential clients trying to get them to start projects that had been shelved for lack of financing. His two courses for Ohio State University (routed by Alister in 1929 and celebrated years afterward by a pair of famous Buckeye golfers, Jack Nicklaus and Tom Weiskopf) were in fact not built until four years after MacKenzie's death.

LEFT: THE 8TH GREEN AT PASATIEMPO. RIGHT: PASATIEMPO'S 15TH. OPPOSITE PAGE: 1942 AERIAL SURVEY APPEARS TO REVEAL NOT ONLY THE BAYSIDE LAYOUT, BUT SOME OF THE LAND'S CONTOUR AS WELL.

Two projects from this period that do deserve special mention are Sharp Park in San Francisco and Bayside in New York. They mark yet another milestone in the evolving MacKenzie style: a willingness to use developing technology (steamshovels and bulldozers) to move large quantities of earth in order to transform flat ground.

Sharp Park was a municipal project located just south of San Francisco in Pacifica at the edge of the ocean. Jack Fleming was assigned the construction of this course, which involved a considerable amount of earthmoving in order to create artificial dune features, similar to what C.B. Macdonald did at The Lido. Sharp Park opened in 1931 to substantial acclaim. A few months later, unfortunately, ocean storms (perhaps an early El Niño) swept over part of the course and wiped out several of the holes. Today, only the inland greens remain true to MacKenzie's design, and the seaside ambiance was sacrificed when a large dyke was erected to keep the ocean back. The only one who really benefited from the design was Jack Fleming. He was so well liked by the city officials that he was offered the job of Director of Parks for the city of San Francisco. Later on he would help the city develop the great municipal course at Harding Park, and establish his own design business in northern California on the side.

New York's Bayside no longer exists, though it is unclear whether its demise stemmed more from the Depression and World War II, or from Robert Moses's plan to erect the Throgs Neck Bridge, linking the Bronx and Long Island, directly into the middle of the course. Until recently the

ONE OF MACKENZIE'S INLAND HOLES AT SHARP PARK GC IN PACIFICA, CALIFORNIA.
OPPOSITE PAGE: MACKENZIE'S SKETCH OF A GREEN AT BAYSIDE LINKS IN NEW YORK.

A. *fond playes route*

B or C. *dubs route.*

course had been completely forgotten except by Robert Trent Jones, who met MacKenzie on site there while Jones was still a student at Cornell University. But the rediscovery of the lost manuscript of *The Spirit of St. Andrews* provides the doctor's own breathless description of the course which was then just finished. Like any golf architect, MacKenzie was quite flushed with pride for his latest work.

Similar to the site at Sharp Park, the ground for Bayside was virtually without undulation. MacKenzie contrived to give it life by creating several swales through the property, both to provide drainage and generate earth to be used in building greens and the foundation for bunkers. (Today's architects dig lakes for the same purpose.) Wendell Miller and Associates was hired to construct the course. Once they started, MacKenzie was in awe of just how fast the work proceeded with modern machinery:

When I arrived on the scene I found over thirty machines, including drag

lines, sixty-horsepower caterpillar bulldozers, scrapers, drainage machines, stone removers, ploughs, disc harrows and others too numerous to mention. Any one of the five larger machines was capable of doing the work of two hundred men.

In five days when we got properly going we had nearly completed the drainage, pulled down over a mile of stone walls and converted them into hillocks, covering them with earth, completed the contouring of four greens with the surrounding hillocks, hollows and bunkers, and partially done eight more.

Miller's success in creating a natural-looking landscape impressed MacKenzie tremendously. When he traveled to Argentina to create a similar course for The Jockey Club, he brought one of Miller's engineers along. One year later, he involved Miller's company from the start in the creation of the Augusta National Golf Club.

SOUTH AMERICA

One of the few places unaffected by the Great Depression was South America, whose republics had just begun to exploit their vast natural resources. So when a call came from Buenos Aires, Dr. MacKenzie quickly arranged to sail through Panama to Argentina. He left in January of 1930 and arrived in the southern summer two weeks later.

MacKenzie's primary commission in South America was for The Jockey Club of San Isidro in the most fashionable suburb of Buenos Aires. However, he also spent considerable time expanding the Club de Golf del Uruguay from nine holes to eighteen. Today, each is the most exclusive golf club in its nation.

The Jockey Club of San Isidro is more than that, though. In fact, it is no less than one of the great sporting clubs of the world. It's difficult to imagine today, but even at the time of MacKenzie's visit in 1930 there were 3,600 members. Its 36 holes of golf—the Colorado (Red) and Azul (Blue) courses, which MacKenzie named after the club's two-colored logo—are flanked on one side by an enormous turf racecourse with grandstands for 30,000 people. On the other side are a large series of practice tracks and polo fields. There are also tennis and cricket in San Isidro, plus a downtown club in Recoleta, the height of Buenos Aires society. But none of these other functions intrude on the 300 acres devoted to golf or the magnificent golf clubhouse.

Except for a handful of new tees, added to keep the Colorado course a viable site for national championships, The Jockey Club is preserved precisely as MacKenzie planned it. The site was relatively flat, so MacKenzie's design began with an elaborate network of shallow drainage swales that snake across the fairways, sometimes doubling as driving hazards. Because of the importance of the drainage and irrigation schemes, MacKenzie enlisted a resident American engineer, Luther Koontz, to supervise construction. (Koontz went on to design 25 courses in the region, including nearby Olivos Golf Club, the country's other top championship course.) But MacKenzie, having no other urgent projects to attend to, remained in Buenos Aires while the dirt was moved, completing his ideas for the greens and bunkers. The contouring took only 21 days. Afterwards, the captain of the club asked him what he was going to do about the bunkering. The doctor replied:

The undulations have created such a varied, interesting, and pleasurable test of golf that we do not require a single bunker. Nevertheless, for the sake of appearance and for the purpose of creating more spectacular thrills, we will give you a few bunkers.

All the dirt excavated from the drainage swales was utilized to form mounded greens' complexes that distinguish each hole, overcoming the otherwise featureless terrain. There are steeply terraced "MacKenzie" greens, such as the par-5 tenth on the Red course, with a small flagstick placement at the front left and a shallow terrace at the back right, four feet higher and guarded by a deep bunker. There are "buried elephant" mounds the size of an elephant's head in a few greens (the largest of which divides the double green at the ninth and 18th holes of the Blue course). There are narrow panhandles on greens like at the short third and 17th of the Red course, leaving only a 30- to 40-foot-wide target between bunkers on either side. And finally there is the Red 16th, whose shallow punchbowl green is guarded by three eight-foot-tall mounds, foreshadowing the eighth at Augusta National.

The total effect is a bit like a bumper pool table—a largely flat, tightly mown playing field governed by mounds and extensive plantings of pines and hardwoods. The design is certainly MacKenzie's, and exceptionally well preserved at that, but something of his naturalist spirit is missing in the obvious artificiality of the greens here. Perhaps Koontz,

the engineer, was too insistent on perfect construction, or else he missed the point of MacKenzie's intention to make everything look natural. (Having the course covered wall-to-wall in common bermudagrass does not add to its natural appearance, either.) In any case, it's the only blemish on a great design.

The Blue course is somewhat shorter than the Red and less exacting—especially the third through seventh holes, which are crowded across the road near a hippodrome. Noteworthy, however, are its back-to-back par-5 opening holes—further evidence that MacKenzie did not have a preconceived program for the sequencing of holes, even on a flat site where the topography made no dictates. Also noteworthy is the double green next to the clubhouse that's used for the ninth and 18th holes. A four-foot-high "buried elephant" divides the two putting surfaces, and it's the only double green in MacKenzie's body of work. Nevertheless, it is the Red course that makes The Jockey Club worth the long trip.

Two hours by ferry across the Rio de la Plata is Montevideo, capital of the Oriental Republic of Uruguay. The Old City sits on a narrow peninsula that forms a fine harbor.

The setting for the course to be designed at Punta Carretas (GC of Uruguay) was promising. It was only two miles from the city on a promontory overlooking the beach and the city. As at Cypress Point and New South Wales, several holes are sited to overlook prominent landmarks. The third and fourth holes both play downhill directly toward Punta Brava, the southernmost point along the coast, located just below the course. Similarly, the approach to the par-5 14th not only plays toward town but directly toward "El Cerro" on the opposite side of the harbor. It's the very hill that caused a Portuguese explorer to exclaim, "I see a hill" (Monte video) and thereby christen the city. Sadly, trees and shrubs planted along a boundary fence obscure some of the drama of these views.

OPPOSITE PAGE, TOP: THE TENTH HOLE ON THE RED COURSE AT THE JOCKEY CLUB, BUENOS AIRES, ARGENTINA. OPPOSITE PAGE, BOTTOM: THE 17TH ON THE RED COURSE AT THE JOCKEY CLUB.

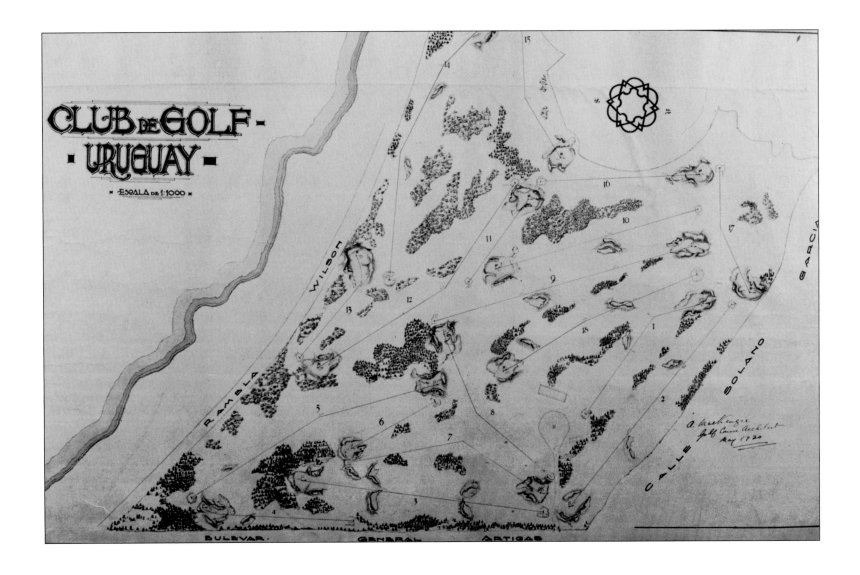

Because the hill of Punta Carretas tilts gently toward the sea, only a couple of its holes were built around distinct features on the ground. If Club de Golf was going to be considered a great course, it would have to succeed on the strength of MacKenzie's bunkers and greens, as was the case with The Jockey Club.

MacKenzie's original plans for the greens at Punta Carretas were eye-popping, with six feet of relief on some of the putting surfaces. But those greens were common bermudagrass, and when the club upgraded to sand-based bentgrass putting surfaces a few years ago, it was decided the original severe contours should be "watered down." "Washed away" is a better way to describe what they accomplished. And since there were only a handful of fairway bunkers in the original design, the course is left with little of MacKenzie's work.

Just as he did in Australia, MacKenzie consulted with other existing clubs while in Argentina. His trip to South America was hastily arranged, however, and therefore less well organized. He made some alterations at the Palermo Club in Buenos Aires and also visited the Mar del Plata course 250 miles to the south, but most of his suggestions there were never implemented.

There are rumors of other MacKenzie associations, but these were at best brief visits. Luther Koontz designed or redesigned 25 courses in the two countries after MacKenzie left, and it is possible that the doctor made suggestions for some of these while he was in the southern hemisphere. Cantegril Country Club in Punta del Este has a handful of greens in the style of MacKenzie, but they weren't actually built until 1940, ten years after the doctor left Uruguay. It is much more likely that Koontz simply adapted some of MacKenzie's style into his own work.

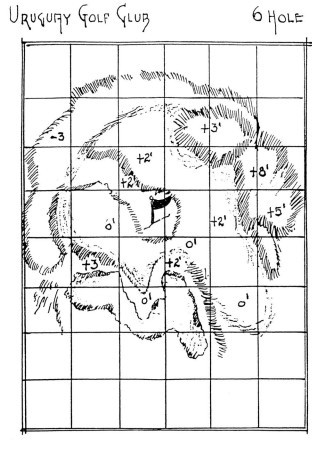

URUGUAY GOLF CLUB   6 HOLE

SECTION   SCALE 8⁺ PER S./Q.
APPROX.

OPPOSITE PAGE: MACKENZIE'S SITE DRAWING FOR PUNTA CARRETAS GC OF URUGUAY. **ABOVE RIGHT:** THE 14TH HOLE AT PUNTA CARRETAS GC OF URUGUAY, WITH THE CITY OF MONTEVIDEO IN THE BACKGROUND. **BOTTOM RIGHT:** MACKENZIE'S GREEN DRAWING FOR THE SIXTH AT PUNTA CARRETAS.

AUGUSTA NATIONAL

After playing both Cypress Point and Pasatiempo in the fall of 1929, Bobby Jones was convinced that Dr. MacKenzie was of like mind on the subject of golf course design. The two had probably met before Jones's trip to California for the 1929 U.S. Amateur—among Jones's memorabilia at East Lake Country Club is a copy of MacKenzie's *Golf Architecture* autographed to Jones and dated 1927. Their first meeting might well have been during Jones's 1927 Open Championship win at the Old Course at St. Andrews. MacKenzie (who had done his famous survey of the Old Course in 1924 and consequently had been asked to make recommendations for cup locations for championship play) was on hand for that event. Very possibly it could have been at the Walker Cup the previous year, also in St. Andrews.

The idea of a club in Augusta was that of Jones's friend Clifford Roberts. Both men frequently visited Augusta, which was Jones's wife Mary's hometown, and they had many friends there who would form the nucleus of the club. Jones was also attracted by the prospect of contributing a championship-quality course to the South, which had relatively few. The deal-clincher was Roberts's discovery of the property. "Fruitlands" was a Civil War era nursery that had been developed by a Belgian named Prosper Berckmans. It contained huge banks of flowering plants, including a double lane of magnolias that led from the entrance to the manor house (today's clubhouse).

Similar to Pasatiempo, the new layout was a multifaceted project: the 365 acres of the nursery were enough to consider two 18-hole courses. Jones and Roberts, however, later settled for just one eighteen. Eventually, a par-3 course and some "cabins" for members were built. The firm of Olmsted Brothers was retained to plan the development and do the landscaping and Wendell P. Miller was selected as the golf course contractor. Though the Depression was now near its full depth, Jones's popularity was enough to get the project moving. Correspondence between the various parties at the early stages still exists.

Memos from Olmsted's project manager to the home office were fascinating. He summed up the preliminary meeting in New York on July 10, 1931:

Roberts outlined to all of us the cooperation he expects pointing out however that the project is primarily for sports and excellence in that respect should not be sacrificed to real estate. Bobby Jones and MacKenzie are to be responsible for the quality of the course from the purely golfing standpoint and we are to be responsible for the lotting, roads, all planting and other Landscape work including details about the clubhouse. Some of MacKenzie's questions indicated that his idea of the Landscape Architect's service is planting flowers about the clubhouse but he expressed no hostility to the thought of a

LEFT: PRIOR TO CONSTRUCTION, MACKENZIE AND BOBBY JONES WALKED THE SITE THAT WOULD BECOME AUGUSTA NATIONAL GOLF CLUB. **OPPOSITE PAGE, TOP:** MACKENZIE'S ORIGINAL 16TH GREEN AT THE JOCKEY CLUB WAS FAR MORE SEVERE THAN IT IS TODAY. **OPPOSITE PAGE, BOTTOM:** THE TALL MOUNDS GUARDING THE 16TH GREEN ON THE RED COURSE USED TO BE PART OF THE GREEN.

AUGUSTA NATIONAL GOLF CLUB
OF AUGUSTA, GEORGIA

Organization Committee

ALFRED SEVERIN BOURNE
ROBERT T. JONES, JR.
GRANTLAND RICE
CLIFFORD ROBERTS
WILLIAM C. WATT

Organization Headquarters

SUITE 201
THE VANDERBILT HOTEL
NEW YORK CITY

TELEPHONE ASHLAND 4-4000

New York, N.Y. July 2nd, 1931

Olmsted Brothers,
Brookline, Mass.

Gentlemen:

I am in receipt of yours of the 1st, and am happy to learn that your organization is familiar with the Augusta territory. Mr. Ruth and others have recommended your firm and I am rather certain that our Committee will want to engage your services.

I enclose preliminary form of invitation, which we expect to put in the mail during the Fall of this year.

For your further information I will tell you that we control 364 acres, which is known as Fruitland Manor, and is located about one and a half miles northeast of the Bon-Air Vanderbilt Hotel at Augusta. We expect to use about one-third of this acreage for an 18 hole golf course and reserve an additional one-third for a second course. The remainder is to be utilized for winter homes that members of the Club may wish to build.

We intend using Dr. Alister MacKenzie as the golf architect and we are at this time planning the first meeting, which is to be held in Augusta, on or about July 14th or July 15th. At that time we want to have both the landscape architect and the golf architect on hand for a meeting with Mr. Jones. The Fruitland Manor Property is unusually beautiful and has a great deal of plant life on it. You will readily appreciate the necessity of the landscape architect working with the golf architect, in order that the property may be further beautified.

                        I wish you would advise me promptly if you can make available on about July 14th a man in your organization who would have charge of the landscaping. I might suggest further, that someone of your firm should meet with me, if convenient, prior to that time.

                    Yours very truly,

                    CLIFFORD ROBERTS

CR:JA

WILLIAM B. MARQUIS
79 RIDGE ROAD
WABAN, MASSACHUSETTS

AUGUSTA NATIONAL GOLF CLUB

REPORT OF CONFERENCE IN NEW YORK   E.C.W.   JULY 10, 1931

Spent nearly an hour discussing the project at the headquarters, suite 201 Vanderbilt Hotel. Mr. Clifford Roberts, chairman of organization committee, Dr. MacKenzie golf architect and Mr. Miller of Wendell P. Phillips Miller Associates, builders of golf courses, I believe.

Roberts outlined to all of us the cooperation he expects pointing out however that the project is primarily for sports and excellence in that respect should not be sacrificed to real estate. Bobby Jones and MacKenzie are to be responsible for the quality of the course from the purely golfing standpoint and we are to be responsible for the lotting, roads, all planting and other Landscape work including details about the clubhouse. Some of MacKenzie's questions indicated that his idea of the Landscape architect service is planting flowers about the clubhouse but he expresses no hostility to the thought of a broader field of our activities and he may ever prove a good cooperator.

I have met Miller before but can't yet place him.

Roberts wants to get things planned out so that work on the course can start this fall and be completed for seeding next June. Clubhouse may not be started until spring.

Architect is Willis Irvine of Augusta. I saw perspective of Clubhouse but no plans.

MacKenzie and Miller going to Augusta, to be there the 14th. Bobby Jones to be there. I agreed to have Marquis there and Miller will get reservation for him to go with them on 1.10 train from New York Monday. Marquis is to meet them at headquarters at Vanderbilt Hotel an hour or so before train time.

Roberts says that the cost of the development has been under written by responsible men and is not speculative or dependent upon the lot sales or club memberships. He and I discussed our methods of charging and he, being a lawyer, seemed to understand. He wants us to handle our end of the job and is satisfied to have us proceed as to charges. He didn't want me to guess at costs now but if after Marquis' visit, we can give some kind of an idea of probable costs, he would like to have it. Better write him confirming the above understanding.

Some things for Marquis attention on preliminary visit:

1 Size up accuracy and adequacy of the topo and check reputation of the engineer. Expect we shall need (a) cross section or other frequent and reliable control on grounds and on plan (b) one foot contours and other detail at larger scale near clubhouse (c) definite locations, etc. of good outstanding trees.

2 See about getting topo tracing and, with Roberts O.K. order additional data needed.

3 See architect and get plans if sufficiently settled.

The intention is to make this the most interesting and attractive and all round first class golf course development possible. An English golf course expert may be called in consultation. The Landscape work should be of the same class—sound and good and appropriate but not extravagant or gaudy.

copy given Mr. Marquis 9/11/31

AUGUSTA NATIONAL GOLF CLUB

Report of Visit   14, 15, 16   July 1931.
By Mr. Marquis

Left Boston night of July 12, left New York 1:10 on the 13th arrived Augusta 11 o'clock morning of the 14th. On trip accompanied by Dr. Alister MacKenzie and Mr. Wendell P. Miller of the Wendell P. Miller Associates. Spent 14, 15 and 16 in Augusta going over the property and conferring with the engineers and architects and working with Dr. MacKenzie and Robert T. Jones, Jr. on the golf course. Other people concerned with this project are Mr. Thomas Barrett, Jr. and Mr. L.A. Berckmans and Mr. P.J. A. Berckmans, Architect's name is Willis Irvin, Engineer is Elroy Smith, address Herald Building, Augusta. Dr. MacKenzie's address is Pasa Tiempo, Santa Cruz, California. Wendell T. Miller, Associates, 277 West End Avenue, New York.

Dr. MacKenzie laid out on the 200-scale map 18 holes and staked this roughly on the ground working but did not offer any suggestions other than that they avoid destroying planting in the valley of the sulphur spring. I said also we should be glad to use the slopes of this valley for home sites, if it proved feasible. I don't believe that he will accomplish this. My impression is that this layout is quite rough and that it will be materially changed when we get a larger scaled more detailed map. I think Dr. MacKenzie will cooperate but he and Jones know that the golf plan is first in consideration so they will probably not want to make changes which will improve the real estate layout at the expense of the golf. The plan now is to get the detailed maps to Dr. MacKenzie in California as soon as they are ready. He will then work on some detailed plans and return to Augusta the end of September. Before he returns, however, he wants enough clearing done on the lines of the fairways so he can tell whether the layout is satisfactory.

I conferred with a Mr. Cassidy representing Elroy Smith, whom I know and have confidence in. Outlined specifications for a map of the entire property at 100-scale and he gave me a figure of $5. per acre. Also outlined specifications for map at 40-scale covering about 30 acres, including the Main Avenue, the old house site and the abandoned hotel site. The figure on this was not more than $300 (See copies our specifications sent to Elroy Smith after my return).

Cassidy promised to have 40-scale plan within two or three weeks and said that the large survey would take probably six weeks. I urged him to shorten this time if possible by getting other engineers to work with him and mentioned this to Mr. Barrett, who gave us authority for having surveys made. Mr. Barrett can probably expedite this work.

Conferred with Mr. Willis Irvin on clubhouse plan and location. I was not very favorably impressed with the plan already drawn because the huge locker room would shut off the rest of the building from the southern views and exposures and thought that some scheme could be worked out which would be better adjusted to the grades and might have some of the space shown in angular wings put over the locker room. The requirements for this clubhouse are very unusual and, therefore, this plan may have to be followed partly, if not entirely.

In a discussion with Mr. Roberts in New York on July 20th he emphasized that as this is to be a golf club primarily they intended to minimize the social features and the serving of meals and simply make the locker building a combined locker and lounge in which they want plenty of light and air and good outlooks. They want room for 400 lockers, some single and some double with about fifteen feet between locker rows. A large lounge in the locker room lighted by a sky-light as well as by windows and small nooks and corners where separate groups of men could congregate. All the rest of the house is to be incidental to this. Kitchen to be in basement with dumb waiter service to pantry and dining room and this service connected through to the locker room. The golf professionals room is to be situated so that members can go from it through to the east or west side of the building, that is, without having to go around outside to get to any of the tees or greens.

On the second floor they want two suites of rooms for manager and locker room man, one business room for Board meetings, and if possible several bed rooms and baths where special people can be taken care of. There are to be no general rooming facilities in the clubhouse. Roberts said that later, if it proved desirable, the Bon Air-Vanderbilt Hotel Company might put up a building for entertaining guests.

On the ground discussed with Irvin and others the advisability of saving the old Berckmans house and remodeling it for some use and later discussed this with Roberts. For sentimental reasons Augusta people would like to see it preserved but Roberts does not care anything about it and says he does not see what practical use could be made of it. I agreed on that. It is not at all modern and would take a lot of money to make it so. The only possible use I can think of is that it might be entirely remodeled for rooms. If this were done very well and the place was furnished with a lot of nice old furniture, it might be interesting to a certain number of members, but most of them would probably be better satisfied in a modern building with all modern conveniences.

As soon as the 40-scale topography is ready, we should think out any suggestions we have for the location of the clubhouse and discuss these with Roberts and probably with Irvin, the latter is a pretty aggressive young fellow, but I believe will cooperate. I suggested this procedure to him and to Roberts.

I did not attempt on this visit to map out any of the areas for lots because Dr. MacKenzie still has to reserve enough land for another eighteen holes and I felt that it wasn't worth while to try to get down to details until we get a larger map.

On water supply, City of Augusta has made a preposition of some $5500 for providing filtered water up Washington Road to Magnolia Avenue entrance, whence the Augusta National Golf Club will have to carry it further. It so happens that the unfiltered water line running from the Savannah River to the Augusta reservoir, cuts across the southeast corner of the property. The plan now is to tap onto this for water for sprinkling the golf course. Miller will, of course, attend to that part of the work. (See note below)

There is no existing sewer which can be used from this property.

Did not inquire about electricity. A transmission line runs up Washington Road and I have no doubt that this will be adequate for clubhouse facilities.

The two Berckmans gentlemen want to have something to do with the carrying out of the plans if possible, and also would like to work out some scheme with the Club for maintenance after the work is finished. This would be very logical, of course, as they know every foot of the land and are familiar with all conditions. We could use them in planting work, and Miller will use them on some of the golf course work. They live on the Mr. P.J.A. Berckmans' property just east of the Magnolia Avenue entrance.

NOTE: The City Engineer's name is W.H. Wise and his assistant is Frank M. White, both of whom I used to know and found willing to cooperate.

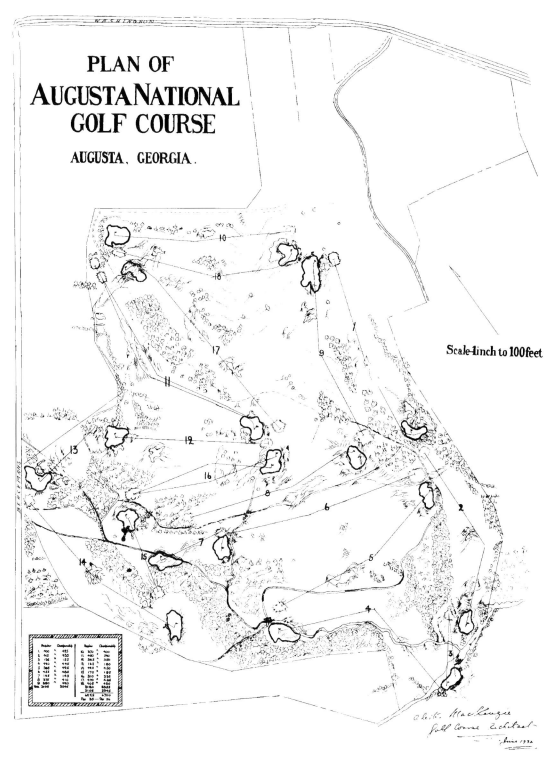

PLAN OF
AUGUSTA NATIONAL
GOLF COURSE

AUGUSTA, GEORGIA.

Scale-1inch to 100feet

THE ORIGINAL LAYOUT OF AUGUSTA NATIONAL GOLF CLUB. TODAY'S "AMEN CORNER" COMPRISED THE SECOND, THIRD AND FOURTH HOLES OF THE DESIGN.

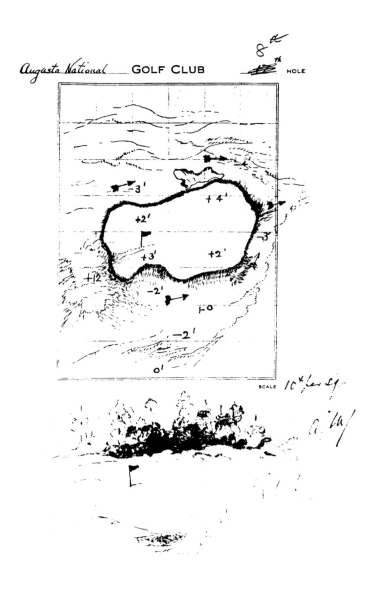

Augusta National GOLF CLUB

8th
HOLE

SCALE

ABOVE: A MACKENZIE SKETCH. **OPPOSITE PAGE:** JONES, MACKENZIE, AND OTHERS
CHECK THE PLAYABILITY OF AUGUSTA NATIONAL'S PAR-5 EIGHTH HOLE.

broader field for our activities and he may even prove a good cooperator...

MacKenzie and Jones met in Augusta on July 14, 15, and 16. MacKenzie laid out a routing on a 200-scale map and then staked the holes in the field with Jones. They then had the centerlines of the holes in wooded areas cleared 60 feet wide before the doctor's next visit in October. By January of 1932, the final plan was set.

A letter from MacKenzie during construction of the course indicated that he was not available to come to the site for a particular meeting. He wrote that, "his associate, Marion Hollins" might come in his place. This was shortly after Roberts had stalled an advance payment on MacKenzie's design contract, so undoubtedly there was "tit for tat" between the two men. But MacKenzie insisted in his letter that "not only are her own ideas valuable, but she is thoroughly conversant in regard to the character of the work I like. I want her views and also her personal impressions in regard to the way the work is being carried out." (He might also have mentioned that, of the three of them, Marion was the only one who could afford to pay for the trip.) Hollins did visit Augusta, and MacKenzie later reported to Wendell Miller that she was favorably impressed with the design.

Construction of the course employed Caterpillar tractors and bulldozers in addition to mules and scrapers. Earthmoving commenced on February 10, 1932 and seeding was complete by May 27. Over that time, 120,000 cubic yards of earth was moved. The most interesting project was the green at today's 12th hole, set beside an old mill and across a swamp. During construction a Native American grave was unearthed, and at one time two tractors and eight mules were mired in the swamp. It was a lot to deal with in the process of moving 5,000 yards of earth to make the green site, which is built over a rock ledge at the far edge of the swamp.

MacKenzie's low regard for professional golfers' opinions on design is well documented, but Jones, the quintessential amateur, was able to avoid his wrath. For his part, Jones was always sure to credit MacKenzie as the architect of the Augusta National course and himself only as an involved observer and president of the club. He was, after all, still only 30 years old (MacKenzie was 62) and, by nature, never quick to draw attention to himself. However, there are some key differences between MacKenzie's design for Augusta and the rest of his work up to that time which suggest Jones's influence. Most importantly:

1. Augusta had radically fewer bunkers than most MacKenzie courses—only 23 originally, compared with 80-100 at Cypress Point or Royal Melbourne.

2. The course was quite a bit longer than any that MacKenzie had built before—a bit over 6,700 yards, versus 6,400 for Cypress Point and Pasatiempo. Of American championship courses of the day, only Oakmont then measured at over 6,700.

3. The key feature of the design were several slopes in the driving zones that could be used to gain added distance if the ball was played to the proper side of the fairway. This feature is still evident today at holes two, nine, ten, 13, and 15. In other words, a reward was given for placing or shaping the drive, rather than a penalty for improperly placing it. This tempered the length of the course for the straight hitter, but makes it play rather short for today's champions. It also coincides perfectly with Jones's description of good golf architecture in his 1959 book, *Golf is My Game:*

There are two ways of widening the gap between a good tee shot and a bad one. One is to inflict a severe and immediate punishment on a bad shot, to place its perpetrator in a bunker or in some other trouble which will demand the sacrifice of a stroke in recovering. The other is to reward the good shot by making the second shot simpler in proportion to the excellence of the first. The reward may be of any nature, but it is more commonly one of four — a better view of the green, an easier angle from which to attack a slope, an open approach past guarding hazards, or even a better run to the tee shot itself. But the elimination of purely punitive hazards provides an opportunity for the player to retrieve his situation by an exceptional second shot.

Though the course opened to substantial acclaim, the Depression made it impossible to sell memberships. In 1933, Augusta National was on the verge of bankruptcy. Clifford Roberts, desperate to generate interest in the course, jumped at the suggestion of visiting United States Golf Association (USGA) official Prescott S. Bush—father of the then eight-

A VINTAGE PHOTO OF THE 11TH GREEN AND 12TH HOLE AT AUGUSTA NATIONAL GOLF CLUB. (HISTORIC GOLF PHOTO/RON WATTS COLLECTION)

year-old future President—that the club might be considered for the site of the 1934 U.S. Open Championship. Bob Jones was also eager to host a USGA event in the South—neither the Open nor the Amateur Championships had ever been held south of Illinois.

After further review, however, the USGA decided it did not want to move the dates of the Open to early spring (it would be much too hot in Augusta in mid-summer), so they declined. But the speculation had convinced Roberts this was just the sort of thing the club needed to kick-start membership sales. So, along with founding member Grantland Rice, an alternative was devised: an invitational event headed by Jones, that could also be billed as Jones's return to competitive golf. And that's how The Masters was born.

As the only major championship to be conducted every year over the same course, The Masters has naturally brought more attention to Augusta National than to any other MacKenzie design. In fact, only two other MacKenzie courses (Royal Melbourne and Moortown) have ever been the site of a top professional event, so it is not surprising that Augusta is the public perception of MacKenzie's design ideals.

Ironically, Augusta National is also one of the most thoroughly *altered* of MacKenzie's designs. Jones respected the opinions of his fellow players immensely, and over the years the club has listened closely to the ideas of former champions on how the design of the course might be improved. Two of the earliest holes to be changed were the seventh and tenth holes, felt by many players to be too easy. The club has also been keen to do anything in its power to improve the excitement of the tournament for its spectators, and this has been the impetus for everything from changing the 16th hole (to bring water more into play) to knocking down the mounds around the eighth green to improve spectator viewing (they have since been restored). In fact, literally every green, every tee, and

THE FAIRWAY BUNKER ON AUGUSTA NATIONAL'S TENTH HOLE IS PERHAPS MACKENZIE'S ONLY ORIGINAL HAZARD STILL REMAINING. BEFORE THE GREEN WAS MOVED TO ITS CURRENT POSITION, IT SAT NEXT TO THIS BUNKER.

every bunker has been rebuilt (if not redesigned) over the past 25 years.

Some critics say that MacKenzie would not even recognize the Augusta National course today because of all the changes. In truth, he never saw the finished course: his last visit there was in April of 1932, just before the grass was planted. (He was hoping to attend the first Masters Tournament, but he died two and a half months before the event.) Then again, it is worth noting that MacKenzie never saw a lot of his other finished creations, either—including everything he built in Australia and South America, Lahinch in Ireland, Crystal Downs in Michigan, and Palmetto in Aiken, South Carolina.

However, the character of the Augusta course, and its razor-sharp edge between a very good shot and a very bad result, is still vintage MacKenzie. Jones's involvement right up until his death ensured that things never got too far away from the original intent of the design. Among the "sacred" parts of the design are two stretches of holes—the third through the fifth and the 12th through the 14th. (The short par-4 third was actually the first hole on the course to be called into question. In 1933, Cliff Roberts wrote to MacKenzie to suggest adding a deep bunker across the front of the green in order to prevent the possibility of

a run-up approach. Bob Jones, however, was not impressed by the idea. In addition, MacKenzie's defense of the hole was strong enough that the change was never pursued.)

Jones apparently gave MacKenzie much freedom to experiment within the design because many of Augusta's green complexes were neither ordinary nor natural. The fifth and 14th are unusual plateaus reminiscent of St. Andrews, with sharp undulations rather than bunkering guarding the front of them. The tilted, bunker-less third and the highly mounded eighth greens are also unlike any other found on this side of the Atlantic. And several greens which have not survived, including the original low green for the seventh hole (which MacKenzie likened to the 18th at St. Andrews), the horseshoe shape of the ninth, and the deep punchbowl of the tenth (which was beside the sprawling bunker in the fairway, rather

ABOVE, LEFT: THE ORIGINAL PAR-3 16TH AT AUGUSTA WASN'T NEARLY THE CHAL-LENGE THAT IT IS TODAY. ABOVE, RIGHT: A RARE POSTCARD OF THE ORIGINAL TENTH HOLE SHOWS HOW THE GREEN WAS SITUATED TO THE RIGHT OF THE SPRAWLING FAIRWAY BUNKER, A FEATURE THAT SURVIVES TODAY. (HISTORIC GOLF PHOTOS / RON WATTS COLLECTION)

THE 475-YARD PAR-5 13TH HAS BECOME WORLD FAMOUS. IN *GOLF IS MY GAME*, BOBBY JONES WROTE: "WE CALL THIRTEEN A PAR FIVE BECAUSE UNDER CERTAIN CONDITIONS OF WIND AND GROUND, FEW PLAYERS WILL RISK TRYING FOR THE GREEN WITH A SECOND SHOT. IN MY OPINION, THIS THIRTEENTH HOLE IS ONE OF THE FINEST HOLES FOR COMPETITIVE PLAY I HAVE EVER SEEN. THE PLAYER IS FIRST TEMPTED TO DARE THE CREEK ON HIS TEE SHOT BY PLAYING IN CLOSE TO THE CORNER, BECAUSE IF HE ATTAINS HIS POSITION HE HAS NOT ONLY SHORTENED THE HOLE BUT OBTAINED A MORE LEVEL LIE FOR HIS SECOND SHOT. DRIVING OUT TO THE RIGHT NOT ONLY INCREASES THE LENGTH OF THE SECOND, BUT ENCOUNTERS AN ANNOYING SIDEHILL LIE. WHATEVER POSITION MAY BE REACHED WITH THE TEE SHOT, THE SECOND SHOT AS WELL ENTAILS A MOMENTOUS DECISION WHETHER OR NOT TO TRY FOR THE GREEN. WITH THE PIN FAR BACK ON THE RIGHT, UNDER NORMAL WEATHER CONDITIONS, THIS IS A VERY GOOD EAGLE HOLE, BECAUSE THE CONTOURS OF THE GREEN TEND TO RUN THE SECOND SHOT CLOSE. THE CHIEF DANGER IS THAT THE BALL WILL FOLLOW THE CREEK. THE MOST DIF-FICULT PIN LOCATIONS ARE ALONG THE CREEK IN THE FORWARD PART OF THE GREEN. A PLAYER WHO DARES THE CREEK ON EITHER HIS FIRST OR SECOND SHOT MAY VERY EASILY ENCOUNTER A SIX OR SEVEN ON THIS HOLE. YET THE REWARD OF A SUCCESSFUL, BOLD PLAY IS MOST ENTICING."

TOP: IN THE MID-FIFTIES, A POND WAS BUILT IN FRONT OF THE SIXTH GREEN, BUT WAS QUICKLY FILLED IN; THE HUMP IN THE GREEN IS CLEARLY VISIBLE HERE.
BOTTOM: THE LONG, NARROW EIGHTH GREEN LAY PARTIALLY HIDDEN IN THE TREES FROM BELOW, SURROUNDED BY TALL MOUNDS THAT PRODUCED A SORT OF GATH-ERING GREEN. **OPPOSITE PAGE:** MACKENZIE'S ORIGINAL NINTH GREEN AT AUGUSTA (CENTER) WAS RATHER HORSESHOE SHAPED AND THE 18TH GREEN TO THE LEFT HAD A LONG, NARROW OPENING IN ITS ORIGINAL DESIGN. (HISTORIC GOLF PHOTO / RON WATTS COLLECTION)

than well past it as it is today), were equally unusual for an American course.

On nearly all of these holes, what makes the design so unusual is the concept of using tightly-mowed slopes as a sort of hazard, so that a bor-derline approach shot runs away from the cup or off the green and leaves a touchy pitch, chip, or putt, often up and over a ridge at the edge of the putting surface. This is a feature of the great links that Jones and MacKenzie so admired, and Augusta is one of few American courses where the man-agement (led for so long by Jones) has remained committed to a firm, fast playing surface (though both MacKenzie and Jones might be aghast at the cost of that commitment today, and the current definition of "fast").

A POSTHUMOUS DESIGN

MacKenzie's redesign of Palmetto Golf Club in Aiken, across the river from Augusta, was completed by Wendell Miller, who boasted that the doctor had trusted his company to complete the new greens without his visiting the site once.

But still on the drawing table in his home was a 36-hole plan for the Ohio State University, originally drawn in late 1929, which was delayed indefinitely due to the Depression. In 1937, three years after the doctor's death, the school finally went ahead with construction of twenty-seven of the thirty-six holes. In their search for someone to supervise con-struction to Doctor MacKenzie's plans, Bobby Jones recommended either Robert Hunter Jr. or the then-30-year-old Robert Trent Jones; he said he was not familiar with Perry Maxwell's work. But in the end, it was decided to hire John S. McCoy, an Ohio State graduate who had worked several years with Wendell Miller's firm, and built MacKenzie's nine holes at St. Charles Country Club in Winnipeg, Manitoba.

The Scarlet and Gray courses, named for the University's colors, were constructed almost entirely with funds provided by the Works Progress Administration and opened in 1938. The championship Scarlet course is home to the University's golf team and became celebrated as one of the nation's best university courses when Jack Nicklaus and Tom Weiskopf were part of the "Buckeye" squad. The shorter Grey course was extended to eighteen holes after World War II.

THE FOURTH HOLE AT PALMETTO GOLF CLUB IN AIKEN, SOUTH CAROLINA. MACKENZIE DIED BEFORE HIS REDESIGN OF THIS GOLF COURSE WAS COMPLETED.

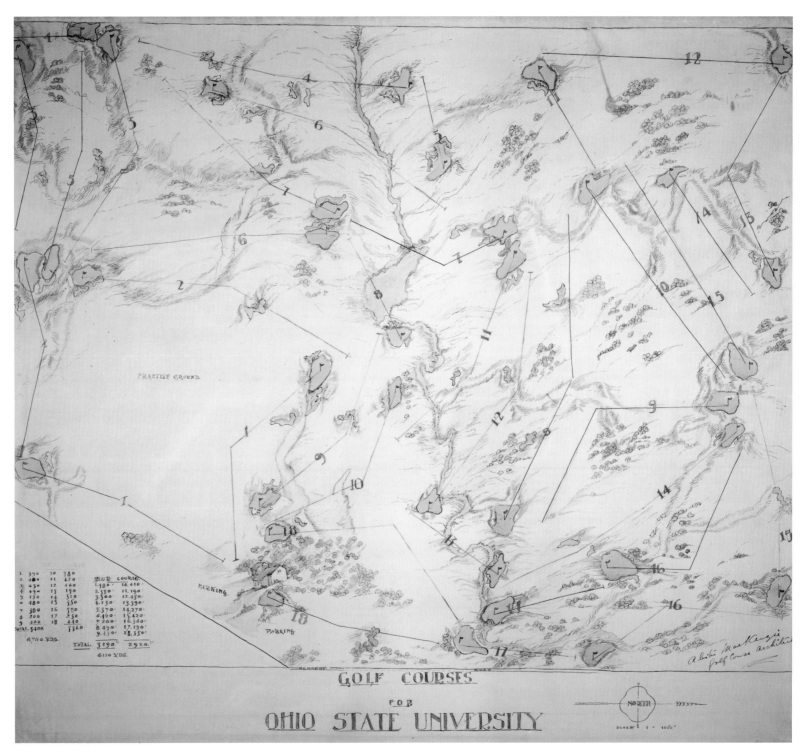

MACKENZIE'S PLANS FOR 36 HOLES AT OHIO STATE UNIVERSITY IN COLUMBUS, OHIO WERE DRAWN IN 1929 BUT THE GREAT DEPRESSION PUT CONSTRUCTION ON HOLD. HE NEVER SAW THE FINISHED PRODUCT. (MICHAEL HURDZAN)

EVEN THOUGH MACKENZIE'S POND (LEFT) HAS NOW BECOME A LAKE, THE ORIGINAL ROUTING PLAN AT OSU IS BASICALLY INTACT. (MICHAEL HURDZAN)

IN 1938, NINE YEARS AFTER THEY WERE DESIGNED, THE SCARLET AND GRAY COURSES AT OHIO STATE UNIVERSITY OPENED. JACK NICKLAUS AND TOM WEISKOPF PLAYED HERE WHEN THEY WERE MEMBERS OF THE OSU GOLF TEAM.

Chapter Ten
The MacKenzie Legacy

THE CORONARY THROMBOSIS THAT WAS TO PROVE FATAL FOR
MACKENZIE STRUCK HIM AT HIS HOME AT PASATIEMPO ON
DECEMBER 31, 1933. HE WAS HOSTING A PARTY FOR HOGMANAY
and there is little doubt that he was wearing his kilt and had a glass in
one hand and a cigarette in the other—a contented Scotsman of the day.
Little active treatment was available for that type of illness in those days,
so he was nursed at home. Hilda and he played bridge each evening with
Hilda's son, Tony Haddock, and Tony's wife. On the following Saturday
(January 6, 1934), Tony went to Santa Cruz to deal with some matters on
Alister's behalf. Hilda brought him his lunch and sat chatting. As she was
tidying up his room, he suddenly gasped and died. He was 63 years old.

MacKenzie's association with Pasatiempo extended beyond his
death. A photo exists of his funeral service being held outside near the
sixth fairway. Yet, the relationship continued even further. Although the
initial death announcement indicated the intention that his remains
should be returned to the ancestral family home in Scotland, it soon
became clear that this was a rather complex transfer. Ultimately, appropriately, his ashes were scattered across the golf course.

Like his contemporary A. W. Tillinghast, MacKenzie not only died
in relative obscurity but in financial distress. Trying to keep up with
Marion Hollins's social circle at Pasatiempo caused him to live, as Fred
Hawtree delicately put it, "beyond his means if not his expectations." His
design fees had to be cut back after the Depression, and even then it was
difficult to collect what was owed. In addition, after he married Hilda,

MACKENZIE WITH HIS STEPGRANDSON PHIL HADDOCK AT PASATIEMPO. **OPPOSITE**
PAGE: AS IT WAS FOR MANY ARCHITECTS, THE DEPRESSION MADE IT DIFFICULT FOR
MACKENZIE TO MAKE A LIVING. CONSTRUCTION OF THE TWO COURSES AT OHIO
STATE UNIVERSITY HAD STILL NOT BEGUN WHEN HE WROTE THIS LETTER, EVEN
THOUGH HE'D COMPLETED THE PLANS IN 1929.

DR. ALISTER MACKENZIE
AND ASSOCIATES

MEMBER OF THE INTERNATIONAL
SOCIETY OF GOLF COURSE ARCHITECTS
[EUROPEAN SECTION]

CYPRESS POINT CLUB
PEBBLE BEACH, CALIFORNIA

RESIDENCE AND HEAD OFFICE
PASATIEMPO ESTATES
SANTA CRUZ, CALIFORNIA
TEL. 2696, SANTA CRUZ
IF NO REPLY TEL. 1600 SANTA CRUZ

OTHER OFFICES
WHITCOMB HOUSE
WHITCOMB ST.
LONDON, ENGLAND

BAYSIDE GOLF LINKS
BAYSIDE, NEW YORK

CARE OF AGNEW & BOEKEL
FEDERAL RESERVE BANK BLDG.
SAN FRANCISCO

ROOM 1609
105 WEST MONROE STREET
CHICAGO

January 16th.1933.

Pasatiempo,
Santa Cruz,
California.

L.W.StJohn Esq.,
Director of Athletics,
The Ohio State University,
Columbus.

My dear Mr.StJohn

        Are there any further developements in
regard to the golf course?

        Even in these hard times every golf course
I have done has been a success for example I recently made
a public course at Bayside Long Island and I am informed
that since it was opened in the Spring they received over
$10,000 a month in Green Fees which I understand is twice
as much as any other course in New York State.

        You will he interested to hear that I have
just had a telegram from Bobby Jones in regard to the opening
of the Augusta National on Saturday last. It reads as follows
"The opening ha been a thorough success despite bad weather
Everyone likes the course wish you were here to hear all
the nice things said about it the whole crowd send regards
and appreciation to you and Mrs Mackenzie Best ever Bob Jones"

        As an indication of the low cost of construction
and maintainance of my golf courses there are only twenty
two bunkers on the Augusta National and only nineteen at
Bayside. This course here at Pasatiempo which many people
consider the best of all inland golf courses is maintained
for $10,000 a year which includes complete fairway irrigation.

        With kindest regards,

                Yours very sincerely,
                a listr mackenzie

her rich uncle—assuming that she would be well provided for—took her out of his will, thus eliminating one expected source of financial security. Not long after Alister's death, Hilda returned to Britain (and not in a first-class cabin).

When he died, MacKenzie was not nearly as well known as he is today. Much of his fame derives from having designed Augusta National, but the first Masters was still three months away. (He had wanted to attend, but it was uncertain whether the club could provide his cross-country train fare. If they could, he offered to camp out in the unfinished clubhouse.) Outside of Australia and California, where he had been rather prolific and had few competitors, his name was largely unknown. In Britain, certainly, Harry Colt and James Braid were better known to the golfing public. In America, it was the same for Donald Ross and Charles Blair Macdonald.

In his last professional brochure, Dr. MacKenzie claimed to have designed "more than 300 courses" around the world. In his 1933 "lost" manuscript, however, the number had grown to 400. No doubt these figures were off the top of his head, rather than the result of meticulous counting. Meticulous counting was anathema to him, as is clear from his highly deprecatory remarks about golfers of the "card and pencil" spirit whose only concern was with what their total score might be. He didn't keep a diary of his work or even copies of many of his plans. His manuscript for *The Spirit of St. Andrews* is his complete memoir and basically all he left, other than his magnificent golf courses. For MacKenzie, what mattered most was not a final score but whether the journey was interesting and exciting.

In *The Spirit of St. Andrews*, MacKenzie took great pride in saying that,

I do not know of a single course out of the more than four hundred we have done which has ever had any drastic changes to the original routing, or even the position of the greens.

In this respect we have always obtained finality, but I know of several where ignorant green committees have shaved down the undulations which created the charm and variety of the approach shots. Not only is this most unwise, but it is as much an affront to the architect as it would be to an artist to alter one of his paintings without his agreement.

In spite of MacKenzie's own scoring, we have only been able to doc-

ument about 150 MacKenzie designs that remain today. Some of the discrepancy is due to the architect's inclusion of courses where he did minimal consulting work (and where his ideas may or may not have been implemented). He also tended to include courses that were designed solely by his partners but were listed by him as part of "their" work. MacKenzie had very little to do with courses such as Pebble Beach and Lake Oswego, which are included in his last brochure. Yet 150 courses is still an impressive number, especially when we consider that his first design came at age 37, he died at 63, and both the First World War and the Great Depression intervened. When you really boil it down, the parallels between MacKenzie's career and that of Bobby Jones are interesting. Jones's biographer, O.B. Keeler, wrote about the "seven lean years" that Bobby suffered through before he won his first major championship in 1923, and of the seven great years afterwards in which he won twelve more majors. MacKenzie's "seven lean years" came between 1919 and 1925. But like Jones he also had "seven fat years," consisting of his overseas work from 1926 to 1933.

Other MacKenzie courses will no doubt come to light, but the number of clubs still unaware seems unlikely to be large.

Since MacKenzie has long left us, the value of his courses is doubled by the fact that so few of them remain intact. Of those, three (Cypress Point, Augusta National—even with its changes—and Royal Melbourne) are often rated among the top five golf courses in the world. As many as a dozen MacKenzie layouts have been rated among the top 100. The total might still be higher if not for the "conventional wisdom" that frequently causes such courses as Cavendish and Melrose—at 5,700 yards each—to be altogether overlooked. What is for certain is that MacKenzie would not have cared, as long as he got the most out of each property. Not only did he refuse to pander to conventional wisdom in his designs, he seemed to defy it deliberately to make a point.

Dr. MacKenzie's work has been credited by historians such as Ron Whitten as possibly having the most influence on modern golf course

OPPOSITE PAGE: THIS ARTICLE RAN IN *GOLFDOM* MAGAZINE A MONTH AFTER MACKENZIE DIED.

FEBRUARY, 1934

Mackenzie, Master Architect, Passes; Leaves His Mark in Golf

By HERB GRAFFIS

DR. ALISTER MACKENZIE,
architect of famous golf courses, died at his home at Pasatiempo, Santa Cruz, Calif., January 6.

Angina pectoris took Mac. About three years ago he became worried about' a persistent heartburn and consulted a doctor in London who told him his heart was sound. A week prior to his death he suffered a painful attack and went to bed under doctor's orders. He had been confined to his bed only three days when the end came. His stepson Anthony Haddon, Mrs. Haddon and their youngsters visited with Mac and Mrs. Mackenzie each day during his last illness. The Mackenzies and Haddons played bridge together each evening while Mac was propped up in bed.

The Saturday morning of his death Tony Haddon went into Santa Cruz to care for a few matters at Mac's request. Mrs. Mackenzie brought up his lunch. These two devoted pals chatted and while Mrs. Mackenzie was putting the sickroom in order, Mac gasped and fell back on his pillow. It was all over.

* * *

You're taking a long chance when you say a man was the "greatest" artist in any line, but there are plenty who would hand "greatest" on Alister Mackenzie as a golf architect and hold up their end of any ensuing argument.

In the United States, in England, Scotland, the Continent, South America and Australia Mackenzie's creative work will stay as long as golf is the golf it is today and has been for a hundred years past.

There probably will be some alterations made but not one in a hundred of them will stand the test of time as well as Mac's original creation.

Mackenzie came to this country first about 10 years ago. He had a high reputation on the other

side; a reputation based on results. He was consulting architect to the Royal and Ancient and the creator of several of the outstanding British courses. During the Great War he had been one of the outstanding camouflage experts and into golf architecture he carried his superb genius for making color masses do tricks to his bidding.

A Versatile Genius

His Cypress Point, Pasatiempo, Bayshore and Augusta National jobs—to name only four examples of his work in this country—gave examples of his art and versatility that contribute greatly to the enjoyment of golf. While Mac was on the Bayshore and Augusta National problems, I had the privilege of frequent contact with him and shall always remember how often he used that word "pleasurable" as the test of golf architecture. These two jobs were entirely dissimilar in their background. Bayshore was built on the Meyer brothers' idea of turning a flat and uninteresting truck garden into the highest type fee course. Augusta National was built on Bob Jones' idea of providing the ultra in private golf courses. Mackenzie being given both jobs tips you off to his rating as an artist.

Golf course architects, like other artists, are not adverse to criticizing questionable points in another artist's work, but I never have heard any of them who did not volunteer the judgment that Mackenzie was the great master. This, in a profession as keenly competitive as golf architecture, is real praise.

One phrase that Mac told me, I've thought was a gem of description of good architecture: "Make it look hard and play easy if the player uses his brains." Mac was strongly against penalizing the dub. It was his idea that the duffer was handicapped enough by lack of distance and control. He also was a pioneer in advocating and employing laborsaving methods in construction and maintenance. He held that the cheaper a good course could be built and kept up, the more courses there would be and the more men ultimately employed in golf.

For a couple of months prior to Mackenzie's death we had been figuring on an architectural department he was to conduct in GOLFDOM and on several articles dealing with course maintenance he had agreed to write.(He had finished the manuscript of a book on golf architecture and maintenance and submitted it to Scribners.

This brilliant Scot, author of classic golf courses, died hard up, with more than $15,000 owed him, which seems a tough finish considering the amount of money spent for American golf courses during the time he was active. Mac certainly deserved a better break for the way in which he served the game.

Mackenzie's Course Principles

Now, as the finale of Mackenzie's work in American golf, we'll take some quotes from letters he wrote several weeks prior to his death.

"He (referring to a commentator on the Augusta National course) states that previous to the Augusta National, my golf courses have always had a wealth of side bunkers, which is untrue. The only one that has is Cypress Point and these are all natural sand dunes made by another fellow, not myself. Over 20 years ago I wrote an article headed "Too many bunkers" and nearly 30 years ago I made Alwoodly and Moortown, which many people consider are the best of British inland courses, without a single side bunker. For 30 years I have been advocating that there should be no purely penal bunkers and that the only reason for bunkers is to give players more interest and more fun."

"All my golf courses have increased in popularity notwithstanding the depression. The reason is that they are different. They have the following characteristics:

"Finally—In the last 25 years no green I have been responsible for has been altered and improved by anyone else. As Bob Jones says in his introduction to my new book: 'All his courses are pleasurable. In

every instance he has placed interest and enjoyment ahead of difficulty.'

"All bunkers are eliminated that do not add materially to the pleasure of my courses. As my courses have only a quarter the usual number of sand traps, the cost of maintenance is correspondingly reduced.

"Natural features of the terrain are used to the fullest extent."

"There is no rough, therefore no lost balls, no weed seeds blowing on the course.

"Construction work is of such character that all tees, hollows, banks and everything except a few yards around the hole are closely mowable with the power five-unit fairway machine.

"Greens are not over watered or over fertilized, so that fine dwarf grasses involving very little labor in cutting are obtained.

"Above all, I realize that more golf courses are ruined by spending money on them than by refraining to do so."

Mackenzie's first book on golf architecture is out of print now. It is interesting to read it and note how many of the policies he advocated in that book and which were received with sharp criticism on publication have been adopted as cardinal principles. Mac also has some highly interesting and provocative ideas about maintenance. Some of them were debatable but he would argue them out with all comers, never admitting defeat, and always willing to continue the debate over the locker-room Scotch in the effort to convert mankind.

Last summer he was working on a book on camouflage, "with (he said) the object of proving that the peace of the world would be assured if all nations were taught to camouflage their defenses."

Mackenzie was a great fellow and a great architect. He did a lot for golf. May his big soul rest in that pleasurable land beyond.

(The first of this series reached GOLFDOM's office only a few days before Dr. Mackenzie's death, probably the last article he wrote. It will appear in an early issue.)

design than any other architect. It could be said the influence was indirect, however, because of all his associates, only Perry Maxwell continued to build outstanding courses after the doctor's death. Certainly, he would be enormously successful today, in a time when dramatic and photogenic designs capture all of the attention. Nevertheless, he might not think much of modern golf architecture, if you consider these observations:

❧ On the fetish of length: *It has often been suggested that an uninteresting hole might be improved by lengthening it, but it would be a safe axiom to adopt, "It will only be made worse and take longer to play. Shorten it and get it over."*

❧ On the creation of water hazards: *Given a free hand, I would use an existing water hazard to the fullest possible extent, but I am very much opposed to creating artificial ones at a cost of thousands of dollars when the money can be used to give much greater thrills in some other way.*

❧ On golf course contractors: *Any contractor who informs a committee that golf courses can be constructed on contract as they would build a clubhouse is either absolutely ignorant of golf course architecture or is trying to*

THE APPROACH TO THE THIRD GREEN AT CAVENDISH GOLF CLUB, BUXTON, DERBYSHIRE, ENGLAND.

hoodwink the golfing public. It would be just as reasonable to expect an artist to estimate the amount he charges for a painting, according to the quantities of paint and materials he uses. . . . It is interesting to note that not a single one of the famous British and American courses have been made in this way.

✎ On alterations to designs (see Augusta National): *It is often suggested that changes in the ball may necessitate alterations to the course, but this is nonsense. A well-designed golf course should suit any golf ball or any class of player. The Old Course at St. Andrews is a classical example. It was the best in the days of the feather, guttie, and the Haskell ball, and Bobby Jones still describes it as the best today.*

✎ On the value of good design: *What does it matter what the fee of the expert is if, owing to his advice, the total cost can be reduced fifty percent and far better results obtained in addition?* [MacKenzie would be appalled to find that today's most famous architects produce the most expensive courses.]

✎ On the interest of running approach shots: *There is a great fascination in playing a shot with a maximum of topspin and seeing one's ball climbing over hillocks, through hollows, curving right to left, or left to right, and finally lying dead at the hole. . . . There is nothing like the same excitement in watching the flight of a ball through the air. Then it is only the result which gives satisfaction. The manner in which a shot is played is a greater lasting pleasure.*

✎ On golf course maintenance: *It is not even necessary that fairways should consist entirely of grasses. There should be a freedom from clover, daisies and plantains, dandelions and other weeds, but others such as yarrow, chickweed, perlwort, moss, and in Britain patches of closely cut heather, make excellent fairways. It is also pleasing to the eye to have varying shades of green instead of one uniform colour.*

It is possible to have too high a degree of perfection. . . . If we have never had a bad lie we are not likely to appreciate a good one, and moreover, the ability to play from a bad lie differentiates between a good player and a bad one.

✎ On the cost of golf: *If more people connected with the promotion and upkeep of golf courses knew that they knew not, the game would probably not cost a quarter as much as at present, and as is the case of motor cars in America, would no longer be considered a luxury but a necessity for the promotion of the health, the happiness and the prosperity of the community.*

And as for the future of golf course design, all involved would do well to remember his final words in *The Spirit of St. Andrews:*

It is of vital importance to avoid anything that tends to make the game simple and stereotyped. On the contrary, every endeavor should be made to increase its strategy, variety, mystery, charm and elusiveness so that we shall never get bored with it, but continue to pursue it with increasing zest, as many of the old stalwarts of St. Andrews do, for the remainder of our lives.

MACKENZIE REVIEWING A COURSE LAYOUT.

Chapter Eleven
"Capability" and "Finality"

IT WOULD BE A BOLD ACT TO CALL 'FINALE' ON THE MACKENZIE STORY EVEN NOW. AT HIS DEATH IN 1934, NO ONE WOULD HAVE GUESSED THAT HE WOULD BE MUCH MORE FAMOUS NEARLY 70 years later. Yet this is the case. When he died, the first Masters Tournament was still to be played and the Augusta National course was yet to establish its reputation, which only built up over the years as one exciting Masters followed another. When it had finally "passed the test of time," the true stature of MacKenzie's work became recognized. In addition, with the arrival of televised golf (ultimately in glorious Technicolor), knowledge of Augusta National spread around the world in a way never dreamed before. Appetite for television views of the Masters extended beyond the ranks of golfers and far beyond the U.S. With each year's tournament, Alister's fame became greater.

MacKenzie was certainly no run-of-the-mill fellow. His artistic individualism, combined with his scientific knowledge—supported by the force of his strong personality and his special brand of benevolent autocracy—made him a man who caused great things to happen around him.

In 1995, something happened that brought MacKenzie's name again to the attention of the golf world: the discovery and publication of his book *The Spirit of St. Andrews*. The publicists, however, perhaps exaggerated the surprise element of this event. It was known from his obituaries in 1934 that such a manuscript had been completed and that Bobby Jones had written the book's foreword. Unfortunately, though, economic and other pressures at that time made publication by his surviving rela-

tives impossible. When it was discovered again after so many years (it had languished in his stepson's papers since 1934), stimulated no doubt by the increasing prominence of MacKenzie's name, the manuscript was resurrected. "Resurrected" is an apt word, because reading the manuscript seems to suddenly bring to life a man long dead, dispensing in a chatty, personal way various recollections, aspirations, and irritations of his life as a course designer, with a sprinkling of his own homespun general and political philosophy. And it tells us some things about Alister that we had not known before.

Many matters in his earlier writings are clarified, explicitly or implicitly. MacKenzie put his thoughts into print roughly every decade that he worked in golf course design. In his lectures to greenkeepers that

was published in 1913, he mentions thirteen years of previous experience in course architecture. No records have come to light of design contracts earlier than 1907-1908, but from shortly after the Boer War, he certainly was involved in discussions—if not arguments—on course design within Yorkshire clubs to which he belonged. He wrote *Golf Architecture* in 1920, and in the early 1930s he wrote *The Spirit of St. Andrews*.

Though details vary, there is remarkable consistency in his message. The prose of his last book is more relaxed and confident than in his earlier

OPPOSITE PAGE: DR. ALISTER MACKENZIE. **ABOVE:** VIEW FROM BEHIND THE FOURTH GREEN AT HALIFAX GOLF CLUB IN ENGLAND.

writing. He is also generous with his comments about fellow architects. This kinder, gentler tone is almost certainly a reflection of the last years of his life being his happiest. Interspersed with his design principles come many references to holes he knew and admired; most frequently they are from the Old Course at St. Andrews, hence the title of the book. But St. Andrews, the "Mecca" for golfers for perhaps hundreds of years, has been much written about, so it is rather on the spirit of *MacKenzie* that the text is most illuminating.

There are more of the "Christmas Cracker"-type anecdotes that Alister had such an affection for. One example: *A Papal bull is a bull kept in the Vatican to give milk to the Pope's children.* In addition, he lets us have his strong views on playing golf and scoring at golf, but goes on to consider golf influencing politics and politics influencing golf. He also expresses frequently, in differing ways, his long held conviction that autocracy is the only sound method of government—at least for a golf club. When he says that, *"In these days there is far too much talk about democracy,"* he was writing at a time when many in western democracies shared his fear that their country would succumb to the creeping cancer of communistic socialism.

Since MacKenzie was writing in the early 1930s, it may be tricky for today's reader to pick up on his golf and political allusions. He mentions "Briand" and "Lloyd George," names not in the forefront of many minds today. In fact, Aristide Briand (1862-1932) was a leading French socialist who had been prime minister of France no fewer than eleven times. As for Lloyd George (1863-1945), he was the British Liberal prime minister from 1916 to 1922 and was known as the "Welsh Wizard." MacKenzie claimed Briand had lost office on one occasion because he was discovered having a putting lesson from Lloyd George. [A French socialist leader cavorting on the putting green with a Liberal British opposite number is the stuff of high treason as seen from the Quai d' Orsay!] MacKenzie also mentions a veritable bag full of American and British politicians who are probably better known but who don't stand in very high esteem today. *"Great minds of the past,"* he calls them. And then he goes on to assert that their political "greatness" could be attributed to their golf!

On the aspect of golf with obvious political connotation—municipal courses—MacKenzie shows an uncharacteristic inconsistency. At times, perhaps when he had just obtained a good design contract for such a course (which didn't happen very often), he extols their virtues uninhibitedly. At other times, perhaps when a contract had gone to another architect, he condemns them all out of hand.

He gives hints of some that might have been MacKenzie triumphs but, alas, the powers in control elected to give the contract to someone else or were unwilling to implement his design suggestions. The course for the Gleneagles Hotel, Perthshire, Scotland, was perhaps the prize he failed to win that rankled him the most. It was a big loss because the facility became world famous. Eventually, six courses were built there. Started by a railroad company when such companies really had serious money at their disposal, there is a suggestion that Alister, ever the champion of efficiency, played his cards incorrectly by overemphasizing the economies he could achieve for the owners.

What will posterity make of MacKenzie and how will it rate him? Posterity is not a permanent state, but in this case it can reasonably be regarded the present, and there is no doubt of his current status. All over the world, golf clubs that had paid little or no attention to what MacKenzie had done at their courses now boast of his contributions. Ranking Alister is difficult because there were no preceding generations in the course design field. Several authors have suggested that he should stand alongside creative figures of the past, such as Holbein and Rembrandt. He has also been compared to Pablo Picasso, a contemporary of Alister, who has already achieved world recognition as a master. Measuring Alister against such men is highly complimentary but they were *artists,* with canvas and paint as their media.

While Alister had much of the artist in him, he was basically an agronomist designer; his medium was the landscape. The outstanding figure from the past who perhaps comes closest to MacKenzie in terms of the medium in which he worked and in what he achieved is Lancelot "Capability" Brown, the doyen of British landscapers. Born in Northumberland near the English border with Scotland in 1716, he lived until 1783. During this period, wealth allowed the development of many grand estates in Britain. Brown started life prosaically as a kitchen gardener but it soon became evident that he had a talent, amounting to

THE 11TH HOLE AT LAHINCH GOLF CLUB, COUNTY CLARE, IRELAND.

genius, for assessing how a landscape might be modified to enhance its beauty. In particular, his talent was—like Alister's—to emphasize natural undulations and produce dramatic arboreal and water vistas. (In *The Spirit of St. Andrews*, MacKenzie explains how his moneyed clients who had land with good water features usually wished to have them removed, while those lacking such natural assets wished to have them created!)

Like Alister, Brown was an agronomist. He also revolutionized England's grand country house landscape design in the mid-eighteenth century much as MacKenzie changed golf course design in the early twentieth century. The ducal and other grand gardens or estates such as Blenheim, Stowe, Kew, and Warwick Castle that Brown designed are now visited annually by thousands of people from all over the globe.[1]

MacKenzie worked—or was prepared to work—in Brown's field of estate and large garden design. His letterhead at one time included "Expert in Landscaping Work." In his 1917 paper "Entrenchments and Camouflage," published in *Professional Memoirs, Corps of Engineers, United States Army* (Vol. 1X, p573, et. Seq.), his name is not specified in the heading but is merely referred to as "a British Officer Skilled in Landscape Gardening." The text, though, contrives to make it clear that Alister is the author.

Brown and MacKenzie also shared an endearing foible: each always used a particular word in an idiosyncratic manner, almost amounting to a malapropism. Brown repeatedly used the word "capabilities" when "possibilities" was appropriate, and it led to his nickname. This was identified when aristocratic clients had discussions together on their dealings with Brown and discovered that each had been told by him, following his initial site inspection, that "Your ground has great capabilities." MacKenzie's inordinate affection for the word "finality," usually used when "permanency" would have been more appropriate, has only come to light while studying his comments on course design work around

the world. Alongside Brown's affectionate nickname of "Capability," it seems apt to link MacKenzie with "Finality."

Cynics may talk of posthumous fame as the greatest joke. But for men like MacKenzie and Brown, who leave pieces of the world's terrain more beautiful, bringing pleasure to generation upon generation, it may be the greatest fame of all.

The fates, which were sometimes very harsh to MacKenzie, were, in the long run, charitable. Perhaps it was not such a bad thing that he was so late in getting started on his true career. Like the tortoise, he overtook the hares.

Yet, the fact that he died at a relatively young age seems sad. Certainly it was for his second wife, Hilda, with whom Alister had only a few years of happiness. But he died while his contentment continued, at the very peak of achievement when his course design work, as well as his golf, was better than ever before. Such an exit is granted to few. It is one which protects a man from being regarded by future generations in the shadow of his performance in the final years of failing powers.

Alister MacKenzie's reputation as a designer of great golf courses is secure.

---

[1] *"Capability" Brown, incidentally, has even been credited by Steel with the design of a golf course: Duddingston in Edinburgh. Since the club was actually formed in 1895, over a hundred years after Brown's death, his connection is that the course was built on the design that he had done for the Duke of Abercorn.*

As a consequence of his original work on the Duddingston site, the course possesses a unique feature in the form of a temple. It is perhaps surprising, considering the frequency with which the names of the Deity and his Son are taken in vain on golf courses, that all courses have not come to include such a feature, providing a suitable place to allow immediate supplication for divine forgiveness.

THE DOGLEG-RIGHT PAR-4 SIXTH AT CRYSTAL DOWNS COUNTRY CLUB, FRANKFORT, MICHIGAN.

Chapter Twelve
MacKenzie's Collaborators

WRITING ABOUT MACKENZIE AND HIS PARTNERS CARRIES AN ELE-
MENT OF THE RIDICULOUS—LIKE WRITING ABOUT GENERAL GEORGE
PATTON'S CHAIN OF COMMAND. ALL THE EVIDENCE INDICATES
that MacKenzie was an individualist who thrived on doing things in his
own, highly personal way. His approach to course design was essentially
that of the solo artist. Early on, the elements of a hole design or course
layout were derived from quick sketches by the master. Eventually,
though, particularly in the globetrotting second half of his career, the
doctor relied on great assistance from others to nurse his designs to
fruition while he continued his travels.

MacKenzie also had a casual "artistic" idea of the nature of partnerships. Whenever he had fresh note paper printed, which seemed to be
frequently, he placed on the letterhead the names of his "Associates" or
"Partners" around the globe, though rarely is there evidence of any for-
mal agreement. In fact, this approach was what eventually dissolved his
first partnership, the firm of Colt, MacKenzie and Alison.

HARRY S. COLT (1869-1951)
BORN: HIGHGATE, MIDDLESEX, ENGLAND
DIED: ST. AMANDS HOUSE, EAST HENDRED, OXFORDSHIRE, ENGLAND

Like Alister MacKenzie, Harry Colt had a university education. He
studied law at Cambridge University, where he was captain of the golf
team, and practiced for several years in Hastings. In 1901, he accepted
the position of club secretary at Sunningdale Golf Club in order to get
into the golf business.

About this time, the development of golf courses in the heathland
belt southwest of London was just starting to boom. Colt, based right in
its center at Sunningdale, received many commissions to lay out courses
in his spare time, including such gems as Stoke Poges, Swinley Forest,
and St. George's Hill. [He also consulted at Alwoodley.] In 1913, Colt
resigned from Sunningdale to devote his full attention to golf architecture. He traveled to the United States and Canada the following year to
lay out several courses. While in America he assisted George Crump
with the routing for Pine Valley Golf Club in New Jersey, where Colt's
design notebook is still a prized possession.

After World War I, Colt established a partnership arrangement with
MacKenzie and Charles Hugh Alison, who had worked informally with
him at Stoke Poges and at some of his other London-area courses. The
partnership, however, was designed only to enlist commissions and
divide them up, not to share revenues or to do co-designs. Through this
arrangement, most of the work in the north of England and Scotland
went to MacKenzie. Alison chose to concentrate his efforts in America,
and Colt, who did not enjoy travel, worked mostly in southern England.
In 1923, a rift developed between Colt and MacKenzie. A few years later
John Morrison took MacKenzie's place in the partnership.

Colt was the first established golf course architect who had not been
a professional golfer. He was an excellent player, however, reaching the

semifinals of the British Amateur in 1906. He was also one of the first to prepare detailed greens and tree planting plans for his designs. He was co-author of *Golf Course Architecture* with Alison in 1920, and co-contributed articles on design for Martin Sutton's *The Book of the Links*. Colt's biography, *Colt and Co.,* Cambuc Archive, was written by architect Fred W. Hawtree in 1991. It included much of the correspondence between Colt, Morrison and Alison during the lean years of the 1930s.

Colt's most prominent designs include Camberley Heath, Stoke Poges, Swinley Forest, St. George's Hill, and Sunningdale (New), all near London; Toronto Golf Club and Hamilton G&CC in Canada; the Country Club of Detroit in Michigan; and Royal Portrush in Northern Ireland.

As with MacKenzie, there now is an eponymous golfing society that keeps his name alive.

CHARLES HUGH ALISON (1882-1952)
BORN: PRESTON, LANCASHIRE, ENGLAND
DIED: JOHANNESBURG, SOUTH AFRICA

Hugh Alison was educated at Oxford, where he was an outstanding cricket player and golfer and the youngest member of the Oxford and Cambridge Golfing Society team that toured America in 1903. After a few years working as a journalist, Alison accepted the position of club secretary at Stoke Poges Golf Club near London. He assisted Harry Colt with the completion of the course, and then worked for Colt in supervising the completion of several other London-area courses.

Following service with the British Army during World War I, Alison entered into partnership with Colt and MacKenzie. Alison soon returned to America, completing virtually all of the courses in North America that carry Colt's name. After the economic collapse of 1929, Alison ventured both to South Africa and the Far East, where in 1932 he designed a handful of landmark courses in Japan. (To this day, in his honor, the deep bunkers he added at Kasumigaseki Country Club near Tokyo are called "Alisons.")

In 1949, Alison returned to South Africa to consult on the remodeling of a course. He stayed to do several more and died there in 1952.

CHARLES ATKINSON MACKENZIE
BORN: 1876, NORMANTON, LEEDS, ENGLAND
DIED: HARROGATE, YORKSHIRE, ENGLAND

Charles was a much more reserved personality than his older brother Alister. But because their wives were such good friends, the brothers socialized regularly at Alwoodley after its formation.

After World War I, Charles began the British Golf Construction Company and continued in the business for twenty years. It was a practice of his brother's to advise all the clubs that he consulted on to hire a specialized golf course contractor. While there is but a hint that Alister specifically recommended his brother's company—something that might have been considered unprofessional—there were few such companies in existence. Consequently, Charles's company often received the work.

Charles was also an aspiring designer and somewhat jealous of his older brother. After the family rift in 1927, caused by the breakup of Alister's marriage, Alister left to work overseas. Charles then managed to attract some design commissions on his own, mostly in northern England. In the obituaries of his brother published in Yorkshire newspapers in 1934, Charles is portrayed as the more successful designer of the two MacKenzie brothers. Quite possibly this is because he was friendly with the obituary writers.

Among Charles's most noteworthy designs are Bingley St. Ives Golf Club, Pannal Golf Club, Scarcroft Golf Club, and Fulford Golf Club in York. These have sometimes been mistakenly credited to Alister, but all were designed and built after his exodus from Leeds.

PERRY DUKE MAXWELL (1879-1952)
BORN: PRINCETON, KENTUCKY
DIED: TULSA, OKLAHOMA

Of Scottish descent, Perry Maxwell settled in Oklahoma in 1897 to recover from an attack of tuberculosis. He began as a cashier at the Ardmore National Bank and eventually rose to vice president. He took up golf about 1909. In 1913, with his wife's assistance, Maxwell laid out a crude nine holes on their farm north of Ardmore and called it Dornick Hills. In 1923, he added a second nine.

The same year, Maxwell made an extended visit to Scotland to see

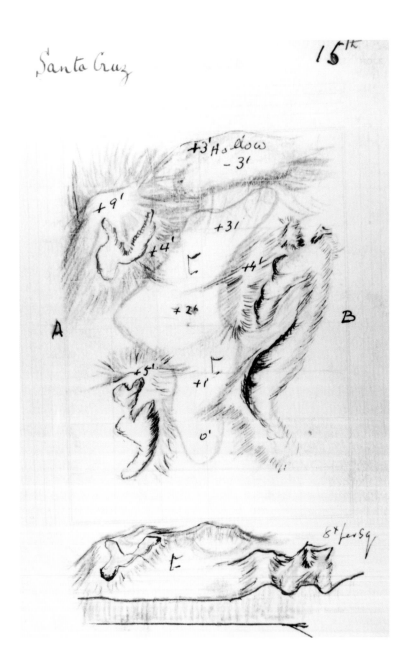

Santa Cruz   *15th*

the classic links first-hand. While there he met MacKenzie and possibly suggested that the two collaborate on projects in the United States. Three years later, on his way to California, MacKenzie stopped to visit Maxwell in Oklahoma. By that time, Maxwell had attracted design commissions in Oklahoma and Pennsylvania. He proceeded to arrange for MacKenzie to be paid as a consultant on his contract for Melrose Country Club near Philadelphia, and it cemented their partnership. Maxwell also arranged for MacKenzie to be celebrated by the Philadelphia press, playing to Alister's ego. It worked; Maxwell became MacKenzie's partner "East of the Rockies" right up until his death, collaborating on the designs of Oklahoma City Golf & Country Club, Crystal Downs Country Club, and the University of Michigan Golf Course.

Of all of MacKenzie's many partners, Maxwell was possibly the one most attuned to Alister's artistic tastes, with a penchant for rugged bunkers and severely contoured greens. The MacKenzie/Maxwell greens at Crystal Downs are some of the most sloping putting surfaces in golf—as are those at Prairie Dunes Country Club, which Maxwell designed a few years after MacKenzie's death. In fact, Maxwell's putting surfaces became so famous that clubs such as The National Golf Links of America, Pine Valley, and Augusta National hired him to install the famous "Maxwell rolls" in a couple of their greens.

Following MacKenzie's death, Maxwell's son, James Press Maxwell, joined him in the business. After his father's leg was amputated in 1946, Press supervised most of the work they did together.

Among Perry Maxwell's most prominent designs are: Dornick Hills, Ardmore, OK; Prairie Dunes, Hutchinson, KS; Southern Hills CC, Tulsa, OK; Twin Hills G & CC, Oklahoma City, OK; Old Town Club, Winston-Salem, NC; and Riverside GC, Austin, TX (formerly the CC of Austin, where Tom Kite and Ben Crenshaw learned the game).

WILES ROBERT HUNTER (1874-1942)
BORN: TERRE HAUTE, INDIANA
DIED: SANTA BARBARA, CALIFORNIA

Robert Hunter had an even more unusual background for a golf course architect than Alister MacKenzie. At the age of 19, he "firmly decided to devote the rest of my days to the care and feeding of the poor." After majoring in sociology at Indiana University, he first went to work at Jane Addams's Hull House in Chicago and then at the University Settlement House in New York.

His first book, *Poverty*, written in 1904, established Hunter as a famous champion of the poor and downtrodden. At the time, Hunter was living a very well-to-do life as the husband of an heiress. This prompted Teddy Roosevelt to categorize him a "millionaire socialist." Hunter was also a neighbor and friend of Mark Twain. In addition, while attending international conferences on socialism, he gained audiences with famous personalities from Nikolai Lenin and Leo Tolstoy to Benito Mussolini. After failing to get elected Govenor of Connecticut on the Socialist ticket in 1910, he lost faith in politics as a solution to the world's problems. He then settled down to an academic career at the University of California, Berkeley.

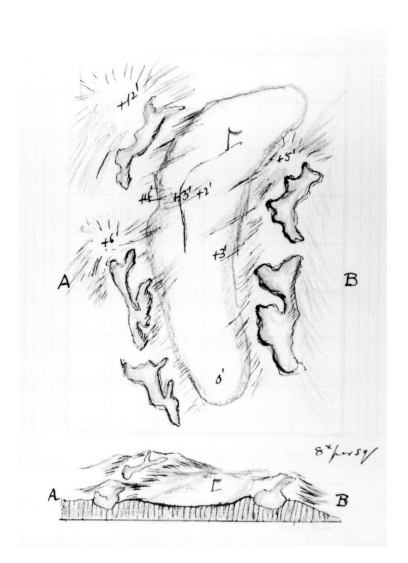

In addition to his many other activities, Hunter was captivated by golf. He took up the game on the advice of a doctor in 1905, after becoming depressed by the subject matter of his book. While in New York, Hunter often played at Shinnecock Hills, Nassau Country Club, and the National Golf Links of America on Long Island. On a European trip in 1912, he spent considerable time on the links of Scotland and England and became very interested in that type of golf. In 1925, Hunter began compiling a book on his hobby of golf course architecture called *The Links*. [As John Strawn wrote, this established Hunter as "the first man who had never been a caddie who was an expert in both poverty and golf."] Impressed with MacKenzie's earlier book on the subject, Hunter contacted him for help in compiling illustrations for *The Links*. Apparently, their correspondence established a warm friendship because it was due to Hunter's urging that MacKenzie set off to the promised land of California to pursue potential projects.

Oddly enough, Hunter never designed a golf course on his own. Prior to his work with MacKenzie, his only experience was at Mira Vista G & CC in Berkeley, California. Willie Watson was recruited to design the course and Hunter served as chairman of the green committee. In 1921, Hunter also tried to bring his friend Walter Travis to California to design courses but Travis's failing health prevented it. Hunter's primary role with MacKenzie was as a deputy responsible for implementing

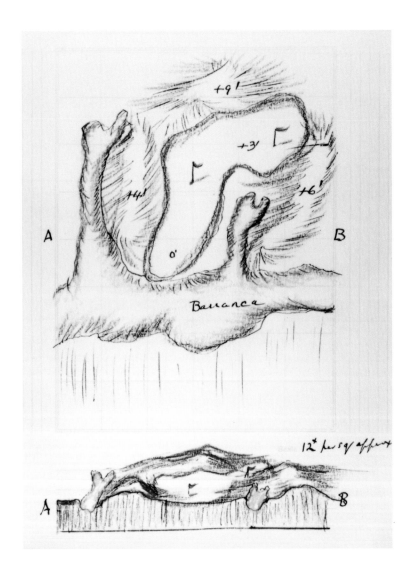

Alister's designs. His son, Robert Jr., formed the American Golf Course Construction Company in order to fulfill construction. Hunter's social contacts, however, and the success of his book brought many potential clients to his and MacKenzie's doorstep. Consequently, MacKenzie gave Hunter full billing as a partner (unlike Jack Fleming who was always only listed a construction foreman).

Hunter's interest in the field would have meant nothing without Alister's practical experience and extensive resume. Working together, though, they were a potent team. Hunter's association with the University of California enabled him to bring in expert consultants on soils and grasses, which added a more professional and scientific aura to the whole process.

Hunter is credited as co-designer of The Meadow Club, Cypress Point, Northwood GC in Guernerville; Pittsburgh GC, a nine-hole layout between Oakland and Sacramento; Green Hills CC in San Francisco; and The Valley Club of Montecito. He moved to Santa Barbara during the construction of The Valley Club and also served as green chairman there until a few years before his death.

H. Chandler Egan (1884-1936)
Born: Chicago, Illinois
Died: Everett, Washington

H. Chandler Egan was one of the most accomplished amateur golfers in America at the turn of the century. He won the U.S. Amateur championship in 1904 and 1905 (the same year he graduated from Harvard) and was a four-time winner of the Western Amateur.

After 1910, Egan moved west and settled on an apple farm in Medford, Oregon. No doubt partly because of his success as a player and partly because he was living in a state that was almost devoid of golf courses, he quickly received commissions to design several courses around Oregon. In 1926, Egan and Robert Hunter were asked by the United States Golf Association to suggest revisions to Pebble Beach Golf Links, the selected site for the 1929 U.S. Amateur. Their changes included a complete overhaul of the ninth and tenth holes, and the rebunkering of many holes. For an encore, Egan reached the semifinals of that '29 Amateur—a newsworthy "comeback" at the age of 45.

Following his return to the spotlight, Egan was added to the letter-head of "MacKenzie and Egan." He replaced Robert Hunter, who had moved permanently to Santa Barbara. Egan collaborated on the doctor's design for the Union League Club in San Francisco (now Green Hills Country Club). Unfortunately, his timing was not very good because the Depression soon cut off any work for the firm. Egan soon returned to Oregon and found a smattering of design work before his untimely death from pneumonia at age 51.

His most prominent designs, apart from the changes to Pebble Beach, are Eastmoreland GC and Lake Oswego CC, both near Portland, Oregon; a second nine for Pacific Grove Golf Links on the Monterey Peninsula; and Indian Canyon GC in Spokane, long considered one of the nation's best public courses.

John Francis Fleming (1896-1986)
Born: Tuam, Co. Galway, Ireland
Died: San Francisco, California

Jack Fleming left Ireland in 1914 in search of a position as a gardener. He wound up landing a job as a laborer on a course being built by Dr. MacKenzie. By 1920 he had graduated to the position of foreman for Charles MacKenzie's construction firm. He then returned to Ireland to supervise the work at Little Island, Douglas, Muskerry, and Monkstown.

Once the job in Cork was finished, MacKenzie persuaded Fleming to emigrate to California, where he was involved with nearly all of MacKenzie's designs between 1927 and 1934, beginning with The Meadow Club in Marin County.

Fleming's son John, the longtime golf course superintendent at The Olympic Club in San Francisco, described his father's role as the "practical construction foreman" for all of MacKenzie's California work (even though another associate, Dan Gormley, was credited by Hunter as the construction superintendent for Cypress Point and Pasatiempo). Hunter, on the other hand, was the "suit" who kept the clients happily informed with progress, and MacKenzie was the mercurial genius who did the design and seldom visited the site afterward. Fleming was also primarily responsible for staffing the construction jobs, bringing several friends from Ireland to supervise individual courses in 1928 and 1929

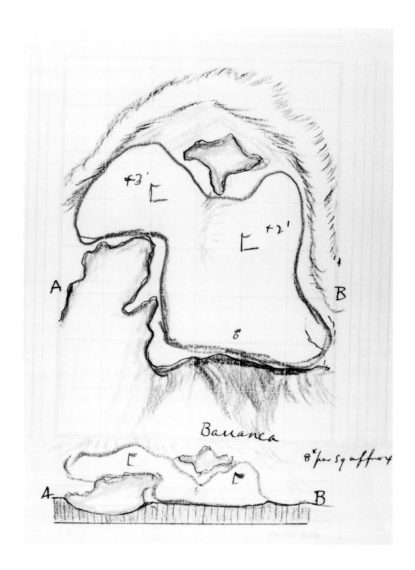

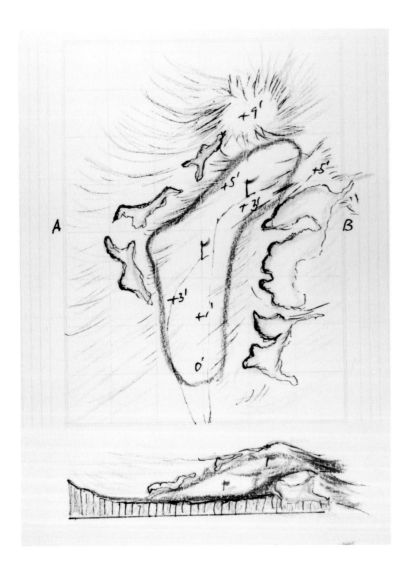

when they had four projects underway simultaneously.

After the Depression began, Fleming settled in as the Director of San Francisco Public Parks, for which he had been contracted to build Alister's Sharp Park Municipal project. He continued in this role until his retirement in 1962. Throughout his construction career, Fleming continued to dabble in golf course architecture, designing and building several short courses around the Bay Area in the 1940s, and then more than twenty more designs during the 1950s and 1960s.

Fleming's solo work includes significant remodeling of Willie Watson's Harding Park Municipal course in San Francisco and the addition of a third nine there which bears his name.

ALEX RUSSELL (1892-1961)
BORN: AUSTRALIA

Alex Russell won the Australian Open in 1924, two years before MacKenzie arrived in that country. He was admired for more than his golf, however: Russell was the confidential secretary to Australian Prime Minister Bruce when he wasn't on the links. Because of his "day job," Russell made several trips to Great Britain. He became familiar with the great links courses.

Russell and another member, A. T. Brown, had actually been deputized to lay out a revised course for Royal Melbourne in 1924. When MacKenzie agreed to travel to Australia, however, Russell was asked to work with him and ensure the implementation of the doctor's ideas.

That Russell and MacKenzie got on so well should be no surprise, for they had much in common. Twenty years MacKenzie's junior, Russell was also a Cambridge man and had played on the golf team. During World War I, he served as a major in the Royal Artillery. A man of letters, Russell was also a man of wealth, residing at "Mawallock" in Beaufort where he maintained his own practice course.

MacKenzie made Russell a partner almost immediately and took him around to other Sand Belt clubs that asked for their advice. The two men are listed as co-designers for the West Course at Royal Melbourne, Yarra Yarra Golf Club (built the next year), and Lake Karrinyup in Perth, the site of which Alister never actually visited. There has been speculation that Russell corresponded regularly with Dr. MacKenzie about design matters, especially bunkering. Russell visited Britain often on state business and they are believed to have discussed the design of Yarra Yarra and Lake Karrinyup during those trips. Strangely, though, Alister's *Spirit of St. Andrews* does not mention Alex Russell or indicate that he ever received any reports about the success of their courses in the southern hemisphere.

Russell laid out Royal Melbourne's East course in 1930 and it opened in 1932. Six of its holes are now included in the famous Composite course used for championship play. He is also credited with several solo designs, the most famous of which is Paraparaumu Beach, near Wellington, New Zealand.

MICK MORCOM (1876-1937)
BORN: AUSTRALIA

Michael "Mick" Morcom was the greenkeeper at Royal Melbourne Golf Club from 1905 until 1937. During that time he also assisted with the construction of Dr. MacKenzie's West Course and participated in the construction of MacKenzie's designs for the bunkering of Kingston Heath and Victoria. Morcom was often assisted on these projects by his son, Vern. Later on, Vern became a golf course architect.

Morcom and MacKenzie spent much time together during Alister's visit to Australia, and Morcom eventually built some of the most beautiful bunkers in the history of the art. In fact, his bunkering influence extended beyond the courses on which MacKenzie consulted. The bunkers on Russell's East Course at Royal Melbourne, Yarra Yarra, and at Woodlands Country Club nearby are definitely Morcom's, while those at Commonwealth Golf Club were certainly inspired by Morcom if not actually built by him.

Mick Morcom also did some design work on his own, notably the municipal Sandringham course across the street from Royal Melbourne, and the Yarra Bend public course which opened in 1928.

When Morcom retired in 1937, he passed on the greenkeeper job at Royal Melbourne to his assistant Claude Crockford. Crockford held the position until 1975 and helped give Royal Melbourne the reputation as the best conditioned course in the world.

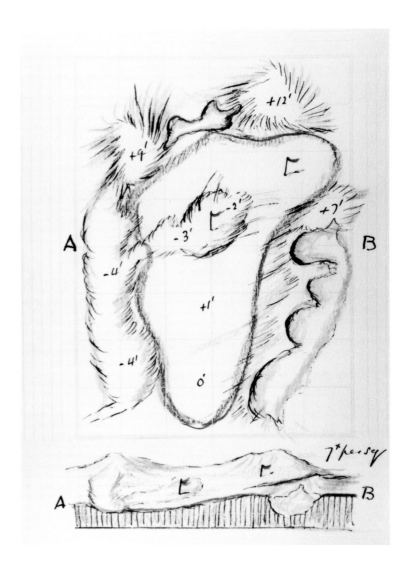

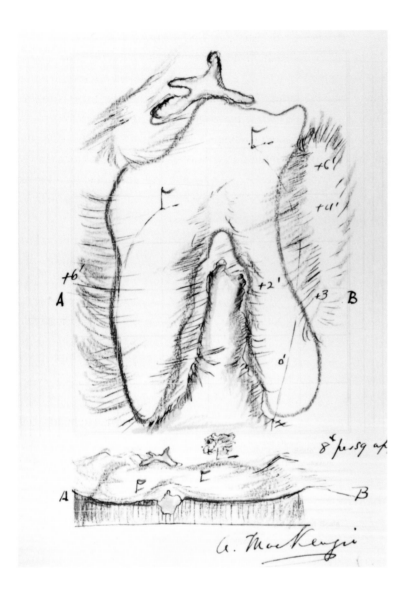

Luther Koontz

When MacKenzie was asked to go to South America in 1930, he brought along an engineer named Luther Koontz from Wendell Miller's golf construction company, with whom MacKenzie was working at Bayside Links in New York. Argentina's Jockey Club was built over a very flat site, and Koontz handled the planning and supervision of construction for MacKenzie's design. Koontz remained in Argentina afterward and designed more than twenty courses there and in Uruguay. Dr. MacKenzie has been rumored to have participated in the design of other courses on the continent, but it is more likely that these are Koontz's work, perhaps with some use of MacKenzie's name; it is unlikely that MacKenzie corresponded with Koontz any more than he did with Alex Russell on future projects in Australia.

Among Koontz's other work are Olivos Country Club, ten miles from The Jockey Club, which is Buenos Aires' other most prominent championship venue; and Cantegril Country Club in Punta del Este, Uruguay, which he revised and expanded to eighteen holes in 1940.

MARION HOLLINS (1892-1944)
BORN: EAST ISLIP, NEW YORK
DIED: PACIFIC GROVE, CALIFORNIA

During the construction of Augusta National Golf Club, unwilling to make a site visit himself despite the insistence of Clifford Roberts, Dr. MacKenzie suggested that "his associate, Marion Hollins," make the trip in his place. Roberts was not happy with a substitute, but Marion did visit the site. She reported back to MacKenzie that she was quite impressed with the design.

That was the only time that Marion was referred to as an "associate" of Dr. MacKenzie. But as both his client and patron, Hollins had a considerable influence on the design of both Cypress Point and Pasatiempo. In fact, it was Hollins who was mainly responsible for the famed 16th hole at Cypress Point, which Marion had convinced original architect Seth Raynor of its feasibility by driving a ball across the ocean to the green site. While she gave MacKenzie all the latitude an architect needs, she was also constantly there to hear him out and ensure that everything was accomplished as he thought best.

Before moving west, Marion had won the U.S. Women's Amateur Championship of 1921—even though polo was her first passion and better sport. In 1922, she founded the Women's National Golf & Tennis Club at Glen Head, New York, collaborating with Devereux Emmet and Seth Raynor on the design. Soon after she moved to the west coast to become the head real estate salesperson for Sam Morse's Del Monte Properties Company on the Monterey Peninsula, owner of Pebble Beach Golf Links. In time, Hollins convinced Morse of the advantage of the company owning another course along the coast. Morse gave the responsibility of founding the new course—eventually called Cypress Point Club—to Hollins.

ROBERT TYRE (BOBBY) JONES, JR. (1902-1971)
BORN: ATLANTA, GEORGIA
DIED: ATLANTA, GEORGIA

Like Marion Hollins, the great champion Robert Tyre [Bobby] Jones, Jr., was more patron than partner to MacKenzie. As such, however, Jones was heavily involved in the concept and design details of the Augusta National Golf Club, and he personally approved any changes to the course in subsequent years.

Like MacKenzie, Jones was well educated. He earned a degree in engineering from Georgia Tech and another in English literature from Harvard. He then went to law school at Emory University and passed the bar exam after one year. But Jones's amateur golf career overshadowed his academic pursuits. After a successful and well-publicized few years as a junior golfer, Jones broke though for his first major championship in the 1923 U.S. Open at Inwood Country Club in New York. Seven years later, his major championships totaled 13, capped off in 1930 by his victories in the British Amateur, British Open, U.S. Open, and U.S. Amateur.

As early as 1926, after taking a job to sell housing lots at the Donald Ross-designed Bobby Jones Golf Course at Whitfield Estates in Florida (now Sara Bay Country Club), Jones had become fascinated with golf course architecture. During the height of his success he was constantly being approached about lending his name to golf course ventures. The only two he took an interest in were the #2 course at his home club of East Lake Country Club in Atlanta and Highlands Country Club in North Carolina (a course that was being designed at the same time by Donald Ross for some East Lake investors).

Jones's fascination with the Old Course at St. Andrews drew him naturally to MacKenzie, who had written so knowingly about it, and whose 1924 survey map of the Old Course occupied a prized place on Jones's office wall. MacKenzie probably met him at some point during Jones's 1927 Open Championship victory at the Old Course (MacKenzie walked the fairways with Bobby's confidant and biographer, O.B. Keeler). The two got to know each other even better in 1929 when Jones played at Cypress Point and Pasatiempo with Marion Hollins after his shocking first-round defeat in the Amateur Championship at Pebble Beach. In 1931, when Clifford Roberts and Jones decided to build a golf course, Jones selected MacKenzie for the job.

Despite his golfing prowess, Jones believed the ideal course should be easily playable for the average member. Starting with that premise, he and MacKenzie agreed that the Old Course was the ideal from which to model their design. In turn, this encouraged MacKenzie to return to thinking economically, to create a radically low-key design that featured only twenty three bunkers, yet was one that nevertheless provided challenging play for the masters of the game.

MacKenzie's Best Golf Holes

Par-3s:

11th at Lahinch, 139 yards.

A wonderful true short hole playing between two large dunes, aligned to give a view of the point at the mouth of the river beyond. The better part of the green is tucked behind the dune on the left, defended by a small pot bunker cut into the toe of slope. The green is quite undulating, one of only two on the course that have never been softened from MacKenzie's original contours.

15th at Kingston Heath, 155 yards.

The only hole on this Australian course that MacKenzie built from scratch, it is a rare great uphill par 3. There are nests of bunkers to the right all the way from the tee, and a single deep bunker up against the left front of the green, which is narrow at the front and then wraps around the left-hand bunker as it widens at the back. You have the choice of playing to this narrow tongue of green or taking an extra club, but the green is sharply tilted back to front, and there is a steep bank down off the back of the green from where it is impossible to make three.

10th at Moortown, 190 yards.

The famous "Gibraltar," named because its green was built atop a rock outcropping. The enterprising MacKenzie took the seed money

from the founders of the club and built this one hole to convince prospective members to join, helping to launch his career. Similar to the famous Redan at North Berwick — although Dr. MacKenzie claimed not to have seen the Redan until years afterward — one can play to the entrance at the front right and hope for the ball to run to the left, or play a bold shot over the deep left front bunker.

16th at Cypress Point, 219 yards.

The most dramatic hole in golf, playing diagonally across a cove of the Pacific Ocean out to a green set on the point. In some conditions even a full drive would not be able to reach the green, so players are offered the option of a safe tee shot over 120 yards of water to the base of the peninsula, where a downslope will scoot the ball ahead into the narrowest part of fairway. From there, they have the chance to play a 50-yard pitch and get up and down for their three. In stroke play discretion is usually called for, but in a match the first player to dare and succeed seizes the advantage. And in non-competitive situations, the thrill of trying for the green is almost irresistible.

Par-4s:

9th at Cypress Point, 291 yards.

A dramatic short par 4 built atop a ridge of dunes. The long and narrow green angles well off to the left, rewarding a long tee shot down the right which flirts with a steep drop into sand. It is possible to reach the entrance of the green from the tee, but to miss with a driver leaves a very awkward half-shot approach, often from a sandy lie. Many players lay back with medium irons off the tee to give themselves a full wedge second shot, but even then the tee shot must land along a narrow isthmus of fairway.

3rd at Royal Adelaide, 301 yards.

A straightaway, driveable par 4 built years before such holes were in fashion. A crest at the 220-yard mark in the fairway means only the top of the flag is visible from the tee, heightening anxiety for those wishing to hit driver. The green is tucked against the bank of the "crater" to its right, and a small ridge to the left of the green leaves a very narrow entrance for the running approach.

7th at Crystal Downs, 335 yards.

Players must choose on the tee whether to drive into a deep valley (leaving a half-blind second shot), or lay up to the edge of a drop-off at 190 yards and a clear view of the green. A poor lay-up will miss the narrow plateau of fairway and leave an awkward stance and sometimes a long second shot. This is believed to be the first of many boomerang-shaped greens that MacKenzie built late in his career. The prototype is the best of the group — located in a natural hollow, it allows players to putt around the right-center bunker using the sideslope at the elbow of the green, instead of having to chip over the bunker from one part of the green to another.

14th at Augusta National, 420 yards.

A very difficult hole without a single bunker, representative of the late period of MacKenzie's career. The green includes an abrupt rise at the front and a pronounced tilt from left to right, and it is critical to get the ball up the front slope, or three putts are inevitable. At the same time putting across the slippery green from the left or behind the hole is frightening. Despite the lack of visible hazards, there is only one reasonable spot in which to miss the green and escape with par.

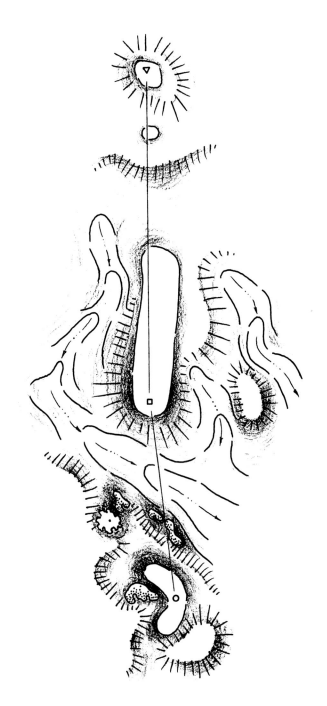

SEVENTH AT CRYSTAL DOWNS. (COURTESY DON PLACEK, RENAISSANCE GOLF DESIGN, INC.)

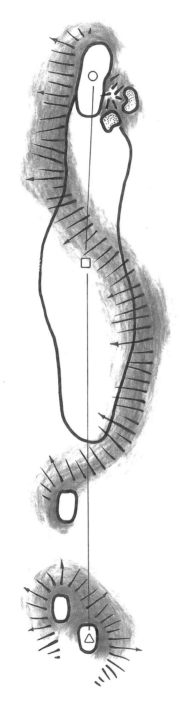

#9 LAHINCH 381 YDS. PAR 4.

16th at Pasatiempo, 385 yards.

MacKenzie named this as his favorite hole before his death, and it is certainly among his most dramatic and challenging tests. Both drive and approach must carry a deep barranca which runs across in front of the tee, continues down the left of the fairway, and then crosses again close beside the green on the right. The crowned fairway gives a bit of roll to weak players' drives, but forces longer hitters to play perilously close to the trouble on the left, or risk going through the fairway into trees. The three-tiered green is one of the most severe MacKenzie greens still in existence, with more than seven feet of rise from front to back.

15th at Alwoodley, 415 yards.

A strong dogleg to the right, with an out-of-bounds fence very close to the corner of the dogleg. The green is set a bit away from the boundary, with a rise in the green set diagonally along the line of play shedding short second shots off toward a bunker on the right.

9th at Lahinch, 381 yards.

From the back tee, high atop a dune, the drive is downhill to a terraced fairway with a severe dip on the left side. Even if one tries and fails to make the carry, leaving a half-blind second shot, the angle to the long and narrow green is a distinct advantage. "Safe" drives to the shelf on the right leave an almost impossible second shot, past a stiff bunker at the right front of the green; most shots which clear the bunker will then carry over the shelf of the green down toward the tenth tee far below.

10th at Cavendish, 450 yards.

One of three stout par 4s that force strong players to respect a course measuring only 5,800 yards on the scorecard. The second shot is one of the toughest Dr. MacKenzie ever built, uphill across a small ravine with the entrance fairway offset to the right of the green.

11th at Royal Melbourne (West), 455 yards, par 4.

This dogleg-left plays around two staggered fairway bunkers at the bottom of a valley. The downslope from the tee is tilted from right to left, so short hitters' tee shots may bounce around the bunkers to achieve the best angle for the approach; but the slope runs out at 240 yards, so long hitters must play a bolder line over the bunkers in order to get a good angle at the flag.

4th at Royal Melbourne (West), 470 yards.

The tee shot is blind but well defined, up over bunkers at the crest of a hill, 30 feet above the tee. A long and straight tee ball will gain considerable run on the back side of the hill, while any shot hedged to the left will run well away to the left, leaving a much longer second shot on this dogleg-right. To get home in two, the long approach shot must flirt with bunkers set along the edge of the fairway on the right, where the ground falls steeply away into trees. A large bunker at the left-front of the green stymies third shots after a safe second shot away from the trouble on the right.

Par-5s:

13th at Augusta National, 485 yards.
Quoting Bob Jones in Golf Is My Game:

"We call thirteen a par five because under certain conditions of wind and ground, few players will risk trying for the green with a second shot. In my opinion this thirteenth hole is one of the finest holes for competitive play I have ever seen. The player is first tempted to dare the creek on his tee shot by playing in close to the corner, because if he attains his position he has not only shortened the hole, but obtained a more level lie for his second shot. Driving out to the right not only increases the length of the second, but encounters an annoying sidehill lie.

Whatever position may be reached with the tee shot, the second shot as well entails a momentous decision whether or not to try for the green. With the pin far back on the right, under normal weather condi-

tions, this is a very good eagle hole, because the contours of the green tend to run the second shot close. The chief danger is that the ball will follow the creek.

The most difficult pin locations are along the creek in the forward part of the green. A player who dares the creek on either his first or second shot may very easily encounter a six or seven at this hole. Yet the reward of successful, bold play is most enticing."

3rd at Alwoodley, 505 yards.

A subtle debut for MacKenzie, this long hole plays across a high plain without a single fairway bunker before arriving at a natural punchbowl green which is offset slightly to the left of the fairway.

5th at New South Wales, 500 yards.

As dramatic a hole as there is in golf, up over a high ridge line and then fantastically downhill to a green set on the promontory of the Cape Banks at the entrance to Botany Bay. In downwind conditions it is easily reachable in two shots, but when played into the wind, the second shot has to be launched over the crest of the hill just in front of the player, where the wind will then play havoc as it descends.

8th at Crystal Downs, 550 yards.

A terrific natural hole with no need for fairway bunkers. Short drives land in an undulating bowl of fairway, leaving a difficult stance for the long second shot, where placement is key. The second shot is uphill over a valley, with a narrow shelf of fairway on the right the preferred landing zone. All other spots will leave a sharply uphill and sidehill lie, making it difficult to pick the correct club for the approach to a very small green guarded by a deep hollow at the left front, and a bunker to the right.

Appendix of MacKenzie Designs

New Designs

[plus major revisions, including routing changes]

Alwoodley GC, Leeds, England (with advice from H.S. Colt), 1907

Augusta National GC, Augusta, Georgia (with Robert Tyre Jones, Jr.), 1933

Blackpool Municipal GC, Stanley Park, Blackpool, England, 1925

Blairgowrie GC, Blairgowrie, Perthshire, Scotland (Rosemount Course), 1934

Bury GC, Bury, Lancashire, England (new course over site of previous layout), 1920

Cavendish GC, Buxton, Derbyshire, England, 1925

Claremont CC, Oakland, California (revision), 1929

Cleckheaton & District GC, Cleckheaton, West Yorkshire, England (new course for existing club), 1920

Cork GC, Little Island, Co. Cork, Ireland (expansion to 18 holes, constructed by C. A. MacKenzie and Jack Fleming), 1927

Crystal Downs CC, Frankfort, Michigan (expansion and redesign of a 1926 layout, with Perry Maxwell), 1932

Cypress Point Club, Pebble Beach, California (with Robert Hunter, constructed by Jack Fleming), 1928

Darlington GC, Durham, England (largely changed today from original design),1914

Didsbury GC, Manchester, England (including five new holes, constructed by C. A. MacKenzie), 1921

Douglas GC, Pulrose, Isle of Man, England (constructed by C. A. MacKenzie), 1921

Galway GC, Blackrock, Co. Galway, Ireland (revision of 1895 layout, by Colt, MacKenzie & Alison; conflicting reports on MacKenzie's involvement), 1925-1930

Garforth GC, Leeds, England, 1913

I.F   POLO   ATHLETIC FIELDS   CEMETERIES   PRIVATE ESTATES   FROST PREVENTION   AIRPORT!

WENDELL P. MILLER
AND ASSOCIATES
CONSULTING ENGINEERS
XXXXXXXXXXXXXXXXXXX
NEW YORK, N. Y.

ENGINEERING SPECIALISTS
IN DRAINAGE
IRRIGATION
SOIL CONDITIONING
AND TURF DEVELOPMENT

SURVEYS, ENGINEERING DESIGI
SPECIFICATIONS
SUPERVISION OF CONSTRUCTIOI
CONSTRUCTION

77-20 Austin St.,
Forest Hills,N.Y.
Mar.31,1934

Mr.L. W. St. John,
Director of Athletics,
Ohio State University,
Columbus, Ohio.

Dear Mr.StJohn;
                    Your letter of Mar.22nd was not
forwarded to me in Augusta last week because I was
expected back in New York several days sooner. When
I wired you Friday night I was quite certain that
we had Doctor Mackenzie's green plans for your course
in our files. A thorough search of the files and
records fails to bring them to light however. From
some correspondence with the Doctor early in 1930
I find that all the plans he had sent me except that
of the general plan were returned to him in California.
                    Therefore I have written Mrs.Mackenzie airmail
asking her to search the Doctor's files for your plans.
If she cannnot find them among his effects, we have
enough information here from which to complete the plans.
No doubt you will recall the Doctor's conversation with
you in which he said that his green plans were never to
be considered as anything but a guide to the engineer,
and were not intended to be followed in detail. Because
of this instruction to us, the actual shape and contour
of the greens on all the courses we built for him, were
determined to a great extent by our own organization.
This resulted in our being trined in the Mackenzie ideals
to such a point that he felt it safe to intrust the
construction of the greens for the Palmetto Club, at
Aiken entirely to us without, once coming to the course
to check our work. The Aiken people say we built them
a better bunch of greens than those on the Augusta National.
                    I wish it had been possible for you to come
to Augusta for the Tournament last week, both to see the
golfcourse and to observe the play. It is doubtful if any
golf course in this country ever created the serious
discussion among pros, amatuers and golf writers that was
involked by this course. The best thing about it was that
the Professionals said it was most interesting course in
America, while the old duffers are just as crazy about it.
There is no doubt but what Mackenzie would have busy
remodeling golf courses to bring them in line with the
Augusta National had he lived..,

THE LARGE NINTH AND EIGHTEENTH (BACKGROUND) GREENS AT CLAREMONT COUNTRY CLUB CIRCA 1915. (COURTESY CLAREMONT COUNTRY CLUB)

THE MUCH SMALLER NINTH AND EIGHTEENTH GREENS AT CLAREMONT COUNTRY CLUB, CIRCA 1933), AFTER MACKENZIE RE-DESIGNED THE COURSE. NOTE THE BUNKERING OF THE 18TH IN THE BACKGROUND. (COURTESY CLAREMONT COUNTRY CLUB)

THE RE-DESIGNED EIGHTH GREEN AT CLAREMONT COUNTRY CLUB. (COURTESY CLAREMONT COUNTRY CLUB)

CLAREMONT COUNTRY CLUB'S ELEVENTH GREEN, CIRCA 1933. (COURTESY CLAREMONT COUNTRY CLUB)

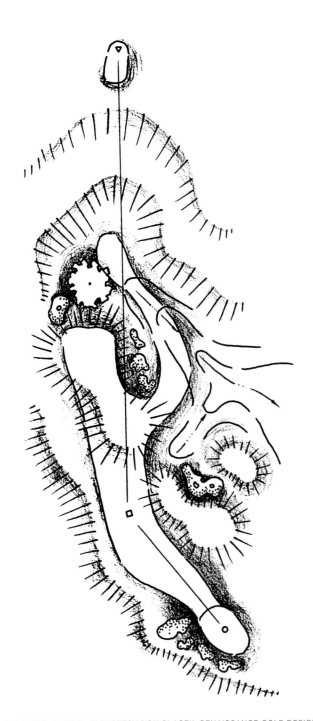

FIFTH AT CRYSTAL DOWNS. (COURTESY DON PLACEK, RENAISSANCE GOLF DESIGN, INC.)

GC del Uruguay, Punta Carretas, Montevideo, Uruguay (expansion and redesign of an 1895 layout, with Luther Koontz), 1934

Grange-over-Sands GC, Grange-over-Sands, Lancashire, England, 1920

Green Hills CC (formerly Union League Club), Millbrae, California (with Robert Hunter and H. Chandler Egan), 1930

Hadley Wood GC, Barnet, Hertfordshire, England, 1921

Hazel Grove GC, Stockport, England (constructed by C. A. MacKenzie), 1920

Hazelhead Municipal GC, Aberdeen, Scotland (No.1 course), 1927

The Jockey Club, San Isidro, Argentina (Red and Blue courses, with Luther Koontz), 1931

Lahinch GC, Lahinch, Co. Clare, Ireland (revision of 1891 Tom Morris layout), 1927

Low Laithes GC, Ossett, West Yorkshire, England (constructed by C. A. MacKenzie), 1925

Malone GC, Belfast, Northern Ireland (design on new site), 1920

Marsden GC, Huddersfield, West Yorkshire, England, 1920-1934

The Meadow Club, Fairfax, California (with Robert Hunter), 1927

Melrose CC, Philadelphia, Pennsylvania (collaboration on Perry Maxwell design already under construction), 1927

Moortown GC, Alwoodley, Leeds, England, 1909

Morecambe GC, Bare, Morecambe, Lancs, England, 1923

ELEVENTH AT CYPRESS POINT. (COURTESY DON PLACEK, RENAISSANCCE GOLF DESIGN, INC.)

Muskerry GC, Carrigrohane, Co. Cork, Ireland (revision, including eleven new holes), 1920

New South Wales GC, La Perouse, N.S.W., Australia (design supervised by Colonel Bertram of Royal Sydney), 1926 (major revisions to layout by Eric Apperly, 1937)

Northwood GC, Guerneville, California (nine holes), 1929

Oakdale GC, Harrogate, Leeds, England, 1913

Ohio State University GC's, Columbus, Ohio (Scarlet and Gray courses; routed in 1929, but not built until 1938, four years after MacKenzie's death)

Oklahoma City G&CC, Oklahoma City, Oklahoma (with Perry Maxwell), 1928

Old Links GC, Bolton, England (new course over site of previous layout), 1922

Palmetto GC, Aiken, South Carolina (expansion and revision of 1895 layout by Herbert Leeds), 1932

TOPOGRAPHIC MAP
SHOWING A PORTION
OF
DEL PASO PARK
OCCUPIED BY
AMERICAN GOLF COURSE
CONSTRUCTION COMPANY

CITY OF SACRAMENTO
ENGINEERING DEPARTMENT
DATE FEB. 3 1932   SCALE 1 IN.= 00 FT.

FRED KLAUS CITY ENGINEER

THE MACKENZIE 18 AT HAGGIN OAKS IN CALIFORNIA
WAS ORIGINALLY CALLED SACRAMENTO MUNICIPAL
GOLF COURSE. (COURTESY CITY OF SACRAMENTO
GOLF DIVISION)

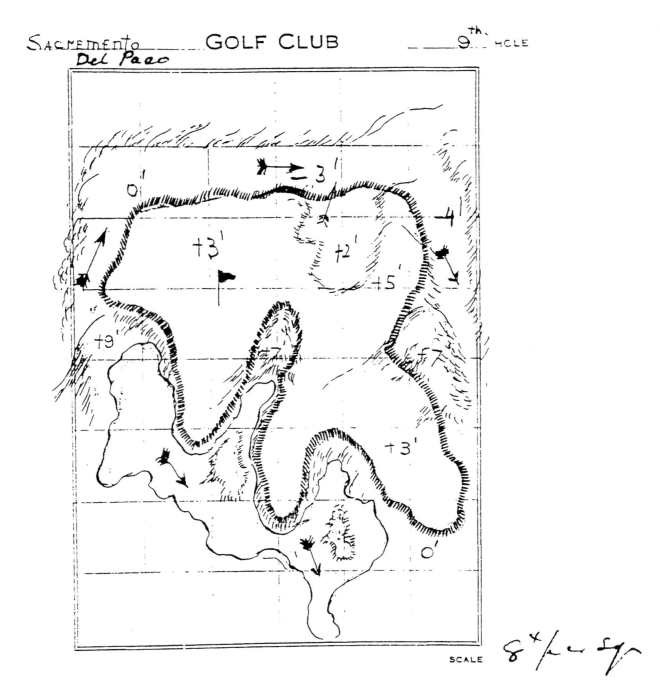

SACRAMENTO GOLF COURSE IS NOW CALLED THE ALISTER MACKENZIE COURSE AT THE HAGGIN OAKS COMPLEX. (COURTESY CITY OF SACRAMENTO GOLF DIVISION)